NEWS FROM THE END OF THE EARTH

JOHN HICKMAN

News from the End of the Earth

A Portrait of Chile

HURST & COMPANY, LONDON

First published in the United Kingdom by
C. Hurst & Co. (Publishers) Ltd.,
38 King Street, London WC2E 8JZ

Printed in Malaysia

ISBNs 1-85065-378-X

To my family, not least the youngest members
Luke, Sebastian and Thomas,
and particularly to Jenny, who
put up with it all

CONTENTS

ILLUSTRATIONS

(All the photographs included in the book have been made available by El Mercurio, *Santiago, and are reproduced by kind permission.)*

MAPS

PREFACE AND ACKNOWLEDGEMENTS

It is an extraordinary fact that a country such as Chile, with which Britain had very close links throughout most of the nineteenth century and the first quarter of the twentieth, should have receded in our national consciousness by the end of the First World War, and almost disappeared from it by the end of the Second. When I first heard from my bosses in the Foreign and Commonwealth Office in 1981 that I was to be posted there as British Ambassador, I was almost as ignorant about it as most people in Britain but I did at least have the advantage of having spent the previous three years in Ecuador in the same continent. It was thousands of kilometres to the north of Chile but also on the west coast facing the Pacific Ocean. So I knew where to find my new destination on the map and a few other things about it.

I knew, for example, that one of Chile's founding fathers, Bernardo O'Higgins, was the son of an Irish-born father and partly educated in England. I knew also of the important role which Britain and Britons, often soldiers and sailors no longer needed by their own country after the end of the Napoleonic Wars, had played in the struggle of the Latin American colonies to win their independence from Spain and Portugal. One hundred years later the Pan-American Centennial Conference, celebrating the centenary of that great movement to independence, declared:

> .... Great Britain lent to the liberty of Spanish America not only the support of its diplomacy, represented by Canning, but also an appreciable contingent of blood, and it may be asserted that there was no battlefield in the War of Independence on which British blood was not shed.

These men were, in one sense, mercenaries or soldiers of fortune. In the British Isles most were soon forgotten. But in South America brilliant figures such as Thomas Cochrane, Earl of Dundonald, Commander-in-Chief of the Chilean Navy (and later also of the Brazilian Navy), and William Miller, gallant commander of marines in Chile and later of Peruvian land forces, were still much honoured for their contributions to the freedom of all the countries they had served. In the same way, British merchants and entrepreneurs who had established themselves in the new Latin American republics as fast as Spanish authority and trading monopolies were removed, had been challenged by other foreign competitors and often eclipsed in these markets within a century of building up their early overwhelming dominance.

Some of these changes were the direct result of two World Wars. Investments had to be sold to pay for them, or companies were forced to concentrate on markets in other more accessible parts of the world. Competition from European rivals had developed over time, but far the greatest impact was naturally made by the rapidly growing financial and commercial strength of the United States – the only true winner in both those devastating wars. In the latter part of the twentieth century Japan had also become a formidable economic competitor in Latin America as elsewhere.

As to the state of Chile itself, I had read the cynical little story told by Claud Cockburn about a competition invented by the sub-editors of *The Times* in the 1930s to see who could write the most boring headline for the paper. His contribution – 'Small Earthquake in Chile. Not Many Dead' – won the prize. Natural disasters are normally front-page news, so it was not earthquakes – even small ones – which Claud Cockburn and his colleagues found tedious so much as their happening in Chile. Was it the relatively small size of Chile which failed to impress them or its extreme remoteness from Europe? For whatever reason, Chile was a far-away country of which they knew little.

This bland apathy was eventually broken down by events in Chile in the early 1970s. In November 1970, and at his fourth attempt, a Socialist politician, Dr Salvador Allende, became President at the head of a left-wing coalition dominated by Marxist, or near-Marxist parties. He had the narrowest of margins over the two rival candidates (36.2 per cent of the vote against 34.9 per cent for the right-wing candidate, Jorge Alessandri) but, despite strenuous efforts by the United States, Allende was eventually confirmed in power by the Chilean Congress in accordance with the usual constitutional process. In his victory speech Allende promised to be 'the first president of the first really democratic, popular, national and revolutionary government in the history of

Chile'. In the event, after three years of increasingly tense and violent confrontation between Allende's government and its opponents, the armed forces ousted him in a bloody *coup d'état* in 1973.

This seemed to be the familiar pattern of military coups in South America in which ruthless generals overthrow democratic governments – usually with the support of shadowy foreign business interests and political cabals either inside the country or abroad. Most observers looking at Chile from afar in 1973, including myself then occupied with South East Asian and Far Eastern problems, thought that the overthrow of Allende had almost certainly been stimulated by Washington in one way or another and perhaps planned by the CIA, and that this coup only differed from the normal pattern in that the repression which followed was more brutal than most and the military regime more willing to perpetuate itself indefinitely. By the time I took up my new post in Santiago in 1982, General Augusto Pinochet had transformed the armed forces government established in 1973 into what was in practice a personal dictatorship based on the Army of which he was Commander-in-Chief. He had designed a new constitution to legalise this system and been elected as President by referendum, but there was almost nothing left of Chile's long democratic heritage.

This snapshot of the situation in 1981 reflects most of my personal knowledge of what had happened in Chile up to that time. I suspect there were few foreigners who were much better informed, apart from a handful of academic and media specialists and diplomats directly involved with the country. However, I soon began to discover that my understanding of the Chilean situation was at best fragmentary and superficial.

I spent the next five years studying the country at close quarters from the ring-side position of a diplomat accredited in Santiago. The advantages which that gives – inside information and personal access to people of influence and power – were counter-balanced, of course, by the inhibitions imposed by diplomatic convention and other restrictions which tend to distort the judgement of the privileged insider. But any bias I acquired from those factors was, I believe, corrected by the impressions gathered by my family, including three grown-up children, at least one of whom was usually living with us in Chile and moving in circles very different to those which diplomats and their wives normally inhabit. And, after our appointment ended and we rather reluctantly returned to live in England, I was able to revisit Chile often and maintain personal friendships there.

Of course I continue to learn. After fifteen years' acquaintance with the country I at least know how little I know. There is no end to the process, and the country itself changes so that there is more to grasp and fit into a continuously evolving picture. The Chile which finally emerged as a restored democracy at the end of the Pinochet regime has a different political ethos to the democracy which Allende tested to the limit in 1970–3 and which the military finally dismantled. Over the same period there has also been an economic revolution in Chile which has made it a model for the whole of Latin America and even for some countries beyond. Larger numbers of foreigners have, therefore, paid a little more attention to that long, thin country at the end of the earth since the Allende period; but many in Britain, the United States and other Western democracies still see it mainly as the subject of film dramas and documentaries about jack-booted dictators – a typical backdrop for 'faction' or the entertainments of Graham Greene or John Le Carré.

This book offers an outsider's view of Chile's situation in the final decade of the twentieth century and how it has reached this point; how it was born as an independent republic, grew stronger and expanded its boundaries in the nineteenth century and has survived the turbulence of our own times. Inevitably I have given a good deal of attention to relations between Chile and English-speaking countries. My view may be Anglocentric, but I hope that Chileans who read this book will excuse that bias. It is addressed primarily to *gringos* rather than to Chileans and to armchair travellers, business people and tourists who visit the country and anyone else wanting to know more than can be found in a guide-book.

Most of the first seven chapters are historical narrative based on authoritative and recently published sources (to which I am much indebted), but with a few personal reflections and opinions added to leaven the loaf. The last five chapters, which include the period since 1982 when I first got to know Chile at first hand, contain rather more original and personal material. In the final part of the book I have also drawn freely on conversations with many Chileans during frequent visits over the past ten years.

These contacts have kept me in touch with the way the country has developed, and on that basis I try to look ahead and guess how it may fare in the first years of the twenty-first century.

All that said, I know that I have not always maintained the dispassionate attitude I originally planned to adopt. Chile is not a country from which it is possible to stay detached for long. At first sight or soon after, all my family (and I more than any) fell for it and there are few who fail to respond to the irresistible, often strange but always strong appeal of that astonishingly varied landscape and the people who live there. I hope that my feeling for this far-away country will show through – now and again – in this book.

Acknowledgements

I owe most to my Chilean and other friends from whom I have learned about the country over the fifteen years since I first went to live there. It would hardly be possible to name them all individually. However, I must single out those who have helped me directly by patiently answering questions and recording interviews; and particularly those who have read and commented on various chapters in draft.

I have been fortunate to be able to draw on the experience of my predecessor as Ambassador in Santiago, John Heath: and two of my successors, Alan White and Frank Wheeler. Victor Bulmer-Thomas, the Director of the Institute of Latin American Studies at London University, also gave valuable advice – as did Eduardo Crawley, the managing editor, and others on the staff of Latin American Newsletters.

The practical support given by Antofagasta Holdings PLC for various journeys to Chile, and within the country, was very welcome. For this, and much else, I express my thanks to my friends, Andrónico Luksic and Philip Adeane, the Chairman and Managing Director of the company. Other good friends, Marco and Monica Cariola, Benjamin and Sylvia Davis, Eugenio and Elspeth Yrarrázaval Peter and Julia Kennedy, Germán and Maria Elena Claro, and Tomás and Monica Puig also helped a lot during my visits to Chile.

The staff of the libraries of the Foreign and Commonwealth Office, the Hispanic and Luso-Brazilian Council and the Institute of Latin American Studies in London, and of the *Biblioteca Nacional* in Chile, were always patient. Guillermo Canales, Director of the Centro de Documentación of *El Mercurio* in Santiago, helped me generously with the choice of photographs. Kevin Lyne and others in the Research Department of the Foreign and Commonwealth Office and John Bowler of the Economist Intelligence Unit were equally helpful.

The book would never have been written at all without the word processing skills, intuition and determination of Nickie Johnson in deciphering my handwriting and putting the result onto discs.

In the United States, two distinguished historians of Latin America, Paul Drake of the University of California and Simon Collier of Vanderbilt University, read several chapters each, gave me valuable insights and saved me from various errors.

In Chile, José Miguel Barros gave much time and care to commenting on several chapters and advising on others. Hernán Cubillos, a former Foreign Minister, was equally helpful and several other people who served in Chilean governments of the 1970s and 1980s provided valuable information about events in those years. I thank Pablo Baraona, Carlos Cáceres, Roberto Kelly and Ernesto Videla in particular for their contributions.

Among other distinguished Chileans who generously replied to my questions about the period since 1988, I am especially grateful to President Eduardo Frei Ruiz Tagle, former President Patricio Aylwin, Foreign Minister Jose Miguel Insulza, Andrés Allamand, Genaro Arriagada, Sergio Bitar, Edgardo Boeninger Alejandro González, Eduardo Ortiz and Maximo Pacheco. Finally, I have had much help and encouragement over many years from successive Ambassadors of Chile in London and members of the Embassy.

Naturally none of the Chileans and others who have so kindly helped me, in their official capacities or privately, is responsible in any way for the opinions I have expressed or any factual errors in the book.

Marlborough,
February 1998 J. H.

GLOSSARY OF SPANISH TERMS

afuerino	casual farm labourer
alcalde	mayor
antiplano	high plateau
asentamiento	settlement (agrarian reform unit)
Audiencia	colonial appeal court and administrative tribunal
cabildo	municipal council
cacique	tribal chief or party boss
callampa	shanty town
camanchaca	coastal fog
campesino	peasant, countryperson
chicha	fermented juice of grape, apple or *frutilla*
chilote	inhabitant of Chiloé
cordón industrial	'industrial belt'
cueca	Chilean national dance
dieciocho	September 18 (national day)
empanada	meat pasty
encomendero	holder of an encomienda
encomienda	grant of Indians to a Spanish conquistador
fundo	farm
gobernador	governor of a provincial district
gremio	(1) trade guild in colonial times; (2) association (usually of the self-employed)
hacendado	landowner of a hacienda
hacienda	great estate, ranch
huaso	peasant owning a horse
inquilino	tenant-labourer on a hacienda
intendente	provincial governor

interventor	temporary administrator
junta	committee (of military officers)
latifundista	estate owner
liceo	high school, secondary school
mestizo	of mixed Spanish/Indian parentage
minifundio	small peasant holding
mirista	member of MIR
momio	right-winger ("mummy")
oficina	(1) nitrate working; (2) office
pampa	northern desert
parcela	plot of land
partido	(1) colonial administrative subdivision; (2) political party
paseo	walk, stroll
patrón	boss, landowner
población	shantytown or marginal community
protesta	protest (1983-86)
quebrada	ravine
roto	urban labourer
salar	salt flat
salitre	nitrate
salitrera	nitrate working
toma	land seizure (literally, a "take")

ACRONYMS

AFP	Administradora de Fondos de Pensión	Pension Fund Administration (1980s onwards)
ASICH	Acción Sindical y Económica de Chile	Chilean Economic and Union Action (Catholic union movement)
CAP	Compañía del Acero del Pacífico	Pacific Steel Company
CERA	Centro de Reforma Agraria	Agrarian Reform Centre (agrarian reform unit)
CEPRO	Centro de Producción	Production Centre (agrarian reform unit)
CIA		Central Intelligence Agency (United States)
CNI	Central Nacional de Informaciones	National Information Centre (secret police, Pinochet regime)
CODELCO	Corporación del Cobre	Copper Corporation
CORA	Corporación de la Reforma Agraria	Agrarian Reform Corporation
CORFO	Corporación de Fomento de la Producción	Production Development Corporation
CTCH	Confederación de Trabajadores de Chile	Confederation of Workers of Chile (trade union confederation)
CUTCH	(1) Central Unica de Trabajadores Chilenos (1953) (2) Central Unitaria de Trabajadores	(1) Sole Workers Centre (trade union federation) (2) Unitary Workers' Centre (trade union federation)
DINA	Dirección de Inteligencia Nacional	Directorate of National Intelligence (secret police, Pinochet regime)

ENU	Escuela Nacional Unificada	Unified National School (Allende government)
FACH	Fuerza Aérea de Chile	Chilean Air Force
FOCH	Federación de Obreros Chilenos	Federation of Chilean Workers (trade union confederation)
FPMR	Frente Patriótico Manuel Rodríguez	Manuel Rodríguez Patriotic Front (Pinochet regime)
FRAP	Frente de Acción Popular	People's Action Front (left-wing coalition, 1950s-1960s)
GAP	Grupo de Amigos Personales	Allende's paramilitary bodyguard
INDAP	Instituto de Desarrollo Agropecuario	Agricultural Development Institute
ISAPRE	Institucion de Salud Previsional	Health Insurance Institute
MAPU	Movimiento de Acción Popular Unitaria	Unitary People's Action Movement
MIR	Movimiento de Izquierda Revolucionaria	Movement of the Revolutionary Left
ODEPLAN	Oficina de Planificación Nacional	National Planning Office
PCCH	Partido Comunista de Chile	Chilean Communist Party
PDC	Partido Demócratacristiano	Christian Democrat Party
PEM	Programa de Empleo Mínimo	Minimum Employment Programme (Pinochet regime)
PN	Partido Nacional	National Party
POJH	Programa Ocupacional para Jefes de Hogar	Work Programme for Heads of Household (Pinochet regime)
POS	Partido Obrero Socialista	Socialist Worker Party
PPD	Partido por la Democracia	Pro-democracy Party
RN	Renovación Nacional	National Renewal party
SNA	Sociedad Nacional de Agricultura	National Society of Agriculture

SOFOFA	Sociedad de Fomento Fabril	Society for Manufacturing Development
UDI	Unión Demócrata Independiente	Independent Democratic Union
UP	Unidad Popular	People's Unity (Allende coalition)
VOP	Vanguardia Organizada del Pueblo	Organised Vanguard of the People (extremist group)

Chile

Arica
NORTE GRANDE
— 20°S
Antofagasta
Copiapó
NORTE CHICO
La Serena
— 30°S
Valparaiso
SANTIAGO
CENTRAL CHILE
CENTRAL VALLEY
Concepción
Temuco
Valdivia
SOUTH
—40°S
Chiloé
FAR SOUTH
—50°S
Magellan
Straits
Tierra del
Fuego
500 mi / 800 km
Venezuela
Guyana
Colombia
Ecuador
Brazil
Peru
Bolivia
Paraguay
Chile
Argentina
Uruguay

1

SKETCH OF A LANDSCAPE WITH FIGURES

'That one may better know where Chile lies one should mark the two poles of the heavens, one the North pole-star, the which is a fixed star that is seen in Spain, and is the axis of the sky, and the other the South pole-star that is the axis of this new world, the which has no fixed star but at thirty degrees a constellation of four very beautiful stars in the form of a cross, whereby the sailors steer as in Europe by the North pole-star.'

– Padre Diego de Rosales (1535-1652)

Between the vast emptiness of the Pacific Ocean to the west and the massed peaks of the Andes to the east, the mainland of Chile stretches for 4,300 kilometres, north to south, along the western coast of South America. It is like a long twisted sash, or a battered sword hanging from the belt of the continent, with its blade aimed at the heart of Antarctica. A long sword, extending over 38 degrees of longitude, more than half the total length of the continent and more than a tenth of the whole of the earth's perimeter. This is as far as from New York to San Francisco, from Lisbon to Moscow, or from Norway to Nigeria.

With an average width of less than 160 kilometres (and nowhere much more), there are many places in Chile from which the Andes and the waters of the Pacific can be seen simultaneously. Thus, despite its great length, the total area of the country, excluding its Antarctic territory, is only some 756,000 square kilometres. The slice of Antarctica claimed by Chile is a triangle extending from its base at the 60° parallel to a point at the South Pole itself. This vast, if virtually uninhabited, territory covers another 1,250,000 square kilometres. (The Chilean claim, like all others, is frozen by the Antarctic Treaty. It also overlaps with both Argentine and British claims but, if included in full, Chile's total national territory would be larger than Mexico's.)

To the north, Chile has a border with Peru; to the east with both Bolivia and Argentina. However its real physical frontiers are the South Pacific, the Andes and, in the extreme south, the Drake Passage joining the Atlantic and Pacific Oceans. These great natural barriers isolate the country on both western and eastern flanks and in the south. Thus Chile has many of the characteristics of an island at the far edge of a continent and Chileans have developed the feeling of separateness and self-sufficiency that all islanders have.

In the north it is the Atacama Desert, stretching from the coastal strip to the Andes in a vast plateau of rock and sand and almost devoid of vegetation, which separates the country from the rest of the world. Only towards the end of the nineteenth century was the northern frontier pushed back to Arica as a result of the War of the Pacific between Chile on one side and Peru and Bolivia on the other. The causes of this war do not concern us at this point but their original source has always been latent in those vast northern deserts where the dull brown and grey shades, which are all that can be seen in full daylight, are transformed into a kaleidoscope of colours – yellow, violet, purple and red – when the slanting evening light falls on the hillsides. Land that seemed at first to be sterile now reveals itself as rich with minerals of all sorts. Those were the prizes for which men ventured into and explored the Chilean and Peruvian deserts, and for which they ultimately fought.

There are places in the Atacama Desert where no rain has ever been recorded. Most of the water which reaches it has to flow down the *quebradas* (ravines) which bring snow water from the mountains when the thaw comes. However, these are just occasional streams and there is only one more or less permanent river, the Loa, which joins the sea between Antofagasta and Iquique. Other streams, formed also by snow water or by the very infrequent rainfall in some areas, may run at times for considerable distances, only to disappear at last in the vast salt flats (*salares*). In this vast desert, the Norte Grande, there are only a few oases with underground water tables, which still serve as staging posts and provide the only cultivable land for a small farming population.[1]

[1] The most famous is the small town of San Pedro de Atacama, where the Spanish *conquistadores* stopped on their way through the desert. It is now an

There are three main physical features which run north to south. In the west, behind a narrow coastal strip, there is a broken range of hills with an average height of about 1,000 metres, but some rising to about 3,000 metres in the middle of the country (near Santiago). To the east of it is the second major feature, a much wider desert plateau. In northern Chile this is known as the *pampa*, but when the deserts finally come to an end and rainfall is higher, this hinterland becomes a long and fertile north/south valley, broken occasionally by transverse valleys bringing rivers, torrential at some seasons, down to the Pacific.

Further east again the mountain range of the Andes is the third longitudinal feature of the landscape. There are many peaks rising as high as 6,000 metres, some of which are active volcanoes; in total there are about 600 along the entire length of the Andes, and some even in the Antarctic region, of which forty-seven are active. Of the land area of Chile 80 per cent is mountainous and the major part of it is volcanic in origin.[2] Less than 20 per cent is suited to agriculture.

The highest peaks in the Andes are around 7,000 metres above sea level, namely Ojos del Salado, north of Copiapó, and Aconcagua just across the border with Argentina and a little north of Santiago. Heights decrease towards the south. In the skiing fields east of Santiago the mountains still reach 5,000-6,000 metres but there are few over 2,000 metres south of Temuco, which is roughly equidistant between Arica and Tierra del Fuego. From Temuco southwards, one of the loveliest regions of Chile has been created by glaciation or volcanic activity producing a series of beautiful lakes stretching for hundreds of kilometres down into Patagonia. This lake district is similar to that in Switzerland but on an even

---

important centre for pre-Colombian archaeology and unfortunately is becoming a major tourist destination.

[2] In some parts of Chile (La Ligua, not far north of Valparaiso, is one example), seismic shocks or tremors can be felt almost every day. More serious earthquakes occur unpredictably in one part or another but often with epicentres off-shore due to the meeting of the South American and Nazca plates. In the twentieth century, the worst were those near Valparaiso (1906) when 2,300 people died; in Chillán (1939) affecting all of the area between the Maule and Bío-Bío Rivers with 5,600 dead; in 1960 throughout the south but worst of all in Valdivia; and in Santiago and the Central Valley (1986), with only about a hundred fatalities but serious damage.

grander scale and less spoilt, even in our own age, by the works of man. Snow-capped mountains tower behind the greenest of pastures and orchards, forests full of splendid native trees, and lakes of all shapes and colours. The deep flowing rivers of the south do not die in summer like those further north but flow strongly all the year.

Further south again the coastal range of mountains descends into the Pacific and forms an immensely complex archipelago of islands which starts with the large island of Chiloé and continues 2,500 kilometres further to the Strait of Magellan and beyond, leading finally through a maze of channels and twisting fjords to Cape Horn. In much of Patagonia the Andes fall directly to the broken coast line and great glaciers join mountains and sea together, forming impossible barriers to movement by land. This wilderness of islands, fjords, rivers and cold rain forest is perhaps the least habitable part of the whole country, its stormy climate making it even less hospitable to humans than the northern deserts. Before it ends there are also two vast and impenetrable ice fields which stretch from the coast inland to the Andean watershed and separate the major part of the Chilean mainland from the windswept plains on the Magellan Strait. (The only land link is through Argentina.)

South of the Strait there is the sparsely populated and windswept island of Tierra del Fuego and hundreds of even more remote islands, splintered by the two oceans which meet around them. The continent finally ends on the 56° parallel at Cape Horn island, mountainous and battered by unrelenting storms. Until the Antarctic continent began to be explored in the last years of the nineteenth century, Cape Horn was the end of the known world – *Finis Terrae.*

Climate is another important factor in Chile's natural make-up. Until it peters out at Chiloé, the coastal range of mountains prevents damp marine air from crossing into the inland valleys where rainfall is therefore lower and temperatures are higher by day and cooler by night than on the coast. The barrier formed by the Andes has even more important effects. It insulates the country almost entirely from continental conditions and causes much higher rainfall and more snow on the western side. Another result of the topography is that average temperatures decrease gradually towards the south while rainfall increases sharply. Average annual rainfall in Iquique is 2.1mm; in Santiago 362mm.; in Valdivia

2,488.7mm.; and at Puerto Aysen, in Patagonia, 2,865 mm. At Puerto Edén, still further south, 4,000 mm. of rain can fall in a year.

However,the most important and probably best-known climatic factor is the Humboldt current, a powerful oceanic cold stream emerging in the extreme south and running northwards in a band about 100km. wide. This current lowers the temperature in coastal areas as far north as the Equator. Nowhere in Chile (or Peru) has a tropical climate equivalent to what is found at similar latitudes on the eastern side of the continent. The Humboldt current produces cold seas and cool coastal temperatures, and due to the juxtaposition with warmer air inland, it creates fogs known as *camanchaca* particularly on the coast in the more northerly parts of the country.

For human beings the best and most attractive part of Chile is the great central depression between the coastal range and the Andes which stretches for some 1,400 kilometres from Copiapó, where the desert ends, to Temuco. This beautiful and productive territory is the heartland of the country, the 'Central Valley', and contains the rich land which encouraged settlement from the earliest pre-Colombian times until today. From Copiapó to the Aconcagua River north of Santiago, it is still a transitional zone between the true deserts of the Norte Grande and the mediterranean belt with its rich soils and equable climate, cool and rainy in winter and warm in summer. Even this transitional zone (the Norte Chico) is relatively attractive and suited to human purposes, particularly in the increasingly frequent and well-watered valleys of the main rivers. However, the richest part of the Chilean heartland, between the Aconcagua and the Bío-Bío rivers, is the welcoming land which the *conquistadores* occupied after their arrival.[3] It eventually became the principal wheat-growing region for all colonial Spanish America and briefly for California and Australia as well. In more recent times, it has also been one of the most

[3] Until the end of the sixteenth century, when the frontier between colonial Chile and the Araucanian Indians was established on the Bío-Bío, there were a few settlements (known as the 'seven cities') further south as well. From then until the mid-nineteenth century, the Araucanian (or Mapuche) Indians preserved their territory and independence against all attempts to subdue them and the only Spanish or Chilean outposts were two precarious settlements at Castro (Chiloé) and Valdivia.

favoured parts of the world for cultivating all kinds of fruit and vegetables and some excellent wines. There are few temperate crops which cannot be grown to the highest standards in the Central Valley of Chile.

The extravagant contrasts and variations in Chile's geography are at least as striking as the range of natural conditions and landscapes which we find from Baja California to Alaska in North America. To travel through the deserts of the Norte Grande; the transitional zone of the Norte Chico; the fertile Central Valley; the frontier region of forests and farms south of the Bío Bío; the lake district further south again; the islands, fjords and glaciers of Patagonia; the plains of Magallanes and Tierra del Fuego; and the massive range of the Andes is to know a whole natural world within one country.

This long, narrow land was occupied by a variety of relatively primitive Indian peoples, some agriculturalists and others hunter gatherers or pastoralists, when the Inca invasion arrived in the fifteenth century. The first inhabitants of Chile have left little trace except in the extreme north where pre-Inca remains and artefacts have been preserved in the arid deserts, particularly mummified bodies and funerary objects in the tribal cemeteries. However most of these early cultures were overwhelmed and subjugated after 1470AD by the organised force of the Inca empire moving south from Cuzco in the Peruvian highlands. The Inca expansion spread as far as the Maule River 35°S, but was halted there by the resistance of the Mapuche peoples and their allies.

The Incas brought political and social organisation to Chile for the first time. However it had little time to take root, and only seventy years later their civilisation was in its turn swept aside by a new invasion originating from another continent and another kingdom – Spain. This is where Chile's recorded history begins.

According to the great Chilean poet Pablo Neruda: 'Chile has an extraordinary history because it was invented by a poet.' He was speaking of the first of a succession of poets inspired by the country, Alonso de Ercilla y Zuñiga, who came to this New World as a soldier, fought in the free-booting campaigns of the *conquistadores*, and in 1569 produced the first volume of his long and powerful epic poem about the Spanish struggle against the Mapuche, or Araucanians as the Spaniards called them. It was this poem, reprinted several times in the next sixty years, which gave Spain and the rest of Europe the very first news ever published about a conflict which was to continue intermittently for three hundred years. Alonso de Ercilla saw the Mapuche and the country they fought for from the view point of an invader: but, knowing them, he came to understand and admire their courage and recorded it memorably in *La Araucana*:

Chile fertíl provincia y señalada
En la región Antártica famosa,
De remotas naciones respetada.
Por fuerte, principal y poderosa:
La gente que produce es tan granada,
Tan soberbia, gallarda y belicosa
Que no ha sido por rey jamás regida
Ni a extranjero dominio sometida.[4]

Ercilla's overwhelming praise was not for the Spanish warriors but for their Araucanian foes; and other writers in later years, not least Neruda himself, have celebrated the fierce and noble qualities of the people who resisted the foreign invaders for so long. Many elements go into the making of national character, but Chile's was greatly influenced by admiration for the heroism of their Araucanian forbears. Indeed most Chileans must have both *conquistador* and Araucanian genes in their blood today.

But the bare facts of genetics, history and geography are not enough to define a country. It is also an idea in the mind for which we have to look to that country's native-born poets. Neruda himself has evoked it lyrically in many different ways. Of his southern homeland, on the edge of Araucanian territory, he writes:

> Under the volcanoes, beside the snow-capped mountains, among the huge lakes, the fragrant, the silent, the tangled Chilean forest.[...] This is a vertical world: a nation of birds, a plenitude of leaves.[...] Farther along, each tree stands away from its

[4] 'Chile my scene; a fertile land remote, Hard by the border of antarctic seas, Home of a stiff-necked people, bred to arms, Renowned in war, by neighbour nations feared; whole hot-distempered blood alike rebels. At rule domestic and at stranger yoke. No king among themselves they own, nor e'er Have bowed the knee to foreign conqueror.' (Translation by Walter Owen, Buenos Aires, 1945)

fellows.[...] They soar up over the carpet of the secretive forest, and the foliage of each has its own style, linear, bristling..., as if cut by shears moving in infinite ways.[...] High up red *copihues* dangle like drops from the magic forest's arteries. Anyone who hasn't been in the Chilean forest doesn't know this planet.[5]

And of the sea, his eternal obsession:

> The Pacific Ocean was overflowing the borders of the map. There was no place to put it. It was so large, wide and blue that it didn't fit anywhere. That's why it was left in front of my window.[6]

But not even Pablo Neruda expressed the Chilean exile's feeling for his country with more passion than José Antonio de Rojas. In the last years of Spanish colonial rule, de Rojas and other young Creole patriots began to think of Chile as an independent entity. Obliged to live in Spain but longing to return to Chile, de Rojas wrote to his friend Manuel de Salas:

> Friend, that is *the* country. I have always had this idea and every day what little I see here confirms it. As you yourself say, Chileans do not need to do more than *want* to be happy for them effectively to be so. They have nothing to desire – Nature lavishes everything with open arms in that most beautiful of kingdoms.[7]

It was an unconscious echo of words written more than two centuries earlier by the first Spaniard who felt himself to be a Chilean at heart, Pedro de Valdivia.

[5] Pablo Neruda, *Confieso Que He Vivido —Memorias*, translated by Hardie St Martin (London, 1977).

[6] Pablo Neruda, *The House in the Sand: Prose Poems*, translated by Dennis Maloney and Clark M. Zlotchew (Minneapolis, 1990).

[7] Quoted by Simon Collier, *Ideas and Politics of Chilean Independence, 1808– 1833* (Cambridge, 1967).

2

COLONY AND NATION (1540–1875)

> 'And let the merchants and other folk who wish to come and settle here be told to come. For this land is such that there is none better in all the world for living and residing in; this I say because it is flat, very healthy and pleasant; it has no more than four months of winter, and even then it is only when the moon is at quarter that it rains a day or two, and all the other days the sunshine is so fine that there is no need to draw near a fire. The summer is so temperate, with such delightful breezes, that a man can be out all day in the sun with no ill effects. It abounds in pastures and fields and in yielding every kind of livestock and plant imaginable; much fine wood for building houses and an infinity of fire wood for use in them, and mines very rich in gold, the whole land being full of it. And wherever men may wish to take land, there they will find the wherewithal to build and water, wood and grass for their beasts; so that it seems God made it on purpose to be able to hold all within the palm of His hand.'
>
> – Pedro de Valdivia, letter to Emperor Charles V, 4 September 1545

Pedro de Valdivia was the first European to establish a settlement in Chile. In February 1541 he reached the small hill known as Huelén beside the River Mapocho which seemed to offer him and his small band of followers a position capable of being defended against the Indians who were already harassing them. With the typical self-assurance of the Spanish *conquistadores*, Pedro de Valdivia called the place his capital and named it after the patron saint of Spain – Santiago del Nuevo Extremo. (He had indeed reached further south than any European, with the single exception of Fernando Magellan who in 1520 discovered the sea passage from the Atlantic to the Pacific Ocean.) The spot where Valdivia made his first camp on 12 February, the day of Santa Lucia, became known as the Cerro Santa Lucia. It is in the centre of what is now a great city and from there he wrote his report to the Emperor Charles V in Spain urging him to send settlers to populate this newest of Spanish territories in America.

Primitive settlement

There were, of course, earlier settlers. Since about 10,000 BC a succession of migratory groups had reached and moved southwards along the coastal strip of what is now northern Chile. The first who have been clearly identified were the Chinchorro people based around Arica whose culture flourished around 6000 BC but who have left little trace of their existence except the huge number of mummified bodies which have survived millennia in the totally dry desert environment. The Chinchorro were hunter gatherers, but after about 2000 BC their successors turned slowly to primitive agriculture and the domestication and herding of the native camelid animals – llamas, alpacas, vicuñas and guanacos.

Two of the outstanding cultures of the next period were the Atacameño in the northern *altiplano* (high plateau) and the Chango fishing culture on the coast. The Aymara, who also lived in the *altiplano* as herdsmen and still do, are related to the people of the powerful Tiwanaku empire based around Lake Titicaca (in modern Bolivia) who spread into huge areas of northern Chile from 300 AD reaching their highest level about 1300 AD. They developed new techniques of cultivation, such as the use of terracing and irrigation canals. In historical times the growing sophistication of these cultures led to trade and other contacts between the coast, the *altiplano* and the *sierra* (mountain) peoples. The Tiwanaku culture, and the Diaguitas who were primarily agricultural people in the valleys from Copiapó down to Santiago, also produced new designs in ceramic decoration, the striking use of colour (red, white and black), and more sophisticated textile production. They even learned the use of hallucogenic drugs for religious ritual and other purposes. From about 1100 AD well-established and largely autonomous settlements appear both at high altitudes and on the coast. The quality of ceramic and textile design become even better and *pukaras* (fortified settlements) are found in a number of the principal centres of population.

The greatest of the pre-Colombian civilizations which reached

Chile was that of the Incas. From the year 1470, at the height of their empire's power, they pushed down from modern Peru across the deserts extending their influence as far south as the River Maule, 180 kilometres south of Santiago. They too brought improved methods of farming but their arrival was more in the nature of a foreign invasion. The Incas built roads, imposed their authority wherever they went and maintained effective communications with their base, Cuzco. This meant that a relatively sophisticated form of centralised government reached Chile in the fifteenth century – not much later than in many parts of Europe and much earlier than in North America.

The Spanish conquest

The period of Inca dominance was short-lived. In 1532 the first and decisive trial of strength between the Spanish, led by Francisco Pizarro, and the Incas under a new leader, Atahualpa, took place at Cajamarca in the highlands of northern Peru. In a dramatic surprise attack, Pizarro's force of 150 men defeated Inca armies numbering 40,000 and possibly more. They captured Atahualpa whom they subsequently ransomed for a huge treasure but nevertheless murdered. Before long, however, rivalry and treachery also grew among the *conquistadores* and particularly between Pizarro and his brothers, and the original partner with whom Pizarro had embarked on the conquest of Peru, Diego de Almagro. It had long been understood and agreed by the Emperor Charles V that Pizarro would assume control of the first new territory to be won by the Spanish in South America, while Almagro was authorised to conquer more remote lands which he would govern independently in the name of the King.

As a result of the successes achieved in Peru, the Spaniards had grown rich on the gold and silver seized from the Incas, but these were not men to be quickly satisfied and return home with their fortunes. In July 1535 Almagro set out from Cuzco with a force of 570 Spanish cavalry and foot soldiers and accompanied by some 12,000 Inca troops and followers. They hoped to find another equally rich Peru beyond the deserts. By the following year Diego de Almagro, after moving south from oasis to oasis with his Inca guides, had reached the Central Valley of Chile but with terrible losses and without finding any evidence of the abundant gold which the guides had promised. Thousands of the Indians accompanying them had disappeared or died in the deserts. Almagro and the surviving Spaniards, less than 100 in all, returned disillusioned to Peru in 1537.

In 1540 Pedro de Valdivia resumed the drive south with a smaller force. Although opposed at times by Indians who now distrusted the Spanish interlopers, they finally reached the River Mapocho, at the point which was to become Santiago. Valdivia was an exceptional soldier who could use his sword or his pen with equal skill, and his appeal to the Emperor for reinforcements earned an effective response. The small group of pioneers was eventually joined by hopeful recruits arriving from Peru and Spain. With the exception of the priests who had come to spread the Catholic faith, nearly all were strongly motivated by hopes of making a quick fortune. Spanish America provided the sixteenth-century gambler with the same sort of golden prospect (and at somewhat better odds) as the lotteries of the late twentieth century. However, so far, Chile did not look like a good bet for Pedro de Valdivia or his followers. The one obvious exaggeration in his report to Charles V was the optimistic (but probably sincere) statement that this new country had 'mines very rich in gold, the whole land being full of it'. There was gold in some parts of the Andean foothills, and much further south as well, but no evidence exists that Valdivia knew specifically of the existence of any of the sources. At best he relied on the word of his Inca guides who knew what the Spaniards wanted and were very ready to promise it to their new masters.

Within seven months the Indians of the Mapocho valley had destroyed the first settlement, and the early years were a continual struggle to survive, but slowly Spanish strength increased and Valdivia, now Governor of Chile, started to push back the frontiers of this new outpost of the Spanish Empire. He looked to the north first and in 1544 founded the city of La Serena at the northern limit of the fertile Chilean heartland, 470 kilometres from Santiago. The first settlement of La Serena seems to have disappeared, but it was refounded by Francisco de Aguirre in 1549 and became a key point in the new colony with the critical task of keeping the route to Peru open. Aguirre therefore became the governor of all the territory between Choapa and the Atacama desert, and in the process of establishing Spanish control of the area he eventually brought a number of Mapuche Indians from well south of Santiago to work the land and the alluvial gold deposits that had been discovered in the rivers which watered it.[1]

This policy of moving conquered people *en masse* from one part of the territory to another, started by the Incas, was also widely adopted by the Spaniards. In the case of La Serena it was apparently necessary because the conquest of the hinterland, particularly the fertile Elqui valley where the Diaguita Indians were established, had decimated their numbers and reinforcements were needed simply to produce sufficient food for the survival of the remainder and of the Spanish garrison. The movement of populations was also a convenient means of destroying the tribal structure and the will of Indians still determined to resist Spanish authority. From an early stage in the conquest, the Spanish also introduced the *encomienda* system whereby all the Indians in a given area were forced to work the land or mines, virtually as serfs.

The Mapuche (Araucanians to the Spanish) were nevertheless to prove over the next three centuries that they were one group of people, and the only one in the New World, who were able to survive the impact of Europeans and European weapons. Until they faced the Mapuche, the Spaniards found that their technological advantages (firearms and the horse) enabled them to overcome any force which the indigenous American population could bring against them. The astonishing dominance of tiny bands of Spaniards, armed with terrifying weapons and mounted on horses (previously unknown in the continent), against vast armies of Inca soldiers had been demonstrated many times in Peru. Initially this held good for Pedro de Valdivia in Chile. Having established the northern communications of the new colony, he moved south in 1550 and founded another new 'city' at Concepción, 516 kilometres from Santiago on the Bío-Bío River. From now on Valdivia was confronted and bitterly resisted by the Mapuche, but despite their resistance, he pressed on to found other settlements, notably one which he named Valdivia

[1] Francisco de Aguirre also conquered a large part of what is now north-west Argentina, to the east of the Andes. He was a larger-than-life figure even among the extraordinary ranks of the *conquistadores*, not least for boasting that he had sired at least fifty children known to him (and no doubt more unknown). When brought to book by the Church and forced to recant, he argued that his service to God by producing *mestizo* children outweighed his sins.

after himself on the coast more than 800 kilometres south of Santiago. They were all called 'cities' and immediately authorised to establish *cabildos* (councils) to run their own affairs. The men who had fought in each of these little campaigns were usually rewarded with *encomiendas* and land grants (and if not given them, they seized them).

Valdivia's successors went even further south, founding settlements as far from Santiago as the island of Chiloé, but they eventually over-reached themselves. In the closing years of the century, a concerted Mapuche rebellion swept away the entire Spanish presence south of the Bío-Bío River. The first blow in the Mapuche's eventual reconquest of this huge area was struck in 1553. A Mapuche chief called Lautaro, who for a time had been Valdivia's servant and learned about Spanish military tactics from first-hand observation, emerged as leader of his own people and forged an alliance of the normally fragmented groups which was strong enough to defeat the Spaniards at the battle of Tucapel where Valdivia himself was killed.[2] Thereafter the victorious Mapuche advanced almost to Santiago but were finally defeated themselves by a force rallied by Francisco de Villagra. Lautaro, in his turn, was killed there.

Had it not been for Villagra's last-ditch victory, the Spanish colony in Chile would have disappeared. With Lautaro's death, however, the Mapuche moved south again and the Bío-Bío became the frontier for the next three centuries. The Spanish were able to hold out continuously only in Castro, on the far-away island of Chiloé. There was sporadic guerrilla warfare along this frontier and periodical Spanish efforts to reoccupy and pacify the territory to the south, with no lasting success until the sustained drive in the latter part of the nineteenth century to enforce the central government's authority by military means. The Mapuche remained a widely dispersed but independent people, harder to conquer precisely because they were more loosely bound together and

[2] One account says that the Mapuche poured liquid gold down Pedro de Valdivia's throat so that he should die in a way that symbolised the greed of all the *conquistadores*. Another early historian, Diego de Rosales, says that the Mapuche ate their enemy's heart. Undoubtedly these battles were fought with extreme brutality and cruelty on both sides. The admiration for Araucanian valour and even nobility expressed in the epic poem *La Araucana* by Alonso de Ercilla did not stop the Spaniards enslaving their prisoners – and vice versa.

thus more resilient. They had all the qualities needed to become expert guerrilla fighters. They were both adaptable and ingenious. While at first overawed by Spanish technical superiority, the Mapuche quickly became great horsemen themselves and learned how to use the hit-and-run raid and similar tactics against the better armed and organised but less flexible Spanish troops.

The colony

By the early seventeenth century, the Spanish population of Chile had grown from Pedro de Valdivia's band of 154 to perhaps 10,000. The Indian population, thought to have been possibly 1 million when the conquest began, had shrunk to about 500,000 and there were possibly as many as 40,000 *mestizos* (people of mixed blood). But the colony remained essentially military because of the need to campaign constantly against the Araucanians. There was also an intermittent threat from British and Dutch pirates attacking coastal settlements from the sea.[3] The so-called 'colonial period' of Chilean history supposedly begins in 1600 but the country was far from stable and, apart from the threat of hostile attack, economic development was frequently interrupted by crop failures and natural disasters such as earthquakes. Chile was the most remote and the poorest of all the Spanish dominions, and the Crown was obliged to make regular financial contributions to meet the cost of maintaining sufficiently strong forces on the frontier, i.e. on the Bío-Bío River in the south, to hold the Mapuches in check. It was the only colony in Spanish America which had to maintain a standing army for this purpose.

The basis of the Spanish system of colonisation was the *encomienda* and the *hacienda*. A successful Spanish commander would receive an *encomienda* applying to all the Indians in a defined area who would usually provide the labour to work the *hacienda* for the benefit of the *encomendero*. In theory *encomenderos* accepted obligations to Christianize and civilize their Indian 'wards'. In the eyes of the Spanish church and officialdom, this was adequate theological

[3] Francis Drake harassed the coast of Chile in 1578 and Castro (Chiloé) was actually occupied by the Dutchman, Baltazar de Cordes, in 1600. These were only the most successful of a much larger number of foreign incursions into Spain's 'private' ocean and empire.

and social justification for the system, but in practice the *encomienda* was usually treated simply as a licence to exploit Indian labour. Many Spanish churchmen in the Americas, such as Bartolomé de las Casas, and the civil authorities in Spain, campaigned strongly against the abuses perpetrated on the Indians but brutality was commonplace and even royal decrees to protect them were usually ignored. In effect the system of *encomienda* was often no better than slavery. The *conquistadores* had not come to the Americas to work but to enrich themselves by every available means. In Chile, particularly after the loss of territory in the south, this came increasingly to mean by farming *haciendas* with Indian labour.

As we have seen, the original indigenous population of Chile is estimated to have been as high as 1 million, which the conquest certainly reduced by about half, partly through war and labour exploitation but mainly as a result of epidemics of measles, smallpox and typhoid. Another important ethnic change came through the inter-breeding of the Spanish invaders with native women. Only one Spanish woman – his mistress Inés de Suárez – arrived with Pedro de Valdivia and many years were to pass before a significant number of other women were tempted to travel from Spain to this remotest of its colonies. Meanwhile the intermingling of the blood of the Spanish and the Indian races went on as fast as in most freshly conquered territories – and perhaps faster than in some.[4] The result was the emergence of the *mestizo* population which has been the preponderant racial element in Chile ever since. The number of pure-blooded Indians or pure-blooded Spaniards inevitably decreased proportionately as *mestizo* strains grew.

Other factors affecting population levels were the result of migration. Harsh working conditions, particularly in the mines in the north, not only killed many of the Indians but encouraged them to migrate to areas where they could not be captured and forced to work in the mines as slaves. In the seventeenth century much of the Aymara people in what is now Bolivia emigrated to the Chilean *altiplano* to avoid working in the great silver mine

[4] Nor was this simply the result of the invaders' need to reproduce, to build families in the new country or to satisfy sexual need. The process worked in both directions and the Indians, particularly the Mapuche, regarded Spanish women as the greatest prizes to be gained in the intermittent guerrilla warfare of the coming centuries.

of Potosí. Later a large number of Mapuches migrated to the pampas of Argentina to join in the hunting of wild cattle which was becoming profitable there even in the late seventeenth century.

The development of new ethnic patterns in the seventeenth and eighteenth centuries had political effects. The Indian and *mestizo* majorities tended to live, generation after generation, in rural *haciendas* which were usually ruled by the descendants of the original *encomenderos* or others of purely Spanish blood who had arrived more recently. In time these families formed a distinct landed class which dominated the economic and social life of the colony and felt it should have an increasing influence on the governors and other officials, all of whom were sent from Spain or from the Vice-Royalty of Lima to rule the colony. This imported ruling class were known as *peninsulares* (from the Iberian peninsula) and much mistrusted by the local landowners who, over time, found that their interests diverged from, or were in direct conflict with, those of the Spanish Crown and its administrators. Chile was also, in a sense, a colony of a colony since its government did not derive authority directly from the monarch in Madrid but indirectly through his Viceroy in Peru. Chile's fundamental importance for the Spanish Crown centred on the strategic need to defend the southern approaches to the New World against interlopers. When King Philip II learned that English, French and Dutch pirates were seeking to break into the Pacific through the back door of the Magellan Straits, or round Cape Horn, he responded by ordering the greatest Spanish navigator of the day, Pedro Sarmiento de Gamboa, to establish settlements at either end of the Straits.[5]

This preoccupation of the Crown in Spain was not by any means so overriding for the home-grown establishment in Chile. With the passage of time these landowners became more detached from their original mother country and felt more loyalty to the country of their birth. They reacted like all settler communities after a few generations and as the North American colonists were to do in their adopted country. In Chile they were known as *criollos*. As such, their preoccupations were more likely to be the protection of their estates from Indian attacks than keeping

[5] The story of this ill-fated attempt by Spain to prevent other countries from penetrating the Pacific is one of the strangest consequences of Drake's exploits.

foreigners out of the Pacific. They also objected to the inadequate supply of imported goods which they could only obtain from Spain under the strict mercantilist policy imposed from Madrid; and complained at the efforts of governors and peninsular officials to enforce Royal decrees intended to protect the Indians from exploitation. Despite these growing causes of dissatisfaction felt by the *criollo* landowners, there was little or no overt change throughout the seventeenth and eighteenth centuries. The Spanish Empire, like the Roman Empire before it, continued to exist and even to maintain a kind of momentum long after the original explosion of vitality and will which had created it. It took a series of momentous events outside Chile, indeed outside Latin America entirely, to start the chain reaction which brought profound change to the continent in the early nineteenth century.

By the end of the eighteenth century Chile was essentially a rural society and economy, but the relaxation under local pressure of restrictions on direct trade in European products had allowed some commercial development particularly in Santiago.[6] By 1780, Santiago's population had reached 25,000 and in the first decade of the nineteenth century it was a city of 34,000. The colonial system ensured that political and economic power was firmly concentrated in the hands of a small élite class and some of these people were now beginning to be intensely aware of events further afield. The successful rebellion of colonists against the British Crown in North America and the foundation of the United States as a new, free nation stimulated revolutionary thoughts in other parts of the world. The outbreak of the French Revolution added to the ferment of new ideas and a number of young South American *criollos* embraced them enthusiastically. The outstanding personality among these patriotic idealists was Francisco de Miranda, born and educated in Venezuela but drawn later to the United States and later resident for several years in England, where he absorbed the liberal ideas of the time. Miranda in his turn influenced the son of an Irish-born Viceroy of Peru and a Chilean mother, Bernardo O'Higgins Riquelme, who had been sent to England to complete

[6] Where trade was still prohibited by law, contraband boomed to the great advantage of European traders, Chilean consumers and often Spanish servants of the Crown. Given any encouragement by the local population, most European merchant venturers, or corsairs, preferred to trade as smugglers than to make their living more dangerously as pirates.

his education and met Miranda there. The majority of the Chilean aristocracy had only limited complaints about certain aspects of Spanish rule; there was no Boston Tea Party in Valparaiso. However a few men like O'Higgins were inspired with the ambition to rid their native countries of the increasingly moribund hand of Spain and, if necessary, to create an independent government in Chile.

Independence

In 1809 their opportunity arrived when Napoleon Bonaparte invaded Spain and replaced the Bourbon King Ferdinand VII with his own brother Joseph. It was a brutal demonstration of *realpolitik*. Spanish authority was shown up as weak even in Europe and on 18 September 1810 a group of prominent *criollos* set up an independent Junta in Santiago. The first intention of this group was simply to reject the authority of the Viceroy in Lima but to continue to recognise the King himself as a political symbol and the unifying link with Spain. However the movement towards independence gathered force with the appearance of a charismatic and ambitious military leader, José Miguel Carrera. He and his brothers rejected the continuing link with the Spanish Crown, proclaimed complete independence and introduced a new constitution. Faced with the certainty of an onslaught by the Royalist forces directed from Lima and despatched to suppress this revolt, the Carreras raised an army to confront the Royalists. At this point the young Bernardo O'Higgins came to the fore, but the patriot army in which he and the Carreras had the main commands was defeated by the Spanish Royalist forces at Rancagua in October 1814. The bulk of the patriot army and its leaders were forced to flee across the Andes to Mendoza, and Spanish authority was reasserted in Chile for the next three years.[7]

In Mendoza the Chilean patriots joined forces with others commanded by a successful Argentine-born leader, General José de San Martín, who had just completed the liberation of his country

[7] The Carreras were strongly encouraged in their pursuit of a fully independent Republic (with Carreras in control) by the US Consul, Joel Poinsett, who engaged himself actively in their cause. Other foreigners, notably British merchants living in Chile, fought in the patriot army under Bernardo O'Higgins.

from Spanish rule. O'Higgins was already close to San Martín through their membership of the so-called 'Lautaro Lodge' of Freemasons which the latter had founded in Buenos Aires. Under his leadership and with O'Higgins's support, the movement for independence in the south was developing a momentum which would prove too strong to be resisted by the Spanish. In the north of the continent Simón Bolivar had launched his final campaigns in Venezuela and New Granada. In 1817 the Argentine and Chilean forces, united under San Martín as the Army of the Andes, crossed the mountains into Chile at several different points (separated by about 500 miles) in a well-co-ordinated operation worthy of a Hannibal or a Napoleon, descended towards Santiago and defeated the Royalist army decisively in the battles of Chacabuco (1817) and Maipú (1818). In 18 February 1818 independence was proclaimed and Bernardo O'Higgins was appointed as Supreme Director of the new government of Chile. San Martín had first been offered this role by the *cabildo* in Santiago, but he wisely declined it. For O'Higgins it was to prove a poisoned chalice.

Deeply aware that there were still strong Royalist forces in Peru which might again be used against the patriots, O'Higgins concentrated first on organizing an expeditionary force to join San Martín in the liberation of Peru. For this, control of sea communications was vital and he enlisted the services of the Scottish admiral, Lord Cochrane, who had (probably unjustly) been dismissed from the Royal Navy and was now given command of the embryo Chilean Navy. Cochrane, an ingenious and daring naval leader, captured the heavily defended city and harbour of Valdivia, the last significant Spanish stronghold in southern Chile, in a brilliant amphibious attack in 1820. He then sailed north to cut out the *Esmeralda,* the flagship of the Royalist forces defending Callao and Lima, and thus establish Chilean control of the Pacific coast. This enabled San Martín's expeditionary force to maintain itself ashore near Lima and, by negotiation as much as military means, bring about the final liberation of Peru.

With Chilean independence secured, O'Higgins could turn to domestic problems. He had absorbed many of the ideas of the European Enlightenment but, like other Chilean leaders, sought to bring his reforms into effect by autocratic means without consensus. On one recorded occasion he exclaimed: 'If they will not

Bernardo O'Higgins.

Diego Portales.

become happy by their own efforts, they shall be made happy by force. By God! they *shall* be happy.'[8] Not all agreed and he soon found himself at odds with the landed oligarchs who had supported the fight for independence but were content to maintain the rest of the Spanish colonial system (now under *criollo* control) and had no interest in other reforms. O'Higgins became isolated and made the crucial error of threatening – unsuccessfully – to replace Ramón Freire, the commander of the Army based in Concepción, whereupon Freire started to march on Santiago. In 1823 O'Higgins resigned and left for Peru where he eventually died in lonely exile. He had served the country heroically in war, but many of his reforming ideas were anathema to the great majority of the *criollo* aristocracy.

Consolidation of the Republic

Some sort of constitutional settlement was needed quickly, but it was not attained for another ten years. The country was often close to anarchy as a succession of brief Presidencies, military rebellions, failed constitutions and chaotic political conflict continued throughout the 1820s. The efforts of liberal-minded reformers like Ramón Freire, with both federalist and anti-clerical ideas, were finally defeated in 1830. It was said of Freire and his liberal followers that they 'wished to build the Republic on the ruins of the colony', but this was not at all what the Conservative oligarchy or the church wanted. After a brief civil war in 1829-30, the Liberals were defeated and a determined Conservative statesman, Diego Portales, emerged to grasp the reins of power and by decisive action to restore orderly conditions which would allow both political and economic development and, above all, re-establish sound national finances. Portales was never President but served simultaneously as Minister of Interior, Foreign Affairs and War, and dominated the political scene till his death in June 1837.

Although others may have held the Presidency, Portales has the main credit for converting the chaotic Republic of the 1820s into an organized and stable state, albeit with autocratic

[8] Quoted by John Miers in *Travels in Chile and La Plata* (London, 1826), vol. II, pp. 36-7.

powers for the President. He chose able men from all walks of life, regardless of party, demanded high standards of efficiency and honesty and did not allow his policies to be frustrated by constitutional or legal obstacles. The achievement for which Diego Portales is most often remembered is as the moving spirit behind the Constitution of 1833, which lasted (with only minimal changes) till 1925. The 1833 Constitution was in effect an instrument which enabled the conservative landowners to control the country indefinitely. At the same time, while making no concessions whatever to the masses, it also provided tolerable government and stability for the whole country. It maintained the Roman Catholic faith as the state religion and, in Portales' own words, created governments able 'to set the citizens on the straight path of order and virtue'. The climate of peace and orderly government in Chile attracted foreign traders and investors so that the new state, despite its relative poverty, could begin to develop economically. Chile was also fortunate to attract outstanding men from other parts of Latin America, most notably the statesman, educationalist and jurist Andrés Bello. Born in Venezuela, he became the first Rector of the University of Chile and devoted much of his life to the intellectual development of the country. Artists, naturalists and scientists were among the many foreigners who arrived in Chile in the nineteenth century, including Charles Darwin, the French historian Claudio Gay and the Bavarian painter Johann Rugendas.

Against the benefits of political stability and good order which Portales imposed on Chile in the 1830s, there were economic disadvantages. Independence had its price, and the first example of it stemmed from the decision in 1811 to open Chilean ports to all friendly or neutral nations. Despite high import duties, this allowed low-priced imports from Europe and North America to eliminate or damage most Chilean manufacturing. All that survived were the most basic processes related to mining, grain and livestock production. According to one of Chile's greatest historians, Francisco Encina,

> What resulted in these years was not, as usually suggested, an intensification of international trade. Rather what occurred was an exploitation of the Chilean economy by foreign interests. They traded 60% of their goods for silver, gold or copper... avoiding the customs house.[...] Luxury goods went down in

> price while the prices of articles of primary necessity went up.[...] Between 1823 and 1830 some three or four thousand foreigners... sucked the blood from the Chilean economy... while 95% of the Chilean population had retrogressed to the life style of the last third of the 17th century.[9]

Encina's diatribe is an extreme statement of the protectionist philosophy put forward regularly in debates in all developing countries (including Chile) for the last century or more. For Chile at least, experience has in the end been much better than Encina's gloomy view suggests, but only after prolonged experiment.

Before the Republic was much older however, it had to withstand a new external threat deriving from the emergence of a Confederation of Peru and Bolivia created by Andrés de Santa Cruz, President of Bolivia. His rhetoric spoke of rebuilding the Inca Empire; this was fanciful but the combination of the two republics with their mineral resources posed an obvious threat to Chile. By 1837 the armies and fleets of the two sides confronted each other and war seemed imminent. Persuaded eventually that the Confederation could not win, Santa Cruz changed tactics and succeeded in subverting a group of Chilean officers, some of whom seized and shot Portales himself. The Chilean reaction was swift and decisive. Once it was seen that foreign agents had bought the traitors, the nation rallied and gave whole-hearted support to a military expedition under General Manuel Bulnes which invaded Peru, defeated Santa Cruz at Yungay and dissolved the Confederation. This would not be the last time that Chile, like other new and older countries, turned to armed force to resolve international problems. Forty years later it was once more at war with Bolivia and Peru, invaded Peru again and emerged from the War of the Pacific with the spoils of victory.

The economy

Those forty intervening years saw an intermittent but steady process of economic development in Chile itself. Successive Presidents were elected in accordance with the constitution and usually to

[9] Quoted and translated by Brian Loveman in *Chile: The Legacy of Hispanic Capitalism*, (Oxford University Press, New York, 1979), ch. 4.

the satisfaction of the oligarchy, and each handed over office peacefully to the next. As in most of Europe, the franchise excluded landless and illiterate citizens (i.e. the great majority) until the twentieth century. Two decades of Conservative presidents were followed by two of Liberal ones. Policies differed little, except in regard to the thorny question of the position and powers of the Catholic Church.[10]

Critics charge that this much-praised Chilean democratic tradition involved only the governing class and a small electorate, but it was certainly preferable to the chaotic civil wars and rule by military *caudillos* that occurred elsewhere in Latin America. Furthermore, this long period of internal political stability allowed extensive development of the rail, road and sea communications, which were vital links drawing this long, narrow country together into a unified whole. Chile was the first country in South America to pioneer steam navigation,[11] the first to build a railway and among the first to develop a telegraph and telephone system. The mining of silver and copper increased dramatically. Joint stock companies, banks and other institutions grew up to finance trade and economic growth. More than 2,000 schools were built, providing free basic education, and a soundly-based system of higher education started to develop under the aegis of the University of Chile.

From around the middle of the century new industries also got under way, usually by the conversion of old craft trades to modern factory systems. Copper smelting and grain milling were among the first such industries, followed by textiles and food processing. These were natural developments from the basic mining and agricultural output of the country. However, four out of every five Chileans still lived on the land very largely as *inquilinos* (tenants of land who paid mainly with their labour). The *inquilino* system had grown up, superseding the *encomienda*, but meeting the same need for a pool of cheap labour. Even when the landowner

[10] It has to be said that vote-rigging and various other kinds of intervention in the electoral process occurred throughout the nineteenth century, and sometimes in the twentieth. These were, however, no more blatant in Chile than elsewhere. Few European states, and fewer outside Europe, could boast of a better record.

[11] Cochrane brought the first steamship, the *Morning Star*, to Chile in 1818 as a personal venture, an example that did much to stimulate steam navigation.

operated the system humanely, the *inquilinos* remained at subsistence level with little hope of any improvement in their lives. The *hacienda* remained the basis of almost all agricultural production. It was organized, as a rule, as a self-sufficient community in which large numbers of illiterate, Indian and *mestizo* Chileans lived and died, generation after generation. Inefficient though the system was in modern terms, the landowners were successful at various times in exporting wheat, meat, hides, tallow etc. to markets throughout South America and further afield, notably to California during the gold rush there and later to Australia. But the *hacendados* were not merely interested in the commercial success of their estates. They saw themselves as a political and social aristocracy leading and controlling the country and naturally tending to equate the national interest with their own. The middle decades of the century saw much material progress in Chile but it hardly touched the *inquilinos* or the migrant labour force (*afuerinos*) in the Central Valley. The population of Santiago, Valparaiso and other provincial towns grew rapidly with the influx of impoverished peasants (*campesinos*) from the countryside. Many also migrated further north to work in the desert mining camps of the Norte Chico. New strikes of silver and copper provided work for a growing army of unskilled labourers, known as *rotos* (lit. 'ragged men').

For centuries , minerals had been mined throughout the country, but mainly in the northern deserts, by primitive methods. With the stimulus of new capital and techniques, production increased from 20,000 kilograms of silver and 2,725 tonnes of copper annually in the 1820s to 127,000 kilograms of silver and 45,600 tonnes of copper in the 1870s. (Only gold production decreased after independence, falling from 1,200 kilograms in the 1820s to about 270 kilograms in the 1870s.) A high proportion of the copper output was exported in locally smelted 'Chili bars' as they were known, and the national revenue depended crucially on these mineral exports. However, it was, a 'boom or bust' form of economic development and in the mid-1870s the long boom of the mid-Victorian era came to an end in the world at large, coinciding with the collapse of a bonanza in silver production from the Caracoles mine in Bolivia. This extreme volatility applied even more dramatically to another mining industry now beginning to develop, namely sodium nitrate production for use as fertilizers and explosives.

A significant amount of the capital and expertise which produced this economic growth came from Britain, still the work shop of the world. It also dominated Chile's overseas trade, taking between one and two thirds of Chile's exports and providing about half of its imports in most years between 1830 and 1875. Much of this trade was organised by import-export houses such as Antony Gibbs, Duncan Fox and Williamson Balfour. These firms and many others were first established in Valparaiso, which had become by far the most important port not only in Chile but also on the entire west coast of South America. According to an American writing of Valparaiso,

> Trade is practically controlled by Englishmen, all commercial transactions are calculated in pounds sterling, the English language is almost exclusively spoken upon the street and in the shops, an English paper is printed there, English goods are almost exclusively sold, and this city is no more than an English colony.[12]

This was a considerable exaggeration. The census of 1875 revealed that there were 4,109 British people (many Scottish and Irish), 4,033 Germans and 2,330 French in the country (other foreigners amounted to about 15,000, of whom 7,000 were Argentines). What is more, many of the foreigners, British included, lived in provincial mining centres like Copiapó. It is true, however, that among the British were a number of particularly prominent and successful entrepreneurs. Men with names such as Edwards, Lyon, Blest, Ross and Walker played leading parts in the development of many new activities. They and their families established powerful interests in mining, banking, shipping and milling but few played a significant political role. There were, of course, many other foreigners who played leading parts in the economic development of nineteenth-century Chile. For example, two audacious and dynamic North American engineers, William Wheelwright and Henry Meiggs, were responsible for crucial developments in ocean transport (Wheelwright was the moving spirit in establishing the British-financed Pacific Steam Navigation

[12] This was the view of W.E. Curtis expressed in *Capitals of Spanish America* (New York, 1888). It compares with Maria Graham who wrote in *Journal of a Residence in Chile* (London, 1824): 'English tailors, shoemakers, saddlers and innkeepers hang out their signs in every street; and the preponderance of the English language would make me fancy Valparaiso a coast town in Britain.'

Company in 1835), in telegraphy and above all in railway construction.

The leading role played by British enterprise and capital in nineteenth-century Chile was, of course, the result of Britain having emerged in the previous century as the pioneer of the industrial revolution, and after the Napoleonic wars as the world's leading maritime power. However, British pre-eminence in Chile was relatively short-lived: by the last quarter of the century both the United States and the newly united Germany were beginning to challenge Britain as economic power houses, investing and trading around the world.

Another reason why foreigners played a disproportionately prominent part in the Chilean economy was that the traditional interest of the leaders of Chilean society, including its ruling oligarchy, was agrarian. Many of them lived for much of the year on their estates and looked at everything from the point of view of the landowner. Furthermore the Chilean landowning class had been discouraged by Spanish policy during the colonial era from engaging in external trade or related activities. It took time for Chilean entrepreneurs or businessmen to emerge and compete successfully with the foreigners. The most notable exceptions were, perhaps surprisingly, in mining where Chileans such as José Tomás Urmaneta and José Ramon Ovalle had become hugely successful after many years of poverty and disappointment.

The state of the nation in 1875

The economic progress achieved in the long period of stability and order created under the Portalian system also encouraged a mood of national self-confidence and patriotism, at least in the urbanized parts of Chile. However, in the country as a whole life had changed little since independence. The *haciendas* and their population of *inquilinos* were virtually untouched by the new wealth created by the export boom of the mid-nineteenth century. But Santiago and Valparaiso had grown to be cities of, respectively, 130,000 and 100,000 people by 1875 and other towns such as Concepción and Copiapó, and even such market towns as Talca, somnolent in the wine-growing Central Valley, had become prosperous. The cities could afford to build fine theatres, avenues and squares, to put up statues to national heroes such as O'Higgins and Portales, and to introduce trams, gas lighting and other amenities. The rich land owners built themselves grand town houses, often in French architectural styles, where they spent their winters. Beside them a new urban middle class of Chileans established itself and began to press for its own voice in government as well as in the national economy.

In the meantime, the patriotism and national will of the Chilean people was about to be put to another test in the War of the Pacific which started in 1879.

3

A MODEL REPUBLIC (1875-1920)

> 'Chile has for several years won the reputation of the model republic of South America. She has been a law-abiding and peace-loving community, allowing her people the enjoyment of all wholesome liberty, and so conducting her administration and ruling her finance as to be able in the most difficult times to fulfil her engagements, to ensure order and prosperity at home and maintain her credit abroad. It is only natural to look upon her wise conduct throughout the past as a pledge of her equally prudent and exemplary behaviour for the future.'
>
> – *The Times*, London, 22 April 1880

The Times' correspondent sent back a series of long reports from South America at the time when Chile's success in the War of the Pacific seemed almost certain and the major powers wanted to encourage her to be magnanimous in victory. Not all the views expressed by *The Times* were so fulsome in praise for 'the model republic',[1] but the writer certainly intended to pay Chileans a compliment when he spoke of them as 'the English of South America'. Whether or not his comparison of the two peoples was accurate, his high opinion of Chile in 1880 was supported by some clear similarities. Both were orderly and stable countries governed by a political class made up mainly of landowners and entrepreneurs which was beginning to be leavened by the middle class – professional men and leading figures from commerce and industry who had no stake in land itself. Both political systems were supposedly democratic while the franchise excluded a large part of the population. There were two dominant political

[1] *The Times* did not invent the phrase. As long before as 5 June 1858, the newspaper *El Copiapino* wrote: 'Everyone is shouting that Chile is the model republic of South America. What on earth can the others be like?'

Chile's territorial expansion in the 19th century.

tendencies, conservative and liberal which had shared power, usually amicably, for half a century and whose political views differed only marginally. In both countries the aristocratic and commercial élites, when forced to make concessions to the classes below them, had learned the art of conceding just enough in the way of reform to satisfy immediate pressure – but not an inch more.

Perhaps the similarities between Britain and Chile do not go far beyond these political coincidences. According to another commentator (Otto von Bismarck), Chileans were 'the Prussians of South America'. Here again the comparison cannot be taken too far. The essential point was not so much that Chile had absorbed or acquired a few European characteristics, as that her political system and financial status were admired in Europe and North America. However it was still evolving as a nation-state and would continue to change in many respects throughout the century while remaining a country defined first and foremost by its Hispanic origin, blood and tradition.[2]

Another reason for Chile's good standing in European eyes in 1880 was that it had not often succumbed to the general Latin American weakness for military coups and *caudillos.* Most of its fellow republics had suffered under eccentric, usually autocratic leaders, whose rule usually ended in revolutions, civil wars and sometimes total anarchy. One reason for the stability which Chile seemed to enjoy was its simpler ethnic structure. With the important exception of the Mapuche who maintained their independent existence south of the Bío Bío, the indigenous Indian population had been assimilated for many years with Spanish stock so that there were only two elements in the racial mixture: whites and *mestizos*. Chile thus escaped the social and political problems caused by the more complex racial structures found elsewhere in Latin America. This two-tier population also inhabited a reasonably compact block of territory stretching from the southern limit of the Atacama Desert to the 'frontier', the Bío-Bío River. If we ignore the huge region south of the frontier, the Chile of the

[2] One of the strongest of the 'European' genes in the Chilean bloodstream originated from Spain but was not strictly Hispanic. From the late seventeenth century up to and beyond independence, there was strong immigration from the Spanish Basque region, and Basque families (Larrain, Errázuriz, Carrera, Toro, Irarrázaval *et al.*) were prominent in the so-called 'Basque-Castilian' aristocracy which had dominated the country since then.

1870s was only one third the size of the country it would grow to be before the end of the century.

The nitrate era

Economic growth in Europe and North America in the nineteenth century produced periodical surges in international demand for copper and sodium nitrate, which led in turn to increases in the population of the scattered inhabited centres in the northern deserts. As the mineral deposits were worked out or became uneconomic, the workforce of *rotos* and their families moved on. Today the desert is littered with the ruins of long-abandoned mining centres. At the other end of the country a few small and scattered settlements, made up largely of immigrants, were establishing themselves in the areas beyond the Mapuche territory, in the lake district north of Puerto Montt and in the far south on the Magellan Straits. But these centres of fresh immigration in the south, made up mostly of peasant farmers from Germany and other parts of Central Europe around the lakes, or of English and Scottish shepherds and Yugoslav labourers on the sheep stations in the flat plains of Magallanes, were not yet sufficiently large to receive much attention from the government in Santiago. The rate of immigration to Chile was no more than a trickle compared to the influx into Argentina and many other parts of South America.

The silver and copper mines of the Norte Chico had been the motor of Chile's economic growth since early in the nineteenth century. In the latter part of the century the discovery of new deposits of sodium nitrate, combined with the rapid expansion of Northern Hemisphere agriculture, led to a new mining boom which in turn caused a major conflagration and changed Chile and the Chilean people both physically and psychologically. From 1830 small quantities of nitrate of soda were being exported to the United States and European markets for use as fertilizer or explosives. As Peruvian guano deposits began to be exhausted in the 1860s and '70s, new and rich nitrate fields were discovered beyond Chile's frontier in the Peruvian province of Tarapacá and the Bolivian province of Antofagasta. These arid and almost uninhabited desert provinces stretched for more than 1,200 kilometres between Arica and Copiapó, but only a small part of the nitrate deposits were in Chilean territory. The Chilean Constitution of

1822 described the country's northern border simply as 'the Atacama Desert', but no-one had seen any great need to define this precisely until it seemed likely that nitrate would replace guano as the principal source of fertilizer for European and North American farms and was potentially of great value.

After years of claim, counter-claim and frustrated negotiation, Bolivia and Chile reached a compromise embodied in a Treaty of 1866, which established their frontier at 24° South (just south of modern Antofagasta) but also provided that between latitudes 23° and 25° taxes on mineral exports should be shared equally between them. It was a historic agreement for both countries but hardly a wise one from the Bolivian point of view since Chile, with larger capital resources, a more mobile labour force and access to sea communications, was already in a better position than Bolivia to exploit the new nitrate fields and would continue to have the advantage.

Once the Treaty was signed, two Chilean pioneers of the nitrate industry, José Santos Ossa and Francisco Puelma, secured a concession from the Bolivian government to exploit nitrate deposits in what was undoubtedly Bolivian territory at Salar del Carmen. Other nitrate discoveries added to the attraction of the area for Chilean and foreign capital, much of the foreign interest being from British enterprises, initially Antony Gibbs & Company. Agustín Edwards, whose Welsh father had arrived in Chile as early as 1807 and who had already made a large fortune, was the principal Chilean investor. More Chilean labourers flocked north seeking work in the nitrate *oficinas* and, by the mid-1870s 95 per cent of the population of the Antofagasta area were not Bolivians but Chileans. There were another 10,000 Chileans still further north in Tarapacá.

In 1872 the Bolivian dictator, Mariano Melgarejo, who had granted all these concessions, died and the Congress annulled them. Chile protested strongly and, after more lengthy negotiations, Chilean mining rights (now held by a single nitrate and railway company, the *Compañia de Salitres y Ferrocarríl de Antofagasta*) were reconfirmed in a new Treaty in 1874. This also set the common boundary at 24° South and reduced Chile's claim to receipts from the shared zone between 23° and 25° South, but guaranteed that for twenty-five years Bolivia would not raise taxes on Chilean exports. Meanwhile Bolivia and Peru had sought to protect themselves against the threat posed by the rapid rise in Chilean activity in their desert provinces by concluding a secret defensive treaty in 1873 guaranteeing their respective sovereignty against external attack, i.e. against Chile. This rapidly became known in Santiago, although it was never publicly acknowledged by the parties, and the existence of the arrangement overhung all subsequent negotiations.

The War of the Pacific

A potentially dangerous situation came to a head in 1878 when a new Bolivian government imposed a heavy tax on exported nitrate. This was tempting fate since it was clearly in contravention of the 1874 Treaty. For good measure, Bolivia sought to impose the tax with retrospective effect to the date of the Treaty. At a stroke, the Chilean company saw its competitive position *vis à vis* Peruvian nitrate swept away. The shareholders, including some leading Chilean politicians, stirred up popular feeling in Santiago against this unilateral Bolivian action which so directly threatened Chile's national interests. The President, José Anibal Pinto, knew that Chile was ill-prepared for war but was persuaded to demand that Bolivia submit the matter to arbitration with the threat that Chile would otherwise resort to force. The Bolivian President, bearing in mind the 'secret' Treaty with Peru, refused arbitration, cancelled the company's concession and ordered that its assets be auctioned in Antofagasta to pay the overdue tax. On the day of the auction, 14 February 1879, two Chilean warships, the *Cochrane* and the *O'Higgins*, sailed in to land troops at Antofagasta and take control of the port and all the Bolivian coast.[3]

Bolivia found itself incapable of resisting this Chilean thrust by military means and by April had abandoned all the inland mining centres as well as the coastal strip south of the 23° parallel. Peru, already nearly bankrupt as a result of excessive borrowing and the effects of general economic depression in the late 1870s,

[3] The general manager of the Chilean company was an Englishman, George Hicks, who refused to accept the Bolivian decision. He took refuge in one of the Chilean warships in Antofagasta before he could be arrested. It was typical of the Chilean Navy that the two ships used in this operation should have British names.

could not honour its treaty obligation to come to the aid of Bolivia. The Chilean government's financial position and military readiness was little better than that of Bolivia and Peru but it at least had the advantages of greater national cohesion and self-confidence. The Peruvian President, Manuel Prado, sent an emissary to Chile to try to mediate in the dispute but when he admitted that his government could not declare itself neutral in the Chilean-Bolivian conflict, President Pinto found himself under irresistible pressure from inflamed public opinion in Chile to declare war on both countries.

The first phase of the war was fought for command of the sea, the only practical means of communication over the huge distances involved. Chile's naval forces were inferior to the best of Peru's warships, particularly its two iron-clad vessels, the *Huáscar* and the *Independencia,* but they were otherwise equally matched. The Chilean vessels *Covadonga* and *Esmeralda* blockaded the Peruvian port of Iquique from the beginning of hostilities and it was there, on 21 May 1879, that the first major naval action took place. The Peruvian warship, *Independencia*, ran aground while pursuing the *Covadonga* and was forced to surrender. The *Esmeralda*, a wooden frigate, was overwhelmed and sunk by the *Huáscar* but its commander, Capitán Arturo Prat, rammed his opponent and led a boarding party. Prat's hopeless gesture failed but did so with such gallantry (Prat died on the *Huáscar*'s deck) that Chileans regard this unsuccessful encounter as equivalent to a great victory.[4] Five months later the *Huáscar* was captured and the Peruvian Admiral Grau killed in the Battle of Angamos. Thereafter the Chileans had effective control of the sea routes which they needed in order to move their army towards the Peruvian capital Lima.

A Chilean expeditionary force of 12,000 troops then moved into Tarapacá and, after a bloody campaign in May and June 1880, occupied Arica and Tacna. The *Morro* of Arica, a heavily fortified headland overlooking the town, was only captured after a desperately brave defence by the Peruvian garrison of 2,000

[4] There is a monument to Arturo Prat, or a street of that name, in almost every Chilean town. Although he achieved no other military success, Prat is revered by Chileans as much as Nelson by the British and George Washington by Americans. The *Huáscar* is still kept open to the public at the Chilean naval base of Talcahuano.

and a bayonet charge uphill by the Chilean infantry. (The Chilean Army was largely recruited from the tough mining labour force of *rotos*, who made first-class fighting troops.) This was the culmination of a series of engagements in which the Peruvians were pushed out of their southern desert provinces. Chilean public opinion, fired up by these clear-cut if costly victories, clamoured for a further demonstration of their country's power and the government ordered a sea-borne expeditionary force of 26,000 men under General Manuel Baquedano to move against Lima. After two fierce battles in January 1881, this Chilean army occupied the city while the Peruvians had to resort to guerrilla war in the mountains. In effect Chile had won the War of the Pacific decisively on both land and sea and was in a position to lay down its own terms for peace.

By the Treaty of Ancón in 1883, Peru was forced to cede to Chile the whole of the province of Tarapacá outright. The provincial frontier towns of Tacna and Arica (on either side of what is now the international frontier) were to be administered by Chile for a period of ten years, after which their permanent status would be decided by plebiscite. The Peruvian President who signed this treaty had in effect been imposed on his country by Chile and was in no position to mitigate these tough peace terms. Bolivia had dropped out of the war by 1880 and withdrawn entirely to the landlocked Andean *altiplano*; it signed a separate truce with Chile in 1884, leaving the whole of the Atacama and Antofagasta province in Chilean hands. A final Peace Treaty was concluded in 1904, but the dispute continues to this day because Bolivia remains determined to regain access to the Pacific through territory under its own control, a requirement originally laid down by Simón Bolívar when he established Bolivia as an independent state with its Pacific port of Cobija.

The effects of victory

Chile naturally derived huge benefits from its victory. The national territory was increased by a third and the mineral wealth of Tarapacá and Antofagasta (the Norte Grande) more than compensated for the declining returns on the exploitation of copper, silver and iron ore in the Norte Chico. This new nitrate wealth provided over 50 per cent of Chile's revenue for many years to come and was the dominant element in the national economy for the next half-century. Perhaps even more important, success in war against their more numerous neighbours enhanced Chile's international standing and gave Chileans a somewhat arrogant belief in their racial and cultural superiority. As one foreign historian has put it, 'After the War of the Pacific, Chileans of all classes believed more than ever in their national destiny.'[5] However, it was a victory won at a price. Their loss of the huge mineral resources of the northern deserts has left bitter resentment in Peru and Bolivia to this day. It can also be argued that having easy riches tempted Chileans to abandon their previous habits of hard work and rest on their laurels enjoying the fruits of victory.

The world economic recession of the mid-1870s had hit Chile hard. The country was in very poor condition to go to war in 1879 and was only saved by the fact that its opponents and their armed forces were in even worse plight. The economic effect of the war was felt almost immediately in increased demand for foodstuffs, leather, wine etc., to feed the Army which gave a strong stimulus to production in the Central Valley and the south. Coastal shipping expanded rapidly. According to SOFOFA, the *Sociedad de Fomento Fabril* (Society for Manufacturing Development) founded in 1883, more new factories were established between 1880 and 1889 than had existed in Chile before the war. Thereafter the flow of capital investment into the nitrate industry and of tax revenues from nitrates into the Treasury, helped to re-invigorate the economy powerfully in many areas. Agriculture and stock rearing were stimulated although the archaic (and, to modern minds, indefensible) *hacienda* system continued unchanged. Demand for social and political change was also stimulated. After the War of the Pacific, an urban proletariat and a professional and commercial middle class began to make itself heard. Eventually these new classes would change, if never quite revolutionise, the structure of Chilean society and politics.

Chile's prospects looked splendid in the aftermath of her remarkable victory, but the seeds of future problems were already present. One source of economic difficulty was the extreme volatility of

[5] Brian Loveman, *Chile: The Legacy of Hispanic Capitalism.*

the demand for nitrate from Europe and North America. Thus the industry, which now dominated the economy to an unhealthy degree, and provided the lion's share of both national revenue and export income, was at the mercy of the rise and fall of nitrate prices. This made the government's revenue from nitrate equally unpredictable. It also produced unstable conditions among the large population of labourers in the nitrate *oficinas.* The managements would contract new labour or lay off workers with equal rapidity according to short-term movement in sales or price. Nitrate production was based on the pick and shovel, and the Chilean *rotos* who wielded them were learning from bitter experience that their interests could conflict sharply with those of the government and the companies. Volatility in a key industry was also aggravated by the rise in inflation from the moment (1878) when Chile left the gold standard. Until then the peso's value had been stable. Now the age of inflation had arrived and those most vulnerable to it were wage-earners.

However, these emerging problems were not the most obvious issues confronting the country in the 1880s. For the government the major issue at the time seemed to be how best to spend the nitrate wealth and whether to allow private owners to control the industry, including its essential transportation network and infrastructure. After careful study, the Liberal President, Domingo Santa María, decided to allow the nitrate fields to continue to be exploited by private enterprise and to take the government's share of the benefit by means of export taxes. 'Let the gringos work the nitrate freely,' he said. 'I shall be waiting for them at the door.' This decision allowed foreign investors, notably John Thomas North, a self-made Yorkshire entrepreneur working with influential Chilean partners, to gain control of the greater part of Chile's principal industry. North became known as the 'Nitrate King', but the dominant position he had acquired came increasingly under criticism throughout the 1880s and was an important factor in the political crisis which exploded into civil war in 1891.

The arrival of Balmaceda

As in other parts of the world, the main ideological theme which held Liberals together and differentiated their thinking from that of the Conservative Party was anti-clericalism. Santa María finally decided in 1884 to force legislation through Congress to establish civil marriage, registration of births and secular cemeteries, to reduce the Church's role in the educational system and, incidentally, to widen the franchise. Presidents were usually able to use their executive powers to put their policies through and the main organiser of this attack on the traditional position of the Catholic Church was José Manuel Balmaceda, then Minister of the Interior, who was to be Santa María's chosen successor. Balmaceda thus incurred the deep enmity of the Church and its Conservative supporters and allies, and from the beginning of his Presidency in 1886 was opposed by them in Congress. As leading Liberal politicians, both Santa María and Balmaceda had long been critics of the dominant powers of the President under the 1833 Constitution but, being themselves autocratic by nature, both used those powers as freely as other Presidents when they reached the Moneda Palace.

Balmaceda's first Ministry embraced a wide range of political opinion, not only representatives of his own group of the Liberal Party, and was intended to be conciliatory. To placate the Conservative opposition he also moved quickly to restore relations with the Holy See and to have an agreed candidate installed as Archbishop of Santiago. However, he was stubbornly single-minded in pursuing his personal programme for developing Chile as a significant power in South America, founded on a more diverse economic base and with a better-educated population. Being a brilliant orator and a forward-looking political leader, Balmaceda inevitably attracted criticism from lesser men, and his honeymoon with Congress lasted little more than a year.

Instead of using the new nitrate income to return to the gold standard and rid the country of the creeping sickness of inflation, as most of the Conservatives urged, Balmaceda launched a programme of expensive public works, particularly for railway and port construction, modernisation of the armed forces, and major improvements of the state educational system. This brought notable benefits to the country, but opposition to it persisted and the political in-fighting and personal animosities in Congress grew worse. The unity and coherence of the Liberal Party, Balmaceda's original power-base, was breaking up and being replaced by factions jockeying for personal power or advantage. By 1890 the Congressional opposition to Balmaceda was much more numerous and had developed a determination to detach the political parties entirely from the President and to subordinate the executive to the legislature. The conflict rumbled on throughout 1890 and came to a head in a critical dispute with North's Nitrate Railway Company when Balmaceda cancelled its monopoly and entered into negotiation with other interests for a competitive railway to be constructed. North's allies in Congress found this conflict a convenient opportunity to increase pressure on Balmaceda. He in turn became increasingly cavalier in his treatment of Congress.

The civil war of 1891

As the political crisis in Congress deepened, serious discontent broke out in the nitrate fields. Another cyclical downturn led to unemployment while the continuing price inflation slashed the purchasing power of those who still had work. A new problem emerged in the form of a wave of strikes in the port of Iquique, which spread rapidly, involving looting and machine wrecking in many of the nitrate *oficinas*, and ultimately reached Valparaiso and Santiago. Although Balmaceda later agreed to use force to restore order, the violence and resulting casualties added to the atmosphere of crisis. The strike had its origins in the bad working conditions in the north, but it had effects in the capital as well. Balmaceda's opponents in Congress then proceeded to use their main weapon – refusal to authorise the collection of tax revenue – against him. On 1 January 1891 he decreed – illegally – that the previous year's legislation should continue in effect. Having failed to persuade the Army Commander-in-Chief to give it his support, the Congress then called on the Navy, under the command of Admiral Jorge Montt, to resist the President's action. Civil war then broke out: with Congressional leaders on board, the fleet sailed to occupy Iquique and take control of the crucial nitrate export trade and revenue.

Balmaceda approved immediate pay increases for the Army and so assured their loyalty, but for several months there was a stalemate in the conflict. The two sides were separated by the Atacama Desert, since the President had no fleet to transport his army to the north and the Congress had no military force to bring south. However, in time, a new army was raised from the ranks of the miners and nitrate and port workers[6] and transported south to confront and defeat the poorly-equipped National Army in bloody battles at Concon and Placilla on the coast north of Valparaiso. Balmaceda took refuge in the Argentine Embassy in Santiago and on 19 September shot himself. Admiral Jorge Montt was elected as the new President and a new era of Chilean political history began. For the next thirty-five years the Congress and not the President would have the upper hand.

The Parliamentary Republic

As Balmaceda himself said in the political testament he wrote before his death, this change in the balance of power within the Chilean political system replaced the authoritarian but efficient form of government devised by Diego Portales with 'a bastard form of parliamentary government'. Without needing to amend the Constitution of 1833, Congress was able to control every President elected from 1891 to 1920. However, it was not a parliamentary system of the British type in which the Ministry could rely on a majority in parliament. The Chilean 'Parliamentary Republic' operated on the basis of a Congressional resolution that it had 'the right to censure ministers and ministries and that in the event of censure these would have to abandon their posts'.[7] It became very difficult for the President to do more than keep a ministry in being, and since it was rare for one to last longer than a few months, the pursuit of long-term aims over a period of time by coherent policy became virtually impossible. Congressmen devoted themselves to factional politics and extracting benefits for themselves and their friends as the price of support for the President. This form of parliamentary government was almost bound to lead to political stalemate since the Constitution

[6] This militia was equipped with modern Mannlicher repeating rifles bought with the government's nitrate taxes and trained by a Prussian officer, Emil Körner, who had been contracted to modernise the training of the Army, but decided to support Congress rather than the President. Körner's work to modernise the regular Army in other ways had not had time to produce results but eventually turned it into what was seen as the only Prussian army outside Europe. To this day it uses *pickelhaube* helmets and the goose-step.

[7] Robert J. Alexander, *The Tragedy of Chile* (Greenwood Press, Westport, CT, 1978).

of 1833 did not allow the President the possibility of appealing to the electorate over the heads of Congress.

The ultimate repository of power during the Parliamentary Republic remained, as for the whole of Chile's first century of independent existence, the landed oligarchy. New parties – notably the *Partido Radical*, a break-away group of anti-clerical Liberals representing white-collar workers, small merchants and other middle-class elements, and the *Partido Democrático* which sought to represent the growing class of urban workers, artisans, miners, and the like – had emerged by this time but still carried little weight politically. Most of Chile remained rural and most members of Congress represented local political interests and derived their power and financial support from the local landowners who were still able to deliver the votes of all their *inquilinos* and other dependants and effectively rig elections.

While the Chilean parliamentary system failed to respond to the obvious need for political and economic reform, the economy expanded rapidly as a result of the nitrate boom. Important public works and commercial development continued to be financed by this income (and by the foreign loans Chile could command because of its good financial reputation). But little of the nitrate wealth was used to improve the lot of the increasingly large urban working class, and certainly not to benefit the *campesinos*. By the turn of the century Valparaiso had a population of 120,000 and Santiago more than 250,000. Over 40 per cent of the total population lived in towns and cities and this fundamental demographic change underlay the dominant national issue beginning to emerge: the so-called 'social question'. This was starkly illustrated by the contrast between the miserable conditions in which the majority of Chileans lived (and could now clearly be seen to live in the cities) and the obvious luxury enjoyed by a few. While this 'social question' was more and more inescapable and indeed was widely debated by many thoughtful Chileans, the political system totally failed to find practical solutions to it. The replacement of a strong Presidency by sterile impasse between executive and legislature made it all but impossible for any government to respond to the needs of the great majority of the people.

In the first years of the new century serious strikes took place in the main centres of the mining industry and ports such as Iquique, Antofagasta and Valparaiso. A variety of working-class organizations began to appear to support the demands of miners and railway and port workers in particular. The first political party representing workers' interests, the *Partido Democrático*, was replaced by the *Partido Obrero Socialista* (POS) in 1912 and gathered some strength. Its founder, Luis Recabarren, had been elected to Congress in 1906 representing the *Partido Democrático* but had not been allowed to take his seat. Recabarren became a dominant figure in left-wing politics and played a major part also in the development of the first trade union organisation, the *Federación Obrera de Chile* (FOCh), after 1909. Anarchist unions, self-help societies and many other workers' organisations were formed in this period to press by more or less militant means (but chiefly the general strike) for improvements in wages and working conditions.

The outbreak of the World War in 1914 precipitated an immediate economic crisis which added momentum to this militant labour movement, and the revolution in Russia three years later increased it. As the post-war era began, there was already a potentially explosive combination of circumstances in Chile. On the one hand the political system had not been able, indeed had hardly tried, to respond to the demands of the majority of Chileans. The political impasse produced by parliamentary dominance over the executive after 1891 had made matters worse. On the other hand, an increasingly militant labour movement had grown up to articulate the demands of workers. This was based mainly in the nitrate fields of the Norte Grande to which a highly mobile and rootless labour force had been drawn from other parts of the country (and outside it). But there was also explosive potential in the ports and in the tenements of Santiago.

The southern frontier

Chile's southern frontier at the time of independence had been declared to be at the tip of Cape Horn. This was vague as an assertion of sovereignty and Bernardo O'Higgins, writing from his exile in Peru in 1830, was the first to urge the government to act decisively to assert the country's claims in the south. However, the only Chilean settlements south of Concepción at that time were the remaining colonial 'cities' of Valdivia, Osorno and Castro (on the island of Chiloé) which the Spanish Crown had contrived to maintain even after all others south of the Bío-Bío River had been wiped out by the Araucanian rebellion at the end of the sixteenth century. A distance of 2,700 kilometres, from Concepción to the Magellan Straits, was inhabited only by the Mapuche peoples, thinly spread as far as Chiloé and, further south, by smaller numbers of Tehuelche, Ona, Yaghan and Alacalufe Indians. These indigenous inhabitants of Patagonia had continued to maintain their primitive way of life in scattered groups. In 1830 they were the only inhabitants of one-third of the total landmass of mainland Chile.[8]

In the 1820s and 1830s the British survey vessel *Beagle* (in which Charles Darwin sailed on one of her voyages) had carefully charted the southern fjords and canals. In the aftermath of Chile's successful campaign in the 1830s against the Peruvian-Bolivian Confederation, President Bulnes ordered a colonising expedition to be sent by sea from Chiloé to establish a permanent presence on the Magellan Straits. Although discussed before, this had become urgent after the introduction of a regular steamship service to the Pacific coast of America through the Magellan Straits in 1840. A demonstration of ownership was also necessary in view of Argentine claims in Patagonia; also the British had established a permanent colony in the Falkland Islands and France was thought to be contemplating a similar move on the mainland. The sea passages round Cape Horn and through the Straits were obviously going to be still more important with the growth of sea-borne trade and potentially vital for the strategic interests of Chile and its Atlantic neighbour Argentina. The first settlement on the Straits west of Punta Arenas was no more than a stockaded fort established in 1843 and reminiscent of the North American wild west. Later the settlers moved to Punta Arenas itself, which at first served mainly as a penal settlement but grew later into a port of call and supply centre for shipping using the Straits.

By the 1870s sheep had been introduced from the Falkland Islands and large-scale sheep ranching developed first on islands

[8] With the exception of a handful of Alacalufe canoe people who still survive on the west coast of southern Patagonia, all of these tribes were exterminated by disease or deliberate killing by the early settlers arriving from the north in the late nineteenth and twentieth centuries. Vivid pictures of the tribes now extinct can be found in Charles Darwin's account from the 1830s and Lucas Bridges' classic, *The Uttermost Part of the Earth* (Hodder and Stoughton, 1948), describing their fate over the following hundred years.

in the Straits and later on the mainland and Tierra del Fuego. Large investments were made by German, British and other entrepreneurs in those years and many skilled foreigners were attracted to the new province of Magallanes as sheep farmers, artisans and tradesmen. The predominant nationalities were English, Scottish, German and Yugoslav, and the development of Punta Arenas was heavily influenced by its European connections and European ideas. To this day the architecture is more like that of a European than a Latin American town. The province of Magallanes also had something in common with Australia and the North American plains in that very large landholdings were necessary to make stock rearing viable in the prevailing conditions. For example, by 1910 the largest of all the ranching companies controlled 3 million hectares of land. The period from about 1880 to 1914 (when the Panama Canal was opened) was the heyday of Punta Arenas during which, being the first port of call in Chile for travellers from Europe, it was in effect nearer to that continent than anywhere else in the country. Thereafter it became mainly a centre for servicing the *estancias* and shipping large amounts of wool and sheep meat to world markets, but its population was relatively small.

Because the big ranching companies did not allow people to settle permanently on the land they controlled, the bulk of the population of Magallanes were little more than an itinerant labour force. Nevertheless the employment of substantial numbers of workers in the meat-processing plants and on the large sheep stations led to the development of a separate and often extremely militant labour movement in the far south of the country. On occasions between 1910 and 1920 they were brutally repressed by the owners, and Magallanes became one of the main centres of socialist and communist strength in Chile.

The end of Araucania

While the Chilean government was asserting its authority in Magallanes in the latter part of the nineteenth century, a rather different process was also going forward in the lake district 2,000 kilometres to the north. President Bulnes commissioned a German scientist from Berlin University, Bernardo Philippi, to survey the area around Osorno and Lake Llanquihue. On the basis of his findings the Congress declared all unoccupied lands in the area to be state property, and in 1848 Philippi was appointed to recruit immigrants from Germany to settle in this part of the country. A visionary Chilean adventurer, Vicente Perez Rosales, was appointed colonising agent in Valdivia, and the first 212 settlers arrived in 1850. Within ten years several new towns, notably Puerto Montt, had been founded and a vast area of land was made available for settlement in blocks sold by the state to newly-arrived settlers from Germany, Switzerland and France. By 1880 the flow of immigrants had largely ceased and at the turn of the century all the land in this area had been sold off.

The Mapuche (or Araucanians) were not directly affected by these settlements in the area of Osorno, Valdivia and Lake Llanquihue which had genuinely been unoccupied on the arrival of settlers from Europe. Further north it was another story. In 1862 the old frontier established in colonial times between Chile and Araucania was pushed south from the Bío-Bío to the Malleco River. A few years later it had reached the Tolten, 250 kilometres further south, and in 1881 the city of Temuco was founded. These were military operations undertaken to 'pacify' the Mapuche, who never stopped resisting Spanish or Chilean pressures until they were overwhelmed by superior force and modern weapons. The purpose of the policy was not only to establish the government's authority over the Mapuche but also to bring the vast amount of territory previously left to them exclusively into use as productive land and incorporate it into the state. For this purpose further immigration was actively promoted, and the Mapuche were left with no more than half a million hectares of land split into a large number of reservations.[9]

The process was well advanced by 1900 and all but complete by 1912. By the standards of the late twentieth century it was a disgraceful abuse of power to force the Mapuche people off land they had occupied, considered to be theirs and to some extent cultivated for centuries. The reservations, known as *reducciones*, in

[9] One of the events which caused the government to proceed by force in pacifying the Mapuche was the arrival of an eccentric Frenchman who proclaimed himself Emperor of Araucania, Orélie-Antoine de Tounens I, in 1861. Although expelled to France he spent the rest of his life trying to return and raise the flag of an independent Araucania. One of his appointed heirs sought to revive his claim more than a century later.

which they were then confined, were usually on poorer land, often overcrowded and soon subject to soil exhaustion at the same time as the human population was weakened by tuberculosis and other diseases. Those responsible for the forceful imposition of foreign authority and laws on what had long been accepted as the independent land of Araucania, including those who by one means or another acquired Mapuche land, may plead that this was no worse than what was happening at the same time in North America and Australasia as well as in other parts of South America, and had often happened elsewhere in the past. Only time will tell whether that is the end of the story.

For Chile as a whole the consequences of this further huge expansion of the national territory are less depressing. The province of Malleco, for example, became the granary of Chile and the wheat grown there formed the basis of an important milling industry. Further south many other crops were cultivated. The farms cleared and created by immigrants transformed what was previously a heavily forested, lake-studded wilderness into a beautiful agricultural and pastoral region. With German drive and skill, Valdivia became a significant industrial centre, famous for its shipbuilding and timber as well as brewing and milling, until it was largely destroyed in an earthquake in 1960. The north-south trunk railway was extended, stage by stage, in the wake of the colonization process until, in 1915, it reached Puerto Montt – still the final terminus of the railway and the Pan-American Highway.

The first railways had been constructed in the north to connect mines and nitrate *oficinas* to the nearest port.[10] However from an early stage the government saw the need, for strategic as well as commercial reasons, to unify the long Central Valley and to link it more closely to the capital. Subsequently the railway would also serve to link the heartland with the northern mining centres and with new territories in the south, and provide the essential transport to support new industries. Until then the most effective means of transport for most purposes, and often the only viable one, was the coastal shipping service. (This too developed strongly throughout the century and increasingly converted to steam.) The railway age came to Chile almost as rapidly and with equally

10 The very first in Latin America was the line linking the Copiapó mines with the port of Caldera (27°S) constructed by William Wheelwright in 1851.

far-reaching effects as it did in Argentina or in Europe or North America. The one part of the country which had not (and has never) been reached by the railroad was the vast area, one-third of the whole, which lies south of Puerto Montt. The more northerly half of this territory, now the XI Region (itself a huge area) with its capital, Coihaique, was only connected internally with the north by road towards the end of the twentieth century. The southern part (the XII Region of Magallanes) is separated from the rest of the country by an ice-cap which has so far proved impassable so that Magallanes will probably always depend primarily on sea or air communications with the rest of the country.

Conflict in Patagonia

Settlement of the most remote parts of the extreme south was bound to be slow and difficult. It also brought Chile into conflict with Argentina over the exact territorial limits in Patagonia. According to the accepted legal doctrine of *uti possidetis*, the national frontiers were taken to be the boundaries fixed in colonial times between the administrative sub-divisions of the Spanish Empire –in this case the Viceroyalty of La Plata (which became Argentina) and the 'Kingdom' or Captaincy-General of Chile. However, these boundaries could themselves be disputed, as indeed they were when it suited either country to do so. While Chile was embroiled with Peru and Bolivia in the dispute which led to the War of the Pacific, Argentina took the opportunity to advance its claims at the other end of the country and eventually secured Chilean acceptance of Argentine sovereignty over huge areas of southern Patagonia. Under the Treaty of 1881 both coasts of the Magellan Straits were declared to be within Chilean territory, but the Straits themselves were neutralised. The boundary north of the Straits was agreed to be the line joining the highest peaks of the Andes, and inevitably this left room for dispute, particularly where the watersheds between rivers flowing east and those flowing west confused the problem of demarcating the boundary in the most inaccessible areas. (From the eastern end of the Straits the boundary to the south dividing the island of Tierra del Fuego was simply defined as the 68°34' meridian west of Greenwich.)

The 1881 Treaty, and later agreements between Chile and Argentina, provided for any future disputes that could not be settled by negotiation to be submitted to arbitration by 'a friendly power'. Over the demarcation of the southern boundaries, the two countries agreed to refer their differences to the British Crown, which was thereby involved in their disputes not only in 1902 when the boundary was finally agreed and demarcated in the south, but also in a succession of further cases up to 1977. In the late nineteenth century, however, the windswept plains of Patagonia were not considered of major economic value. Until modern times when oil was discovered in the Magellan Straits and off the Atlantic coast of Tierra del Fuego, the government of Chile calculated correctly in preferring to concede to Argentina in the south in order to be free to secure the full benefit of its territorial gains in the north following the Pacific War.

In the 1970s and '80s this old rivalry between Chile and Argentina over territory at the extreme southern end of the continent, and particularly in the Beagle Channel south of Tierra del Fuego, would become once more a major diplomatic problem for Chile. It came near to being a *casus belli* when the military government of Argentina pushed the dispute to the very brink in 1978. But at the end of the First World War, Chile could face the international situation on its frontiers with reasonable confidence and was on tolerably good terms with the most powerful of its neighbours. In the north the Peace Treaty with Peru held,[11] and in 1904 a final Peace Treaty was signed with Bolivia. The boundaries of modern Chile were established, if with underlying resentment and occasionally open dispute on the part of the northern and north-eastern neighbours. Easter Island, 2,350 miles away in the South Pacific, and the nearer islands of the Juan Fernández archipelago were also under Chilean control.

However, Chile's military success in the War of the Pacific and the consolidation of its control of new territories in the next forty years, had done nothing to resolve the desperate social problems facing the country in the post-war era.

[11] The permanent confirmation of the restoration of Tacna to Peru was not achieved until 1929. There are still minor issues to be settled in connection with Peru's right to port facilities at Arica, which remained part of Chile.

4

POST-WAR CHALLENGES (1920-1958)

> 'Meanwhile, life was changing in Chile.[...] On the one hand, the great leader of the petite bourgeoisie, Arturo Alessandri Palma, a dynamic and demagogic man, became President of the Republic, but not before he had rocked the country with his fiery and threatening speeches. In spite of his extraordinary personality, once in power he quickly turned into the classic ruler of our Americas; the dominant sector of the oligarchy, whom he had fought, opened its maw and swallowed him and his revolutionary speeches. The country continued to be torn apart by bitter strife.'
>
> – Pablo Neruda, *Confieso que he vivido. Memorias*

The Russian Revolution of 1917 had sent tremors around the world and Chile was no exception. The Chilean Workers' Federation (FOCH) affiliated itself to the Soviet-led international trade union movement in 1921 and the Chilean Communist Party (PC) was established the next year. It was the first in Latin America, a fact which it always proclaimed with pride. However, the main immediate effect was to split the Left in Chile, and it would be many years before any sort of unity would be restored in the Chilean working-class movement. Nevertheless the 1920s were the years in which left-wing political forces made themselves felt for the first time.

Possibly Chile was not ripe for revolution in 1920 but, if so, it was not because of any wise policies of gradual reform pursued by the various governments which ruled during the Parliamentary Republic. Between 1891 and 1915, as many as sixty governments were formed and lasted on average less than five months. Most were hamstrung by Congress unless there was near universal consensus in favour of a proposed course of action, and, given the nature of factional politics, this was exceedingly rare.

The failure of parliamentary government

The political system as it operated after 1891 had indeed failed to respond to the most basic needs of the mining and urban workers, let alone the *campesinos.* Congress always contained a strong conservative element representing the landed oligarchy and commercial interests, which was certain to resist any measure involving social reform or higher taxation; thus to a degree the failure to tackle the 'social question' was not due simply to political stalemate or incapacity but also to a deliberate determination not to do so. The instinctive response of many of the governments of the parliamentary period to industrial unrest, and certainly to any threat to public order or to property, was to repress it – if necessary by force.

The modernisation of the Army on German lines had been resumed after the civil war. From 1891 the Prussian military mission, set up originally by Colonel Emil Körner, who now became Chief of the General Staff, was expanded and new equipment was acquired for both the Army and the Navy. By 1902 the Army had a strength of 17,500 men compared to 2,500 in 1879. The purpose was, of course, to maintain the country's military ascendancy over its rivals in the Southern Cone, but in practice the main use to which the Army was put was internal. It was sent in by the government to break major strikes at Valparaiso in 1903, Antofagasta in 1906 and Iquique in 1907, and the workers killed or wounded in these confrontations became the martyrs of the growing labour movement.

The intensity of this industrial conflict reflected the cycle of expansion and contraction that had always characterised the nitrate industry and, to a smaller extent, other mining. One immediate effect of depression in the mining industry would be a decline in the demand for foodstuffs and other essential supplies provided to the nitrate fields and ports by the Central Valley *haciendas.* This quickly led to unemployment there as well, so that the hardships were compounded. One means of relieving the misery of unemployment was found in the jobs provided by new public works programmes and particularly the extension of the north-south trunk railway. Until that was completed, travel between the northern and southern extremes of the territory was still only possible by sea (as remained the case south of Puerto Montt until the introduction of commercial aviation). The total extent of Chile from north to south is 4,300 kilometres in a direct line; the journey was usually far from direct, and distance alone was therefore a formidable obstacle. In 1915, however, the rail link finally reached Puerto Montt so that people could travel fairly easily from Coquimbo in the Norte Chico to Puerto Montt, 1,500 kilometres south.

One unforeseen result of this was that the Chilean workers, who had for many years been scattered over a great area, now developed greater common purpose in step with the growth of that feeling of national unity which the government itself had sought to encourage. Government agencies frequently studied the plight of the working classes and proposed reforms, but very little had actually been done to remedy even the most obvious problems before the 1920s. Among the few exceptions were laws to establish Sunday as a day of rest in 1907 and a primitive scheme of insurance against industrial accidents in 1917, but the basic problems of exploitation of labour and extreme poverty were either ignored or evaded by most politicians regardless of party. There was no lack of debate about the 'social question' in intellectual circles. In 1910 Alejandro Venegas, a provincial schoolteacher, wrote angrily:

> We have armies, warships, fortresses, cities and ports, theatres and racetracks... and opulent magnates who live in splendid palaces... but at no great distance there live the people, that is to say nine tenths of the population of Chile, plunged in the most fearful economic, physical and moral poverty, and degenerating rapidly through overwork, poor diet, lack of hygiene, extreme ignorance and the grossest vices.[1]

Impact of the First World War

By 1920 Chile's population had increased to 3,730,000 and the cities, particularly Santiago, Valparaiso and Concepción, had grown relatively faster. Since 1895 the population of Santiago had risen to 547,000 from 300,000 and Valparaiso's to 266,000 from 173,000. Much modernisation and new building had been undertaken on

[1] Alejandro Venegas, writing under the pseudonym 'Dr Julio Valdés Cauge', published his book *Sinceridad. Chile Intimo en 1910*, savagely castigating the failings of the Chilean élite.

the back of the nitrate wealth. Not only private houses but also fine theatres, churches and civic buildings, new railway stations and grand avenues and plazas date from this period. The obvious contrast with the increasingly wretched conditions of life of the urban proletariat was aggravated by rising levels of inflation. Between 1880 and 1922 the value of the peso fell by more than 70 per cent, and the outbreak of the world war in 1914 gave inflation a further boost. In a broader sense, the war marked a turning point in social and economic life, and by the time it ended, although Chile had remained neutral, it felt the effects keenly. For example, the country depended heavily on both Germany and Britain as markets for its mineral exports and as sources for the supply of both consumer and capital goods. This established pattern of trade was interrupted by the war and never fully recovered thereafter. The war also precipitated the widespread use of artificial nitrate particularly in Germany (where it was first invented in 1913) – a development which led eventually to the collapse of the natural nitrate industry.

With the exhaustion of all the major European powers (and the total collapse of Germany), the post-war era brought a permanent shift of economic power from Europe to the United States. By the early 1920s the Chilean economy had become as dependent on the United States as it had ever been on Britain, France and Germany. Even in 1914 American investment in Chile had grown to $200 million, almost two-thirds of the total value of British investments built up over a century. However, the participation of the United States in the Chilean economy was more heavily concentrated on nitrate and copper and iron mining. By 1918 US companies controlled as much as 87 per cent by value of Chile's copper, and trade with the United States had risen to over half of all Chile's external trade. The economic re-orientation brought about by the war also included the introduction of American techniques, equipment and commercial (and even cultural) influence in place of nineteenth-century European models. The process had started before 1914 but accelerated under the pressures of the world conflict.

First Presidency of Arturo Alessandri

In 1919 the world economy experienced the inevitable post-war depression. The nitrate industry ran into a severe crisis and there were serious strikes not only in the northern mining centres but also in Magallanes and Santiago. They were savagely repressed and by the end of the year some towns in the north were under semi-permanent martial law. The presidential campaign of 1920 was therefore contested in a climate of dangerous industrial unrest and political tension. Despite the obvious risks, many thoughtful Chilean voters felt that the time was ripe for fundamental reform. After the long period of stagnation since the civil war of 1891 they were ready to welcome change, and a candidate emerged who seemed to reflect their mood by openly attacking the influence of the oligarchy and promising real economic and social reforms.

Arturo Alessandri Palma, grandson of an Italian immigrant, was brought up on a farm in the agricultural province of Linares, but had made a successful career as a lawyer and been a deputy for the Liberal Party since before the beginning of the century. He served briefly as Minister of Finance in 1898 but his political career had not been particularly remarkable. In 1915, however, he became Liberal candidate for Senator for the mining province of Tarapacá. Facing a local party chief notorious for repressing nitrate workers in the interests of the companies, Alessandri fought and won a furious contest marked by fiery attacks on the corrupt political system (which actually led to a duel with the then Minister of the Interior). This campaign earned him the life-long nickname of 'the Lion of Tarapacá' and his political career was transformed. In the 1920 presidential campaign he had the enthusiastic support of all the parties interested in reform, particularly the Radical and Democratic parties, as well as his own Liberal Party, against a right-wing candidate, Luis Barros Borgoño.

The election was very close and there was an unprecedented level of violence and intimidation by supporters of both sides. Eventually it was announced that Alessandri had obtained 179 votes against 174 for Barros. (At that time presidential elections were conducted by an electoral college on the United States model.) The result was challenged by both sides and had to be referred to the Congress and then to a so-called 'Tribunal of Honour' for a decision. After three tense months, this Tribunal declared Alessandri elected by a single vote and he assumed the Presidency in December 1920.

Alessandri's right-wing opponents, who still controlled the Senate, took every opportunity to obstruct his programme. Even the Liberal Alliance, which had supported him and once seemed enthusiastic for reform, dragged its feet when confronted with the reality of Alessandri's labour and social welfare legislation. When it realised that major improvements in the lot of the masses would require real sacrifice by the governing élites, in the form of higher taxation if nothing else, even the Radical and Democratic parties recoiled from the prospect. In four years Alessandri appointed sixteen different ministries without making serious progress in implementing his programme. He became convinced that only constitutional change would enable Chile to tackle its real social problems.

In his campaign in 1920 Alessandri had proclaimed: 'I want to be a threat to all reactionary spirits and to those who resist all just and necessary reforms.' Despite demonstrations of support for him from many quarters, and the successes of his supporters in the Congressional elections of 1924, he delivered nothing. Matters came to a head in August of that year when Congress deferred its consideration of the proposed reforms in order to vote themselves salaries. At this point a group of young officers appeared in the gallery of Congress to demonstrate the Army's dissatisfaction with this blatant subordination of national interests to the personal interests of the politicians. Their noisy intervention, known afterwards as 'the rattling of sabres', was only one manifestation of military impatience with the civilian authorities: when Alessandri demanded that these young officers be disciplined, their seniors backed them and presented a list of petitions to the President supporting many of the reforms, including action on the budget, social security and social laws and the payment of back salaries to public employees.[2] Within days the President had vetoed the Congressional salary law, and Congress, faced with the threat of military intervention, had conceded all the Army's requests.

Alessandri nominated a conservative general, Luis Altamirano,

[2] Although much less inclined than other South American armies to take a hand in national politics, the Chilean military class had been increasingly dissatisfied with politicians since the early years of the century. In part it was concerned to restore standards and unify the country, and in part reacting against the increasing use of military force to repress strikes and Congressional interference in Army promotion and other internal matters.

to head a new Cabinet after the first demonstration of the Army's readiness to intervene. He now found his authority as President under pressure and, faced with a direct challenge, resigned and left the country in the hands of a government Junta of three senior officers who assumed executive responsibility in his place. However, the young officers also maintained their self-appointed monitoring role as a military Junta in the background. Their leaders were two Army majors who in very different ways were to play important roles in the years ahead: Carlos Ibañez and Marmaduke Grove. In January 1925 they organized a further coup to replace the government Junta, and soon afterwards they invited Arturo Alessandri, by now living in Italy, to return and resume the Presidency. On this occasion, however, Congress was not recalled and Alessandri proceeded to rule by decree for a crucial period of six months from March to September 1925. In April 1925 he started the process of preparing a new Constitution which was approved by a national plebiscite in August.

The 1925 Constitution and the rise of Carlos Ibañez

The new Constitution shifted the balance of power away from Congress. Its main provisions were for direct popular election of the President; an independent tribunal to review election results; and the separation of powers by making Ministers answerable to the President rather than to Congress and preventing Congressmen serving in government posts. The presidential term was extended to six years but with the immediate re-election of the incumbent prohibited. The President was also empowered to appoint *intendentes* (governors) responsible only to the central government to run each of the provinces. Congress kept important budgetary powers, but lost the traditional instruments of influence which had been used so often to obstruct the executive, e.g. refusal to authorise tax collection and the ability to force ministerial resignations. However the 1925 Constitution actually increased Congressional power in other ways by staggering the timing of elections so that no President was likely to hold office and simultaneously control the legislature, and by allowing Congress to select a President from among the two candidates with the highest popular vote if none had a plurality. These provisions ensured that Congress would retain a crucial role in the Chilean political system and that the

President could not become an elective dictator. Another fundamental and highly controversial change was the formal separation of the state from the Catholic Church.

Alessandri was not personally involved in the drafting of the new Constitution, which he left to others, but it certainly reflected to a considerable degree his own ideas and, above all, his conviction that the authority of the executive arm of government had to be strengthened sufficiently to enable Presidents to govern effectively, although subject both to Congressional influence and the counter-balancing authority of an independent judiciary. It was not simply a return to the original model of strong government as designed by Diego Portales. Nor did it overcome the addiction that Chileans had developed to party politics, which had become almost a game to be played for its own sake.

The 1925 Constitution was the principal lasting achievement of Arturo Alessandri's first Presidency. Thereafter, however, he quickly found himself in conflict with the man who had emerged from the crisis in 1924 as the leading figure among the military, Carlos Ibañez del Campo. As Minister of War under Alessandri, Ibañez used the Army to suppress another workers' strike in the nitrate fields at La Coruña at the appalling cost of 600 casualties. Fearing the consequences of an open confrontation with Ibañez, Alessandri resigned again in October 1925, and his elected successor (Emiliano Figueroa Larrain) proved incapable of implementing the new Constitution. In 1927, after less than two years in office, Figueroa resigned and left the country effectively in the hands of Carlos Ibañez. A few months later Ibañez himself was elected by a wide margin. The only candidate to oppose him was the representative of the Communist Party, Elías Lafferte, who won only 4,000 votes (possibly handicapped by government interference with the polls).

Ibañez now had a cloak of constitutional authority and he proceeded to give Chile four years of efficient and honest but increasingly authoritarian government. He was described by the British Minister of the time[3] as the antithesis of the kind of politician who had governed Chile under the Parliamentary Republic and a throw-back to the model of Portales:

[3] Hohler to Sir A. Chamberlain, Santiago, 25 Jan. 1928. *Annual Report on Chile for 1927* (PRO).

> He is a man of few words, very reserved, and a keeper of his own counsels; he is poor... his house is a model of Spartan simplicity; he is one of the very few men in public life in Chile against whom I have never heard a charge of corruption or venality. I believe that he himself is inspired merely with his desire to serve his country to the best of his ability....

Although widely criticised by parliamentarians as a dictator, and not unhappy to be called 'the Chilean Mussolini', Ibañez clearly had the support of the great majority of the electorate (albeit still a small one) in 1927 and continued to enjoy it so long as he delivered effective government and, above all, economic prosperity.

After 1925 the economy began to revive from the post-war depression. Nitrate and copper production recovered and Ibañez was able to launch the largest public works programmes in Chile's history until that time. Much of the national infrastructure (ports, roads, irrigation and sewage systems, public buildings etc.) was built or modernised. Between 1925 and 1930 the educational budget doubled and many deficiencies were remedied. Most of the army of unemployed were back in work by 1928 and industrial and technological progress went forward strongly. The economic record of the Ibañez government was as good as the best that Chile had previously experienced but it was accompanied by more controversial changes, notably the reorganisation of the national police force (the *Carabineros*) as an instrument of internal control in the hands of the President and a counterweight to the Army. Ibañez openly despised parliamentary politics and politicians and used all available means to manipulate the press and Congress, including imprisonment or exile of persistent political critics of the regime. A measure of government control over the labour movement was achieved with the introduction of a Labour Code in 1931 which was highly restrictive by later standards but nevertheless a huge advance on the previous situation in Chile. Under the Code legal trade unions were encouraged and, for the first time, employers had to enter into written contracts with workers and to comply with the relevant legislation on social security etc. The complete freedom of Chilean employers and landowners to treat labour entirely as they liked was now somewhat restricted, but conversely labour and labour organisations were obliged to operate within strict limits.

The Ibañez government represented a break in almost all respects with the parliamentary period. Henceforward Chilean governments would seek regularly to intervene in the economy in one way or another and to increase the role of the state in promoting industrial and technological change, public health and education and shaping the national economic life in many other ways. This approach was maintained more or less continuously until the late 1970s, and the state's new involvement was accompanied by a large increase in the numbers employed in public administration and services such as health and education. These people were drawn from and represented a more confident middle class which was the backbone of the increasingly formidable Radical Party and eventually challenged the old political classes for control of the state. In one sense Ibañez represented a reversion to the ideas of the Portalian state. In another, his government was a precedent for a succession of highly interventionist regimes, and eventually a socialist one which led to the destruction of the 1925 Constitution.

The crash of 1929

The economic prosperity which sustained Ibañez in power was based on a temporary revival of the nitrate industry and the greatly increased level of foreign borrowing. Both came to an abrupt end in 1930. Following the North American stock market crash of 1929, the world economy slid inevitably into depression and slump causing catastrophic falls in international demand for both copper and nitrates. According to a League of Nations report, Chile was hit harder by the shock than any other country in the world. The effect on its vital export trade was devastating.[4] A favourable trade balance of 676 million gold pesos in 1929 became a deficit of 74 million by 1930 and in 1932 the country suspended payments on foreign debt for the first time in a century and left

[4] The trade figures were :

	(In gold pesos)		
	1929	*1930*	*1932*
Exports	2,293	1,326	282
Imports	1,617	1,400	214

the gold standard again. In the three years 1929-32, the Gross Domestic Product fell by almost 40 per cent. Unemployment rose steeply throughout the country but affected the north worst. (In 1932 the nitrate *oficinas* were employing only 8,500 workers, compared with nearly 60,000 only three years before.)

By July 1931 Ibañez's position had become untenable. Against a background of violence in the streets, the middle-class professional organisations known as *gremios* representing lawyers, doctors, teachers, bank employees and other occupations joined together and forced him to resign. In the next seventeen months the country experienced a variety of civilian and military governments of all persuasions, including a period of 100 days from June 1932, when a 'Socialist Republic' was proclaimed by an unstable Junta consisting of the Air Force commander, the colourful Colonel Marmaduke Grove whom we last met as one of the leaders of the young officers' revolt in 1924, and a socialist lawyer, Eugenio Matte. However, they were soon ousted by a supporter of Ibañez, Carlos Dávila, who tried and failed to bring Ibañez back from exile. Neither the Socialist Republic in its various forms nor any of the other nine ephemeral governments could make any impact on the crippled economy which only revived slowly with the worldwide recovery.

In September 1932 this bewildering succession of events was ended by a military *coup d'état* whose leader, General Bartolomé Blanche, called immediately for new elections in October. There were two candidates from the Right who won 26 per cent of the vote; and two from the Left who between them won 19 per cent (with Grove for the newly-formed Socialist Party having 18 per cent). However, Arturo Alessandri emerged the winner with 55 per cent, supported initially by a somewhat shaky alliance of Radicals, Democrats and left-wing Liberals but eventually drawing much more strength from the Right, who saw him as the best defence against the threat from the Socialist and Communist Left. In the Congressional elections a clear tripolar pattern of voting emerged between Left, Right and Centre which was to persist in Chilean politics for the next four decades. However it appeared that, faced with political crisis, the Chilean electorate would usually choose a President who offered strength and stability rather than experiment with new forces. They seem to have voted for Alessandri because he was the most likely to provide steady civilian government and restore a semblance of national unity.

The return of Arturo Alessandri

Arturo Alessandri returned to power on a platform of mild liberal reform. His first priority was to re-establish the idea of democratic and constitutional government and make a clean break with the *caudillismo* which was so common elsewhere in Latin America, and with which democratic Chile had begun to experiment after the military intervention of 1924. The next necessity was to rebuild the economy after the slump and this had to be done by means acceptable both to the Right, who retained considerable influence in Congress, and to a Left wing which had grown in strength, and held office for a moment in 1932. The executive, despite the shift of power produced by the 1925 Constitution, still needed a degree of co-operation from the dominant parties in Congress. Thus landowners were still able to protect their own interests, and primarily the *hacienda* system and the subordination of the *inquilinos* and other rural workers. Over the next thirty years this was tacitly accepted by the Left whose main clients were the urban, not the rural, working class.

In economic matters Alessandri set out to use the new mechanisms of state intervention and regulation introduced by Ibañez to protect industry, increase revenue and thus revive the economy. But his first concern was devoted to implementing the 1925 Constitution and the Labour Code. In both respects he was reasonably successful, but the creation of rural unions was resisted successfully by the landowners who persuaded Alessandri that this would destroy law and order in the countryside. The threat seemed to be confirmed by a violent disturbance in the Bío Bío valley in June 1934, when 100 *campesinos* protesting against eviction were shot down by the *Carabineros*. An efficient and well-armed Republican Militia which had emerged in the turbulent years 1931-2 as a counterweight to the regular armed forces, also enabled Alessandri both to keep the latter out of politics and to counter subversion from the Left.

The rise of the Radical Party

With the shift of the Alessandri administration to the right, the Radical Party found itself needing to form working relationships with the Socialists and Communists with the idea of achieving power, as the moderate element in a left-wing coalition. By coincidence, in 1935, the Comintern instructed the leaders of communist parties around the world to form Popular Front alliances with social democratic parties. In the following year the first Popular Front committee was formed in Chile, and this led to the victory of a Popular Front candidate in the Presidential election of 1938. The new President was Pedro Aguirre Cerda, a right-wing Radical who, ironically, had voted against his party's original decision to join the Front. Aguirre Cerda came to power with a heterogeneous mix of electoral support[5] but the Radicals remained the dominant party in Chilean politics for the next fourteen years. Almost at once, however, he was confronted with a revived challenge in the countryside when his supposed allies, the Socialists and Communists, organised another burst of agitation for the establishment of legal agricultural unions. This immediately compelled the landowners and their pressure group, the *Sociedad Nacional de Agricultura* (SNA), to defend the *status quo*. Aguirre Cerda's response was the same as Alessandri's in 1933. Faced with the threat to law and order around the country and the potentially damaging opposition of the oligarchy, he suspended rural unionisation. This suspension remained in force till 1946 and was accepted by all the politicians in the Popular Front as the price of 'social peace'. *Plus ça change....*

The President also needed support from the Right for the programme of reconstruction needed after a disastrous earthquake in January 1939 in the Central Valley. This caused at least 5,600 deaths and widespread physical damage, leaving as many as 70,000 homeless, which could only be remedied by a massive and costly reconstruction programme. The major instrument created to manage the reconstruction programme was 'CORFO' – the *Corporación de Fomento a la Producción* (Production Development Corporation),

[5] Aguirre Cerda was elected with the support of Communists, Socialists, Radicals, the Chilean Nazi Party and the personal followers of Carlos Ibañez. As a *mestizo* he was despised by the old political élite but as a vineyard owner, nicknamed 'Don Tinto', was well-liked by the rest of the Chilean public.

which became the official mechanism for long-term economic development, relying heavily on external financing by the US Export-Import Bank. Aguirre Cerda's initiative in creating CORFO had far-reaching effects over the next four decades, in which it became the holding company for state participation in a huge range of industries and thus the lynchpin of the whole national economy. At the same time the necessity for CORFO to obtain much of its finance from the EXIM Bank made Chile's economic policy even more dependent on the co-operation of Washington. Between 1939 and the early 1950s CORFO provided one third of all capital investment in Chile, and another third of it came from the EXIM Bank. The United States doubled its exports to Chile and tripled its imports. The participation of Britain and Germany, cut down to size after the First World War, recovered to some extent in the 1930s but was inevitably cut back again during and after the war of 1939-45.

The *inquilinos* and other rural workers, once again, were the chief losers in this period as a result of the tacit agreement of governments – both Alessandri's and the Popular Front – to give priority to the interests of the urban proletariat. This implied keeping the price of food low (and rural labour cheap). After 1939, however, the impact of inflation (which the Popular Front barely attempted to control) and wartime restrictions meant that urban workers did little better. The main beneficiary was the middle class, which moved in increasing strength into government employment. Aguirre Cerda died in 1941 and was succeeded by another Radical from the right of that party, Juan Antonio Ríos. However, even with a Popular Front majority in Congress, the Ríos government passed very little reforming social legislation. His main objective was to overcome wartime shortages by maximising production and import substitution.

Despite the natural pro-German sympathies of some elements of the Chilean public and hesitations about the ability of the United States to guarantee South American security after the disaster of Pearl Harbor, Ríos was eventually persuaded to break off relations with the Axis powers in January 1943 and to align Chile – though still formally neutral – more clearly with the United States and its Allies. This decision gave the country membership of the United Nations and added a political dimension to what was now the inescapable reality of its economic dependence on the United

States. After the war, and even more sharply after the break-up of the West's wartime alliance with the Soviet Union and the beginning of the Cold War, the parties of the Left in Chile were growing more and more critical of the country's excessive dependence on the United States, and particularly of the US copper companies' ability to manipulate Chilean copper production and prices while resisting all attempts to increase tax levels on it. This theme was to become dominant in the politics of the 1960s and '70s.

In 1946 a new Radical leader, this time from its left wing, Gabriel González Videla, became President at the head of an unstable coalition which included the Liberals, the Communists and some Socialists. In the same year the left-wing unity first forged in 1936 between the Communist and Socialist parties broke apart. The Communists seized control of the principal labour federation, the *Confederación de Trabajadores de Chile* (CTCh), while the Socialists, aligning themselves with the US AFL/CIO, formed a new labour organisation and split the Left in the industrial field as well. The *campesinos* were still virtually unorganised. González Videla had promised to allow the formation of rural unions, but he effectively reversed this by accepting new permanent legislation demanded by the Liberal Party which severely restricted the activities of such unions by inhibiting collective bargaining and outlawing agricultural strikes. From within the government, the Communists actively fomented labour conflicts throughout the countryside as well as in industry and the mines. The President finally threw them out of his Cabinet in April 1947, and the next year Congress passed the Law for the Permanent Defence of Democracy (Law 8987) which outlawed the Communist Party and empowered the government to remove its members from the labour movement and even to send them into 'internal exile'.[6]

During the three Radical Presidencies between 1938 and 1952, but particularly during the first four years, there had been important advances in levels of industrial production and overall economic growth, but the reliance of successive governments on heavy deficit financing and foreign loans had fuelled inflation usually at the

[6] The concepts of external and internal exile were not new in Chile and feature in all the country's constitutions in one form or another. One of those who had to leave as a result of Law 8987 was Pablo Neruda, then a Communist senator. As a result President González Videla is probably best known today as the target of Neruda's biting poetic denunciations.

expense of the poorest Chileans. Industrialisation had brought benefits to those immediately involved but the growth of the population and the movement of workers from the farms towards the towns and cities had increased demand for food and other essentials while the total neglect of agriculture meant that food production had stagnated. Chile's total population had grown from 4,365,000 in 1930 to 5,063,000 in 1940 and 6,295,000 in 1950, and more than half now lived in towns. The poor performance of agriculture also meant that Chile, once the bread basket of the west coast of South America which had exported wheat to California and even Australia, now depended increasingly on imported food. Responsibility for this had to be laid mainly at the door of the landowners and their pressure group, the SNA, but neither the Radicals nor the Left had achieved anything for the *campesinos.*

The end of the Radical era

The Radicals had lost their way, and the type of economic policy pursued by them and the Popular Front governments no longer seemed capable of producing sound and non-inflationary economic growth. They had never even attempted to bring about the basic changes in the Chilean body politic which all left-of-centre parties had been advocating for two or three decades. By the time González Videla's Presidency was coming to an end in 1952, there was general disillusionment with party politics. The evident exhaustion of Radical-led or Popular Front governments provided another opportunity for a 'non-political' Presidency. The old dictator, Carlos Ibañez, now presented as 'the General of Hope', seized it. This was the first presidential election in which women had the vote and they predominantly supported Ibañez. Apart from his personal following, he also drew support from a mixed bag of Socialists, Radicals and even Conservatives and a new grouping, the Agrarian Labour Party (PAL), but he was not limited by party or ideological considerations in the choice of Ministers. During his second Presidency, Ibañez made a virtue out of having no defined platform and not too many promises to break, but he did not flout the Constitution openly and was faithful to two electoral promises he had made, which were to have significant effects in the next decade.

The most far-reaching of these took the form of important electoral reforms in 1958 which extended the franchise substantially and made voting both secret and compulsory. For the first time landlords were prevented from controlling the votes of their work-forces in the old way. The percentage of the population registered to vote rose from 10 per cent in the 1930s and '40s to 18 per cent in 1952 and 21 per cent in 1958. Stronger penalties for electoral fraud or bribery (still widespread in 1952) were also introduced at this juncture. This was a serious blow to the political machines operated by the landowners and *caciques* (local party bosses) in rural Chile and removed, or weakened, an important prop of the *hacienda* system. Eventually it enabled Marxists, Christian Democrats, Radicals and other parties to win significant support in the rural areas and heralded the demise of the traditional power of the oligarchy.

The second of Ibañez's critical election promises was to eliminate the Law for the Permanent Defence of Democracy and thus allow the Communist Party to return to national politics and facilitate the organisation of workers throughout the country. This made possible a new electoral coalition of the Left between the Communist and Socialist parties, known as the *Frente de Acción Popular* (FRAP), which became the core of the coalition which nearly captured the Presidency in 1958 and finally brought Salvador Allende to power in 1970.

However, before taking those steps at the end of his Presidency, Ibañez was faced with a new economic crisis. In 1953, following the end of the Korean War, demand for copper and thus Chile's capacity to pay for imports fell by almost 30 per cent. By this time an economic policy based on stimulating domestic industrial development by tariff protection, and encouraging import substitution was no longer adequate. Ibañez called in a US economic team, the Klein-Saks Mission, whose recommendations represented a return to the market-oriented economic policies favoured by the international financial establishment and the IMF in particular. It was duly implemented by the Ibañez government. The new policy made a substantial impact on the rate of inflation, which till then had been out of control, and gave further incentives to private investment, and particularly to investment by the big US copper companies such as Anaconda and Kennecott. But the measures against inflation precipitated another severe recession

President Carlos Ibañez (*left*) and President Juan Peron of Argentina.

President Eduardo Frei Montalva being received in London by Queen Elizabeth II and the Duke of Edinburgh.

which in turn hit the standard of living of most groups in Chile. This lost the government much of the middle-class support Ibañez had enjoyed in the first three years of his Presidency. His popularity depended too much on his personal standing and powers of leadership and therefore, lacking a reliable political base, he had little to fall back on when his economic policies were seen to be failing after 1955. In any event Carlos Ibañez could not stand for election again in 1958.

The failure of Ibañez's economic policy made financial orthodoxy unpopular once more and increased the appeal of the more radical ideas, such as nationalisation and redistribution of wealth, proposed by the Left. On the labour front there had also been a certain rapprochement between the Communist and Socialist parties after the disappearance of the CTCh and the establishment of a single organisation, the *Central Unica de Trabajadores Chilenos* (CUTCh), in 1953. On the basis of their new electoral coalition, the FRAP, they were able to unite behind a single candidate, Salvador Allende, and have a real chance of success in 1958.[7] This was also the first occasion when the Christian Democratic Party appeared as a political force in a presidential campaign, with the emerging figure of Eduardo Frei as its candidate. Luis Bossay stood for the Radicals but their dominance of the centre ground of Chilean politics was already in decline and was now superseded by another left-of-centre party drawing mainly (but not exclusively) on middle-class support.

The candidate of the Right was Jorge Alessandri, one of the sons of Arturo Alessandri, an ex-Minister of Finance under Ibañez and widely respected as a successful business leader. Alessandri stood nominally as an independent, although supported mainly by the Conservative and Liberal vote, and had a sufficiently broad appeal to achieve a narrow lead (31.5 per cent). Allende for the FRAP had the next-largest share of the votes with 28.5 per cent and Frei came third with 20.5 per cent. In accordance with the Constitution, the decision between the two front-runners had to be taken by the Congress since no candidate had an overall majority. Alessandri's election was in due course confirmed by Congress

[7] His candidature in 1952 had been supported by a derisorily small turn-out of Socialists and Communists, about 52,000 in total, which represented only 5 per cent of the vote in that year.

where the convention had developed that the leading contender should be voted into office.

Historians and contemporary writers have made much of the fact that Allende would have had the largest percentage vote (although still only a plurality) if there had not also been a maverick left-wing candidate who took a critical 41,000 (3.3 per cent) of the votes from the Left. It was also notable that the Centre vote was split rather more equally, and with results which were equally damaging for Frei (he had 20.5 per cent of the vote and Bossay for the Radicals had 15 per cent). Perhaps the most significant point, however, was that the tripolar division of electoral strength which has so often condemned Chile to weak or unstable government emerged as clearly as ever in 1958, notwithstanding the presence of two other candidates to complicate the picture. Alessandri now achieved office on a minority vote as Allende was to do in 1970. They and Eduardo Frei dominated Chilean politics for the next fifteen years.

5

THE SWING OF THE PENDULUM (1958-1970)

> 'There are three things working in our favour. First, people are tired of the present political juxtaposition. Second people don't want a rightist government. Third, people don't want a communist government'. – Eduardo Frei Montalva speaking in 1963 and quoted by Leonard Gross in *The Last Best Hope: Eduardo Frei and Chilean Democracy* (New York, 1967)

Under the three Presidents who governed Chile in the fifteen years 1958-73, the political centre of gravity swung continuously from right to left. One of the reasons for this was the fact that the right to vote had been extended to include the great majority of adult Chileans, and this broader electorate was looking for more profound changes. Another reason was the growth in the population of the cities. The population of Santiago doubled between 1952 and 1970, when it reached 2.8 million and a growing proportion were living in the most primitive conditions in the peripheral shanty towns, known as *callampas* (mushrooms) or, more politely, *poblaciones* which provided them with little more than basic shelter. Of course the enfranchisement of these hundreds of thousands of people did not immediately transform the political landscape, but it had a cumulative impact on the middle-class leadership of existing parties and on the kind of policies which they put forward to solve the country's social and economic problems. The Radical Party's recipes had proved to be little more than rhetoric. Other political forces now emerged to replace the Radicals.

In fact sweeping change was in the wind throughout the 1960s in the whole of Latin America. It was perhaps the first decade since the 1920s when people, particularly the young, in all parts of the world decided that the peace and prosperity promised by their politicians were not being achieved and turned eagerly to new prophets and ideologies. Radical and sometimes revolutionary ideas flourished not only in the underdeveloped world but also in Western Europe where they even threatened the stability of wealthy democracies such as France and Italy.

However, this new wave of ideas had not reached Chile when Jorge Alessandri was elected in 1958 on a Conservative platform. In order to appeal to the widest possible range of opinion, he presented himself as a non-party independent, but he was also the candidate of the Conservative and Liberal parties. Apart from the advantage of his family name (a factor which has always weighed heavily in Chile), his greatest political asset was his personal reputation as a man of integrity, admired even by his opponents for his unpretentious, almost austere lifestyle. As President he lived in a modest apartment and walked unaccompanied to the Moneda Palace each day. Having been a businessman[1] with a long and successful career in the post-war period, he presented himself not as a political leader but as the 'Great Engineer' who could regenerate the economy after many years of mismanagement by Radical administrations, and by Ibañez. He realised the great need for practical measures to improve the lot of the workers, and his government was the first to try to tackle the slum conditions of the Santiago *poblaciones* on a scale which was anything like commensurate with the size of the problem. However, his overall purpose was to promote economic growth by opening the economy to market forces and encouraging foreign investment. It was a classic mix of pragmatic economic liberalism with moderate conservatism.

The Cuban revolution and the Alliance for Progress

Whatever his personal inclinations, Alessandri soon found himself under pressure to embrace other changes which were anathema to his Conservative supporters. This unwelcome pressure originated

[1] Apart from his period as Minister of Finance from 1947-50, Jorge Alessandri was Chairman, before and after his time as President, of the major industrial group *Companía Manufacturera de Papeles y Cartones* – the bellwether company of the Chilean private sector, and for fifteen years President of the main big business organisation, the *Confederación de la Producción y del Comercio*.

in a powerful political reaction to the advent of Fidel Castro in Cuba and reached Chile via the United States. For many years the United States' approach towards Latin America had been confined (at least in the Southern Cone) to asserting a general leadership through mechanisms such as Roosevelt's 'good neighbour' policy. After 1945, however, it promoted specific arrangements for collective Latin American defence. This was linked – in theory – to a strong commitment to the principle of non-interference in the internal affairs of any member country. (There had been many obvious breaches of this principle, particularly in Central America, but everyone still paid lip-service to it.) The main structure of collective defence was the 1947 Treaty of Mutual Assistance (the 'Rio Treaty') supported by bilateral military aid agreements, but there had been only a limited flow of official US government economic aid to Chile and little or no attempt to promote internal reform. Most Chileans of the ruling political class would certainly have opposed any such attempt.

Following the Cuban revolution of 1959, and with the prospect of communist influence spreading throughout the hemisphere, US policy began to change significantly. In 1960 the Inter-American Development Bank was created as an 'independent' organization through which official US funds could be channelled to the continent. The process accelerated with the end of President Eisenhower's second term and the election of John F. Kennedy who immediately called for fundamental changes, both social and economic, in Latin America and promised a revolution in US policy to help achieve them. After first launching the idea during his 1960 election campaign, Kennedy followed it up in March 1961 with a major speech calling for an 'Alliance for Progress with Latin America... a great common effort to develop the resources of the entire hemisphere, strengthen the forces of democracy, and widen the vocational and educational opportunities of every person in all the Americas.' His rhetoric was deployed in reply to perceived threats from both Cuba (Castro) on the Left and the Dominican Republic (Rafael Trujillo) on the Right, but it was without doubt Cuba and Fidel Castro that loomed largest for Washington. This dramatic initiative was given substance in the Charter of Punta del Este, Uruguay, a few months later when the United States committed itself to provide $20 billion in aid and investment over ten years to promote economic growth in the continent.

Most significant for Chile was the fact that the United States had called specifically for comprehensive agrarian reform with a view to replacing *latifundia* and *minifundia* by an equitable system of land tenure. From the point of view of President Alessandri it was a mixed blessing that Chile had been picked out by Washington as one of the countries, and perhaps the first choice, which it thought suitable as a showcase for its new policy in Latin America. On the other hand Alessandri's electoral base was not strong and both of the centre parties (the Radicals and the Christian Democrats) were already pressing for fundamental changes in this area. Even some on the Right were prepared to agree that agriculture based on *latifundia* had failed even to provide adequate supplies of food – let alone a tolerable living for the rural workforce. Santiago was, by coincidence, the headquarters of the United Nations Economic Commission for Latin America (ECLA or CEPAL in its Spanish form) which had originated many of the ideas adopted by the Alliance for Progress and which had considerable impact on Chilean economists and political thinkers.

By 1961 Chile was receiving the largest amount *per capita* of US aid given to Latin America, totalling $180 million. The Alliance for Progress had approved a development plan worked out by CORFO which would involve an annual investment of $600 million, of which $250 million was to come from abroad. Chile's share of US aid was so high partly because it included special grants towards the heavy relief programme required after the disastrous earthquake of 1960 in the south of the country.[2] The opportunity offered by the Alliance for Progress obviously could not be ignored, but there was a price attached to it – agrarian reform. It is a question for debate, whether the Alliance was primarily responsible for forcing this policy on Alessandri, or whether it would have come in his own time in any case. What is certain is that after the Congressional elections of 1961, Conservative and Liberal strength in Congress was much reduced and

[2] This was the earthquake which virtually destroyed half of the city and port of Valdivia, an industrial centre second only to Concepción in the south, and did huge damage elsewhere on the Pacific coast.

Alessandri had no option but to depend on the Radicals who, like the Christian Democrats, were already committed to agrarian reform.

In the view of CEPAL (and all liberal thinkers in the Latin America of the 1960s), land reform meant the expropriation of *latifundios* (however they might be defined) and sub-division into smaller holdings to be transferred to peasant farmers. This was also what the Chilean *campesino* wanted and it became the cornerstone of legislation, the *Ley de Reforma Agraria* enacted in August 1962. This law was supposed eventually to involve the expropriation and redistribution of cultivated land, but owners had to be compensated with a combination of 20 per cent cash and ten-year interest-bearing bonds. It was therefore very expensive to apply and the law was used almost exclusively to bring badly cultivated or abandoned land into production as smallholdings in the hands of a few lucky *campesinos*. Alessandri's land reform was derisively described at the time as a 'flower-pot reform' (*reforma de macetero*) but it nevertheless represented the first blow against the *hacienda* system which had been successfully maintained intact by the landowners since independence. It set an important precedent and also provided for real improvements in the living conditions of rural workers.

Apart from this minimal experiment with land reform, the Alessandri Presidency was notable for orthodox management of the national economy, which curbed the rate of inflation in the period up to 1961 but was less successful thereafter (by 1963 it had risen to 46 per cent having been as low as 7.7 per cent in 1961). Internationally Alessandri took part in the first attempt to create a regional common market in Latin America by joining the Latin American Free Trade Area (LAFTA). But neither he nor his immediate predecessor, Carlos Ibañez, had attempted to tackle the fundamental economic problem which confronted Chile in the twentieth century. The governments of the 1930s and those of the Radical Presidents between 1938 and 1952 had, to one degree or another, used state intervention to encourage import substitution and reduce dependence on exports. However, they had all failed to reform the regressive tax system and increase state revenue, and were therefore obliged to rely too heavily on foreign borrowing. By the late 1950s this approach was seen to be inadequate and something more dynamic was needed to provide better economic prospects for a growing, and increasingly urban, population – and to bring the rural population into the twentieth century.

The origins of Christian Democracy

By the time of the next presidential election in 1964, there were two alternative programmes on offer. One was the Marxist version offered by the FRAP coalition of the Communist and Socialist parties; the other was based on the less well-known ideas of the Christian Democratic Party. The Christian Democrats only came together as a separate political party in 1957 but they had been developing as an identifiable force for much longer. Their thinking derived from Roman Catholic social doctrine which went back to the Papal encyclicals *Rerum Novarum* (1891) and *Quadragesimo Anno* (1931) defining the Church's attitude to industrial society and the challenge of Marxism. This had been further developed by the French Catholic philosopher Jacques Maritain and others, and by young Chilean intellectuals who began to apply the social doctrine of the Church to the Chilean situation and to translate it into a political programme.[3] In 1938 a group of them broke away from the Conservative Youth Wing and other established political parties to found a new one, the *Falange Nacional.*

The *Falange* represented one organised response by progressive Catholics to the 'social question' which had dominated Chilean politics persistently throughout the century. In the 1940s, another break-away party, the Social Christian Conservative Party, had been formed for similar reasons. Both the Social Christians and the *Falange* developed slowly as political parties at national level but had considerable impact on political debate at the grassroots in the 1940s and '50s. They played important roles in seeking to organize rural workers' unions under the Church's labour umbrella, *Acción Sindical Economica de Chile* (ASICH) which was opposed both by the Marxist-led unions in the countryside and by all the national political parties. This early experience set the stage for fierce rivalry between Christian Democrats and Marxists for the

[3] Among the new generation of Chileans most influenced by Catholic social doctrine were several future leaders of the Christian Democratic Party: Bernardo Leighton, Manuel Garretón, Radomiro Tomíc and Eduardo Frei.

leadership of the *campesinos*, who were increasingly finding a political voice as the franchise reforms of the 1950s had their effect.

In 1957 the *Falange*[4] merged with the Social Christian Party to create the Christian Democratic Party and Eduardo Frei became its candidate in the presidential election of 1958. From the start the Christian Democrats placed great emphasis on the notion that their movement should have a strong communitarian character. Although this idea was never defined with great clarity, it embraced not only the encouragement of Christian Democrat-led rural workers' unions as already described, but also similar kinds of trade unions in the industrial centres, and social organisations in the urban shanty-towns and among students led by Christian Democratic party members. As the Radical Party had done for many years, the Christian Democrats were determined to be more than a conventional political party and to mobilise broadly-based support at all levels in the Chilean economy and society in favour of an alternative programme offering fundamental change by constitutional means. This thinking was developed as the basis for the programme labelled a 'Revolution in Liberty' which Eduardo Frei presented to the Chilean electorate in the campaign of 1964 and which formed the agenda for his administration after his overwhelming victory in that year. Frei achieved a decisive majority of 56 per cent of the total vote. Salvador Allende, campaigning once again for the FRAP coalition, received 39 per cent and Julio Durán (Radical Party) a minimal figure of 5 per cent.

The Presidency of Eduardo Frei

One of the main reasons for the large margin of Frei's victory over Salvador Allende on this occasion was that the parties of the Right, which had formed an electoral coalition known as the Democratic Front by joining forces with the Radicals before the election, eventually became convinced that their joint candidate (Durán) had no hope of winning. Following a critical by-election defeat some months before, the Conservative and Liberal parties changed tactics and reluctantly put their weight behind the Christian

[4] The Chilean *Falange Nacional* ('National Phalanx') had no direct relationship with the Falange movement founded in 1928 in Spain as a traditional nationalist and 'fascist' political party.

Democrats, as the *mal menor* (lesser evil). Had there been a candidate for the Presidency standing to the right of Eduardo Frei, his share of the vote would have been much lower and Allende might well have finished first in the electoral race in 1964, as he had nearly done in 1958. As it was, Frei had an unusually clear overall majority and was able to assume office with strong popular support.

Frei had always been deeply interested in Catholic social teaching and became President of the Catholic youth of Chile while still a student of law at the Catholic University. Initially a political commentator and journalist rather than a professional politician, he was eventually elected to the Senate during the Ibañez Presidency in 1949 without ever having been a Deputy. He was tall and lugubrious in appearance but his large nose made him a delight to cartoonists and probably increased his popularity. Even if his sweeping majority in the presidential election in 1964 was partly due to the tactical voting of the Conservatives and Liberals, it was also attributable to some extent to his personal charisma and sincerity. When he assumed power he carried with him the fervent hopes of liberals throughout the Western democracies and particularly in the United States. Although he had many political opponents in Chile, he was seen by many observers abroad as the best hope for a non-Marxist future in South America.[5]

Within six months the Christian Democrats achieved an absolute majority in the Chamber of Deputies and won twelve seats in the Senate. All the omens seemed good but perhaps the optimism produced by these victories had its own disadvantages since it led to over-confidence. Both the Right, regrouping as the National Party in 1966, and the Left, which still retained a strong social and economic base in the trade union movement, would be back in contention before the half-way point in Frei's period of office.

Frei and his party probably made their first mistake by refusing to bring the Radicals, who would have been their natural partners, into a governing coalition. Some of the Radicals, with their strong anti-clerical views, would have hesitated to ally themselves with what they saw as a 'confessional' Catholic party, but they were never given the chance to decide. The Christian Democrats, in

[5] According to a US Senate Committee Report of 1975, the CIA provided $2.6 million to support Frei's campaign in 1964 although Frei himself had apparently been unaware of this.

the first flush of victory, were not prepared to share power and its prerogatives with any other group. Some left-wing elements who remained powerful within the party until the latter part of the Frei administration also had ideological objections to bringing the Radicals into government in any circumstances. The scale of Christian Democrat triumphs in 1964 and 1965 also encouraged factionalism within the party. This tendency was particularly strong among the new generation of younger figures who had risen recently to top positions in the movement with attitudes and preoccupations which were more doctrinaire than those of Frei and the original leaders. These younger men had come under the influence of more radical social theorists in Europe, and often had also been influenced by the Cuban Revolution.

The factions within the Christian Democratic Party which caused substantial problems for President Frei and the established leadership (known as the *oficialistas*) were the *rebeldes* and the *terceristas* (the third group). These 'young Turks' became increasingly critical of the Frei government over various issues, and particularly over the pace and character of agrarian reform, labour policy and the government's plans for promoting communitarianism in social, industrial and commercial areas. The underlying strategic motive behind many of these differences was the view, held by the *rebeldes* in particular, that the Christian Democrats should be moving towards an alliance with the Communists and Socialists in the 1970 presidential election.

This emerged clearly in debates over the revision of the Labour Code proposed by President Frei and his Minister of Labour (William Thayer). They wanted to allow workers to establish as many unions and union federations as they wished, thus encouraging the foundation of a rival overall labour confederation to challenge the communist-controlled CUT. Legislation to this effect was effectively blocked by the *rebeldes* inside the Christian Democratic Party, enabling the Marxist parties to maintain their influence over the CUT and thus the overall leadership of organised labour. The one area of labour relations in which Frei and Thayer succeeded in putting their ideas into effect was that of rural unions. The relevant law (*Ley de Sindicalización Campesina*) spelt the end of the landowners' freedom to treat their *inquilinos* virtually as servants. For the first time all *campesinos* could legally organise to defend their own interests within a framework established by government, and could pursue their demands when necessary with strike action. This change in the balance of power in the countryside also enabled a larger number of Chileans to have a political voice of their own instead of being merely pawns controlled by their landlords.

Reclaiming copper

Another vested interest which was immediately attacked by Frei was that of the North American copper companies which controlled almost all the *gran minería* – the major copper mines. Although the Christian Democrats had at first considered the outright nationalisation of the industry, they now moved less dramatically to 'Chileanise' it by acquiring majority interests in each of the companies. Negotiations with the principal US interests (Anaconda and Kennecott) were protracted and the final agreement with Anaconda was not achieved till 1969. By then a new state body, the *Corporación del Cobre* (CODELCO), had been established to supervise the overall development of the copper industry and promote a major expansion of production, the refining of copper ore within Chile and the maximising of the prices obtained on international markets.[6] The expansion of the huge Chuquicamata open-cast mine at Calama, inland from Antofagasta, and the creation of two new mines in this period, combined with the higher prices achieved, helped the Frei government to maintain a healthy balance of payments during the late 1960s. Efforts to diversify by winning new markets and promoting non-traditional exports (petrochemicals, pulp and paper, fish products etc.) made some contribution, but copper and other minerals nevertheless became more dominant in Chile's international trade than ever before.

The 'Chileanisation' of the copper-mining companies controlled by United States capital was not, of course, supposed to be part

[6] Since the Second World War, the US administration, acting with US companies, had been able to control the price of Chilean copper at levels which were normally well below the prevailing international prices. This seems hard to believe in the 1990s but the Chilean copper and nitrate industries were so dominated by US capital up till the 1960s that they could be manipulated to that extent.

of the reforming agenda supported by the Alliance for Progress. In fact US commercial interests were in conflict with the objectives of the Alliance in the case of Chilean copper. To resolve the conflict the US Export-Import Bank granted a number of large loans for new mining development. Notwithstanding that, some critics argued that Chile paid too high a price to secure majority control of the copper companies. However, Frei's policy commanded support in principle from a large majority in the Congress and was only opposed by the Communists and Socialists in the FRAP on the grounds that the measure did not go far enough and should have involved immediate and total nationalisation of copper. Moreover the expansion of the copper industry which was achieved paid big dividends in due course (ironically it was the Allende administration which derived the greatest benefit from this).

Agrarian reform

The Frei government was forced to rely on the support of right-wing parties in Congress to win approval for the Chileanisation of the major copper mines. When their new agrarian reform law came forward for consideration it was, of course, bitterly opposed by the Right and the SNA, and with the FRAP again obstructing the measure for tactical reasons, the passage of the legislation took from November 1965 to July 1967. As finally enacted, it allowed the state to expropriate any landholding of more than 80 hectares of irrigated land. Landowners could also lose all their land if it was badly cultivated or left uncultivated, or if they were held to have maltreated their workers. Most significantly a constitutional amendment passed at the same time allowed compensation for expropriated land to be paid in long-term government bonds, which made the policy of expropriation much more affordable.

The land thus taken from landowners was to be consolidated and farmed collectively in *asentamientos agrarios* (agrarian settlements) so that the *campesinos* could have a period of training and experience and to facilitate investment in the new farming units. At the end of at most five years the *campesinos* living and working in them were to have the right to decide whether the land should be distributed in separate family farms, continue to be run as co-operatives, or be organised under a combination of these systems on a permanent basis. The management of the agrarian reform programme was put into the hands of two organisations originally set up under Alessandri's legislation, the *Corporación de Reforma Agraria* (CORA) and the *Instituto de Desarrollo Agropecuario* or Agrarian Development Institute (INDAP), made responsible for giving financial and technical backing to the *asentamientos*. Under the threat of this legislation, some landlords began to negotiate the transfer of land from 1965 – two years before the law became effective.

The left-wing *rebeldes* of the Christian Democratic Party – led by Jacques Chonchol, who had become President of INDAP, and others on the Left – wished to go much faster and did so by by encouraging illegal seizures of land up and down the country. In 1969/70 there were at least 400 such *tomas*. Chonchol and his supporters were competing hard with the Marxist parties in the mass mobilisation of the *campesinos*, with little regard for legality. These mounting pressures presented the Frei government with severe problems of public order and made it difficult to maintain control of an incipient revolution in the Chilean countryside which landowners resisted with increasing bitterness.

According to figures published by CORA, the Frei administration had, by July 1970, expropriated 1,319 landholdings with a total area of 3.5 million hectares. Some 30,000 families had formed 910 *asentamientos* on 3 million hectares and the other half-million hectares had been distributed finally as co-operatives or family farms. However, the bare figures do not begin to show the impact of the agrarian reform policy on the rural economy or its political effects. Under the *Unidad Popular* government of Salvador Allende the process of expropriation was to go much further – and with more disruptive results – than under Eduardo Frei, but it was Frei and the Christian Democrats who were seen as the principal enemies of the landowning class and, by extension, of rights of property. For four centuries the *hacienda* system had been the fundamental source of political power in Chile. The growth of labour unions in the countryside, now strongly supported by the Christian Democrats as well as by the Marxist parties, had greatly increased the bargaining power of rural workers. Land reform gave some of them a personal stake in the ownership of a family farm or a direct share in the management of a collective – or at least it gave them the feeling of having such a stake. This change had been brought about at the expense of the landowners, but was also seen by many Chileans who were not landowners as an omen of a wider attack on other forms of property. It is not simply a coincidence that in 1966 the political parties of the Right – the old Conservative and Liberal parties – decided to join together to form the National Party, which represented not only the traditional landed oligarchy but also a large part of the town-based upper and middle classes involved in commerce, industry and the professions. Many of these groups were beginning to see themselves as threatened by the Christian Democratic Party (PDC) and their Revolution in Liberty.

Polarisation

Whatever the reaction of the Right in Chile, until 1967 the Frei government was considered a success by most objective opinion. In three years the country's GDP rose by 19 per cent, industrial output by 17 per cent and copper production by 14 per cent. Revenue and government expenditure were both higher, and the balance of payments was healthy. Eduardo Frei was hailed in the United States and Europe as the leader who would show that Chile (and perhaps Latin America as a whole) could achieve a fairer and more prosperous society by democratic means. The Christian Democrat alternative to Marxist revolution was working and the Alliance for Progress had a strong standard-bearer.[7]

However, although Frei's policies had worked well, there were still serious tensions within the PDC and persistent pressure from the Left for faster and more radical change. Wage increases and lower inflation were expected to produce a good showing for the government in the municipal elections in April 1967. In the event, however, its vote dropped from 42 pe cent (in 1965) to 36 per cent. The main gains on this occasion were made by the Right, but paradoxically the reaction of the PDC was to move to the Left. In July the *rebeldes* and *terceristas* won control of the party machine from the pro-Frei group and adopted a new policy

[7] In Peru a reformist democratic President, Fernando Belaunde, came to power in 1962 with somewhat similar policies. These were successful for a short period, but he was ousted by a military coup in 1968.

statement calling in extreme language for more nationalisation and the extension of worker control in other areas.

The Radicals also moved to the left and their right wing was forced to split away and form a new Radical Democratic Party. Then, as Paul Sigmund has put it, 'even the left moved to the left'.[8] At their party conference in November 1967 the Socialists formally defined their party as a Marxist-Leninist organisation, adding: 'Revolutionary violence is inevitable and legitimate.' With this inflamatory rhetoric the Chilean Socialist Party not only outflanked the Christian Democrats but also declared itself to be more extreme even than the Communist Party which continued to support the tactics of the *via pacífica*, the peaceful path to socialism. Yet more ominously, a new and uncompromising revolutionary group dedicated to using terrorist violence to change society appeared in the University of Concepción. This was the *Movimiento de Izquierda Revolucionaria* or Movement of the Revolutionary Left (MIR) which idolised Che Guevara and wanted to create a Cuban-style revolution in Chile. The MIR was to play a major part in the disastrous polarisation of Chilean politics.

Within a year, these developments threatened to wreck Frei's Revolution in Liberty by splitting the PDC itself and inflaming the political opposition. Economic difficulties also damaged the government. The rate of inflation, after falling in 1965 and 1966 began to rise again in 1967. The large investments being made in agriculture and the mining sector were not yet paying off to the full, and private sector investment in domestic industry actually dropped. The Socialist- and Communist-controlled unions were active in promoting unaffordable wage demands, which, with many other factors, contributed to the resurgence of inflation. Prices of both domestic and imported goods had risen; and a terrible drought in 1968 seriously damaged agricultural production and power supply. By the end of Frei's Presidency, inflation had risen to 35 per cent, the highest for a decade. Few wage-earners were able to keep up with such a rate and, perhaps more significantly, many small businessmen and white-collar workers who had previously given their support to the PDC began to be alienated from it.

[8] Paul E. Sigmund, *The United States and Democracy in Chile* (Baltimore and London, 1993), p. 32.

In 1968 Richard Nixon was elected President of the United States in succession to Lyndon Johnson. Nixon had visited Chile the previous year and, unimpressed by the reception he received, decided that the Christian Democrats were not so much reforming as destabilising Chile. Frei rapidly ceased to be the 'last, best hope' and a model democratic leader in the eyes of the US administration; indeed the Alliance for Progress, whatever its merits, was too much the brainchild of John Kennedy to appeal to Nixon and little was heard of it under Nixon's Presidency. What was not allowed to decline, however, was CIA support for anti-communist groups in Chile, including its readiness to influence elections. According to the committee of the US Senate headed by Senator Church (known as the Church Committee) and other investigations undertaken in the 1970s, the CIA spent nearly $2 million between 1964 and 1970 on twenty covert projects in Chile, including subventions to the PDC and the new National Party. Notwithstanding this continued US backing, or perhaps because of it, the Christian Democrats did badly in the Congressional elections of 1969. Their share of the vote dropped to 29 per cent, only marginally more than was polled by the Communists (16.6 per cent) and Socialists (12.3 per cent) combined. The National Party got 20 per cent. On this showing, it seemed all too likely that there would be no outright winner in the presidential elections of 1970 and that the tri-polar pattern would again produce a minority government for a country more deeply divided than ever.

Unrest continued to grow in the countryside and in the urban *poblaciones*. The MIR engaged in a series of bank and supermarket robberies and raids on isolated police posts with open support from the Socialists but condemned by the Communist Party as provocative.

As the end of Frei's Presidency approached, the Right began to seek a strong candidate who would restore law and order and stabilise the deteriorating economic situation. Despite his age (he was already seventy-four), they once more turned to Jorge Alessandri who was legally able to stand again after a period out of office. Frei was prohibited from succeeding himself and it was tacitly understood that the PDC candidate would be Radomiro Tomíc, who had long been heir-apparent to Frei and was a forceful and eloquent politician. Tomíc had decided that to retain power the Christian Democrats must become more radical and he argued that the right strategy for the 1970 election was to form an alliance with the left-wing FRAP on a 'popular unity' programme. He later dropped this approach but continued to present himself as more 'revolutionary' than Frei and to advocate even more extreme measures than Allende in an effort to outbid him. As a result Tomíc probably lost the support of many of the middle-of-the-road voters who had voted for Frei, but failed to gain much new support on the Left.

The Unidad Popular

Salvador Allende had already competed and lost in three successive presidential elections and his own Socialist Party was not easily persuaded to nominate him for a fourth attempt. After much manoeuvring between them, the Communists, the Radicals and three smaller left-wing parties, agreement was reached to launch the *Unidad Popular* (UP) as a coalition with Allende as its presidential candidate. It was a broader group than the FRAP (which had included only the Socialists and the Communists), and it immediately adopted a programme for constitutional change including abolishing the two-house legislature in favour of a single 'Assembly of the People', and replacing the independent judiciary by 'people's courts' with judges appointed by the Assembly. The UP also proposed wholesale nationalisation of all mining, banking, insurance and large industrial or commercial enterprises. Their foreign policy platform involved strong solidarity with Cuba and withdrawal from the Organisation of American States, 'an instrument of North American imperialism', and all bilateral treaties with the United States. This statement of revolutionary aspirations was promoted by Allende and the UP as 'the Chilean road to Socialism'. It was in fact a Marxist manifesto expressed in revolutionary terms and largely lifted from the Communist Party's own programme.

The Communist Party did not press to have its own candidate adopted as the leader of the *Unidad Popular.* As a necessary move in the process of finding a figure who appealed to all its component parties, they took the strange step of nominating Chile's great but eccentric poet Pablo Neruda as their stalking horse. Neruda recorded:

> It was a courageous way to force the others to come to an

agreement. When I accepted I told Comrade Corvalán I was doing it on condition that my resignation would be accepted when I tendered it. My withdrawal was inevitable, I felt.[9]

Neruda was probably the most famous figure in his Party but he knew that the others were highly unlikely to accept any Communist as leader of the UP. Because of its stubborn maintenance of a Stalinist line, even after Stalin himself was discredited, the Chilean Communist Party could not expect to draw much support from outside its own ranks; the Socialists, despite being more extreme ideologically, were likely to have more electoral appeal.

None of the three candidates seemed likely to get the absolute majority required for a clear win. The result of the first round was indeed very close: Allende received 36.3 per cent of the total votes, Alessandri 34.9 per cent, and Tomíc 27.8 per cent.[10] Under the Constitution, Congress now had to decide between Allende and Alessandri, the two candidates with most popular support. Despite precedents which indicated that Congress should elect the front-runner, and Tomíc's personal gesture in immediately visiting Allende to greet him as President-elect, the Christian Democrats were not committed formally to either Allende or Alessandri. The next weeks before the vote in Congress were a period of intense political bargaining, propaganda and covert plotting by Allende's opponents. In order to keep Allende out, Alessandri offered that, if elected, he would immediately resign and leave the field open for Frei to stand in a straight race in which, with his personal popularity and support from the Right, he would certainly defeat Allende. The Christian Democrats rejected this cynical deal and instead demanded that Allende should give a series of fundamental guarantees on freedom of expression, on the operation of political parties and trade unions, on the autonomy of both the legislature and the judiciary and on the preservation of the armed forces from political influence. Some of the Christian

[9] Pablo Neruda, *Confieso que He Vivido: Memorias*. For a moment, however, his candidacy caught fire. He says (in a rare access of realism) that 'fascinated and terrified I began to wonder what I would do if I was elected President of a republic wholly untamed, patently unable to solve its problems, deeply in debt.'

[10] Allende in fact got a lower percentage in 1970 than the 39 per cent he had in 1964, when there were only two strong candidates.

Democrats (but not Radomiro Tomíc) were deeply suspicious of the ultimate objectives of the UP and withheld support for Allende's election until he had signed a Statute of Constitutional Guarantees, which they hoped would bind him and the UP to observe these promises and act only within the Constitution.

CIA involvement

Meanwhile, in the United States the CIA and the high-level 'Forty Committee', which co-ordinated covert action abroad, were reacting frenetically, if belatedly, to the prospect of an avowedly Marxist government in South America. Before the election it had been decided not to provide financial support directly to Alessandri or Tomíc for their campaigns and to spend only a modest $135,000 on anti-Communist propaganda. The International Telephone and Telegraph Company (ITT) was not content with this and provided $350,000 (another $350,000 coming from other US companies operating in Chile) for the Alessandri campaign. This private support, though not approved by the Forty Committee, was facilitated by the CIA station in Santiago – a fact which soon became known in Chile. The full story was published in August before the election. The fact that foreign multinational corporations were known to have intervened in a Chilean election probably nullified any advantage which Alessandri might have gained from their support.

However, with Allende on the verge of becoming President the Forty Committee became more active. The idea of encouraging a military coup to stop Allende was canvassed but discarded (partly on principle and partly on practical grounds). A campaign of propaganda and economic pressure with the same objective was authorised from mid-September. This became known as 'Track I'; but another approach, 'Track II', was ordered simultaneously in Washington by Richard Nixon personally.[11] This involved efforts to stimulate some kind of military action: if not a *coup d'état*, then at least a change in circumstances which would somehow

[11] The only members of the Nixon administration who were parties to this were Henry Kissinger, Attorney General John Mitchell and the Director of the CIA, Richard Helms. Their main point of contact with Chile at the critical time was the owner of the newspaper *El Mercurio* and a great business empire in Chile, Agustín Edwards.

or other prevent Allende's election. For this purpose the Army Commander-in-Chief, General Schneider, who was clearly and publicly committed to observing the Constitution, would have to be removed. It was doubtful whether the kidnapping of Schneider alone would have had the desired effect since his presumed successor, General Carlos Prats, was also loyal to the Constitution. Nevertheless Track II was used to instruct the CIA station in Santiago (without the knowledge of the State Department, the Ambassador or even the Forty Committee) to contact other officers or right-wing civilians to this end. There was no shortage of Chilean plotters ready to act and the story of the CIA's efforts to influence them is a black comedy of confusion and cross-purposes.

Ultimately Nixon and Henry Kissinger, his National Security Adviser, decided on 12 October 1973 to put a stop to attempts to kidnap Schneider (which were by that time being planned by two separate groups). Nevertheless one of them attempted it, almost certainly without Washington's knowledge, on 22 October, with the disastrous result that Schneider, while resisting the kidnapping, was shot and died three days later.

Nixon and Kissinger believed that, if Allende came to power, Chile would become a 'popular democracy' like those of Eastern Europe and Cuba in which there would never be another free election. While Nixon's hatred of Allende was apparently based on visceral anti-communism, Kissinger's attitude was, typically, the result of political calculation. He argued that a Marxist government in Chile would exacerbate instability, encourage anti-US forces in Latin America as a whole, and even reinforce the appeal of 'Euro-Communism' in France and Italy.[12] Whether right or not, the outcome of Track II was the opposite to what had been intended. The murder of General Schneider strengthened the determination of the Chilean armed forces to allow the constitutional process to proceed. On 24 October Salvador Allende was elected President by a large majority at a joint session of Congress.

[12] Seymour Hersh (*The Price of Power*, 1983) quotes Kissinger as saying: 'I don't see why we need stand by and watch a country go communist because of the irresponsibility of its own people.'

An assessment of the Frei administration

The Frei administration changed Chilean society fundamentally. This was what the Christian Democrats had promised in the years before they attained power but the changes and their consequences did not turn out exactly as planned. Frei was above all a democrat devoted to constitutional government, but by 1970 he was being criticised as the Kerensky of Chilean politics.[13]

The 'Revolution in Liberty' was most evident in rural Chile but there were also major changes among the working classes in cities and towns, particularly in Santiago. In pursuit of their idea of promoting communitarian politics to enable people to take a direct hand in local affairs, the government provided support for neighbourhood committees (*juntas de vecinos*), women's organisations (*centros de madres*), housing projects and co-operatives. Both in the countryside and in the towns, many benefitted from these changes, but inevitably there were many more whose expectations were aroused but were impossible to satisfy. Unfortunately the Christian Democrats had inherited problems of inflation, debt and structural inefficiency in the economy which they could not solve in a single period of six years. The mobilisation of grassroots opinion, which was made a deliberate objective by the Christian Democrats in order to create political support for their policies, also created a huge and expectant clientele among the most needy Chileans, who could not then be persuaded to support unattractive but necessary measures to restrain wages, control inflation, raise productivity and so on.

These contradictions made it easy for the Marxist opposition parties to attack the government. The parties of the Right were already fighting hard to defend the interests of their supporters against the effects of agrarian reform (and the wider threat to the established order). Thus, from opposite political positions, both Right and Left used every possible means to obstruct the government's reform programmes – which had, of course, been the usual fate of reforming governments in Chile. By the end of Eduardo Frei's Presidency there was, less typically, a climate of

[13] This jibe derived from the title of a book published in Brazil in the middle of Frei's term of office which was eventually banned from circulation in Chile. It refers to the Russian constitutional political leader whose actions opened the door to the Bolsheviks in 1917.

increasing violence in the form of illegal occupations of land and strikes fomented by the Left; and the Army gave an ominous demonstration of protest in the shape of an aborted coup in 1969.

Nevertheless, the Christian Democrats had improved the lives of many thousands of Chilean workers and given hope to many more that their lot could eventually improve. The reforms which they had actually brought in, and the great drive towards popular participation in the political system, had created both the expectation of further fundamental reforms and a new impetus towards them. Eduardo Frei and his government have to be credited with substantial if sometimes double-edged achievements, but they had also contributed to a dangerous polarisation. The pendulum was now about to swing beyond the point of no return.

6

REVOLUTION AND REACTION (1970-1973)

> 'In those days a condition of latent violence had emerged in the country, a violence which could somehow be felt in the atmosphere. We had always lived far from the world's conflicts, had been the more or less contented and unconcerned inhabitants of a country where nothing ever happened; and suddenly a perverse turn of the wheel of history put us at the very vortex of the whirlwind.'
>
> – Jorge Edwards, *Adios Poeta*

Salvador Allende's victory in 1970 was greeted as the dawn of a new age by his supporters. His opponents felt the first tremor of an approaching earthquake which had already shaken the established order elsewhere in the world. The UP came to power in the wake of a widespread surge of radical, and sometimes revolutionary sentiment. Everywhere a new generation had been beating on the doors of governments and demanding change. In France the student movement had come near to bringing a government down in 1968 and Che Guevara was the cult figure of the age. The left, and liberals in the world at large, thought that Allende's Marxist government might succeed where others had failed.

Salvador Allende

People expected great things of Salvador Allende – but he was an improbable figure as a revolutionary leader. Dapper and even vain about his appearance, he was a *bon vivant* devoted to pretty women, Chivas Regal whisky and other good things of life. After a comfortable bourgeois upbringing, Allende qualified as a doctor and became Minister of Health under a Radical President from 1939 to 1942, but he was also a life-long socialist and enjoyed the heady environment of left-wing politics. He joined the Socialist Party in 1933, the year of its foundation, and in due course became its Secretary General and a leading critic of the faction which advocated working with the Communists. He was elected a Senator in 1945 and for twenty-five years was on good terms with many leaders of Chilean industry, the armed forces and even landowners. This was partly due to his connections as a freemason but he had charisma and even his political opponents found him *simpático* as a man.

After being defeated in the 1952 presidential election, Allende began to move closer to the Communist Party and associated himself enthusiastically with Fidel Castro, maintaining this connection even when Castro turned Cuba into a one-party state. He had close links also with the extreme Left in Chile, not least through his daughter and his sister, both of whom were associated with the Altamirano faction, and his nephew Andrés Pascal Allende, a leading figure in the MIR. Some members of the MIR were in Allende's personal bodyguard, the so-called *Grupo de Amigos Personales* (GAP), and he seemed entirely unconcerned by the contradiction between the MIR's record of revolutionary violence and his own avowed commitment to constitutional politics.

Was Allende a convinced Marxist-Leninist? According to his own public declarations, he firmly believed in pluralist democracy and (unlike Castro) would have handed over power to an elected successor after completing his term of office. Others such as the French Marxist commentator Régis Debray have described Allende as a real revolutionary who simply used democratic means to move towards the ultimate end of subverting constitutional democracy.[1] Debray was a Castroite ideologue who sought to present Allende as a man of similar stamp to Castro. Most Chilean politicians saw him differently. One, a life-long Conservative, summed him up as follows:

> Allende was an old-style politician, but one who, knowing human weaknesses only too well, knew how to manipulate them. It cannot be said that at any time in his long political career he ever achieved great popularity as a political leader. His style and

[1] Régis Debray, *Conversations with Allende: Socialism in Chile.* Debray remained deeply involved with Chile for many years after Allende's fall, and had considerable influence on French policy towards Chile in the 1970s and '80s.

> his character resembled very closely those of a radical socialist of the Fourth French Republic. Ambitious and tenacious, while not absolutely scrupulous, he was definitely a man who was loyal to all those who gave him their political support.
>
> In his public appearances he was arrogant, and looked like a patent leather dandy; while in private he was unaffected and nice. He was a skilful political manipulator. In the forty years that I knew him, and in spite of the intensity of our political battles, I never saw him act with deliberate ill-will, or become the slave of hatred or incurable resentment....[2]

Whatever his deepest motives Allende was certainly determined not to be deflected from the platform proposed by the UP during the 1970 campaign. This involved a massive programme of nationalisation of virtually all major industries and commercial enterprises;[3] the rapid acceleration of land expropriations (and a redirection of the reform process begun under Frei); immediate redistribution of incomes by wage and taxation policy; and a number of fundamental constitutional changes. It was a programme of government which could only be called revolutionary. Allende repeatedly said that his objective was to put the manifesto into effect and make it irreversible.

This would have been almost impossible to achieve by constitutional means even if the UP and Salvador Allende had commanded an effective majority in the Congress, but with only 18 seats in the Senate and 57 in the lower house (as opposed to 32 and 93 for the opposition) they had nowhere near the level of support necessary to enact their legislation. The problems of leading the UP were also compounded by its internal divisions. Throughout the period there were serious differences of view on the tactics to be followed by the government and to some extent on ultimate objectives. These differences were sharpest between the Communists and Socialists, but arose also with minor parties and even between different factions within the Socialist Party.

2 Pedro Ibáñez, *The Chilean Crisis and its Outcome* (1974), cited in R.J. Alexander, *The Tragedy of Chile*.

3 The UP were committed to nationalise the mines, banks, foreign trade, all means of transport and communications, power supply, petroleum, iron and steel and many other strategic industries.

President Salvador Allende at a press conference.

Fidel Castro on a visit to Chile in November 1971, with President Allende.

The make-up of Unidad Popular

Chile probably had the most orthodox Communist Party in all Latin America. In theory it accepted all the classic tenets of Marxism-Leninism, including the dictatorship of the proletariat, the class war and the use of violence if necessary to achieve its objectives. At the same time the Chilean Party was very loyal to Moscow. It was the first outside the Soviet bloc to welcome the invasion of Czechoslovakia in 1968, but was always prepared to adjust its tactics to suit the interests of the Communist Party in European countries such as Spain, Italy and France where the road to power (as in Chile) required it to establish alliances with others. This preoccupation meant that the Chilean Communists always moved with caution towards their objectives. They preferred to work themselves into positions of power and influence within the UP government and operate by Fabian methods rather than by direct action such as take-overs of land or factories by the workers. From the beginning of Allende's Presidency, the Communists contrived to occupy the main economic ministries almost continuously and also a large number of Under Secretaryships in other departments. They did not expect to achieve their goals within a single presidential term but nevertheless retained their eventual objective of establishing a Soviet-style dictatorship in Chile.

The Socialists, as already noted, were nothing like as well-disciplined as the Communist Party. Socialism contained several factions often bitterly feuding with each other. One, led by Aniceto Rodríguez who had been narrowly defeated by Allende in the struggle for the presidential nomination,. was overtly Marxist-Leninist in ideology, but preferred to follow as far as possible the electoral or constitutional path. However, in January 1971, Rodríguez was superseded by Carlos Altamirano who led a more extreme 'Leninist' faction which was convinced that the UP would have to obtain total power in order to bring about revolution. It refused to be restrained by a web of 'bourgeois legality'. Notwithstanding his admiration for Castro, Allende himself had usually sided with the 'electoral' faction of the party. The Altamirano faction kept control of the Socialist Party till September 1973 and profited greatly by its success in the municipal elections of 1971 when it won 22.4 per cent, only marginally less than the

Christian Democrats and well ahead of the Communists with 16.9 per cent. This strengthened Altamirano's voice and influence as against Allende's in the debate about tactics within the UP.

In practical terms, differences between them centred usually on the pace of change, with Altamirano pressing for more extreme measures on all fronts to accelerate the revolution, and on tactics. While Allende sought to persuade opponents to accept UP policies, the Altamirano faction had no time for political manoeuvring of the traditional kind. They were not only ready to ally the UP government openly with the MIR but also totally opposed to any kind of compromise with the Christian Democrats or the middle classes whom they saw as no different from the conservative National Party.[4] In both respects, Allende's views were usually closer to those of the Communists than to those of the people who dominated his own Socialist party.

The minor partners in the UP were the Radical Party, which split and split again in 1970 and 1971, becoming a much reduced shadow of its former self, and a number of other small groups, such as the *Movimiento de Acción Popular Unitaria* (MAPU) and the *Izquierda Cristiana* (IC) which had split away from the Christian Democratic Party. The MAPU eventually became an openly Marxist party and allied itself with the extreme left wing of the Socialists and the MIR, while the *Izquierda Cristiana* kept somewhat nearer to its Catholic roots. Among these minor partners only the MAPU had much influence on the direction of UP policy, but their very existence added to the underlying incoherence of the government. Superficially, however, the UP at least appeared to be bound together by rhetoric. Different sections of it had very different ideas about how to achieve the objectives and what priority to give them, but they all appeared to be aiming at nothing less than a revolution.

The class war

In the early days of the UP government its aspirations were chillingly summed up by Carlos Altamirano: 'The bourgeois state in Chile

[4] Well-off landowners, professionals and commercial leaders who were still strongly represented in the National Party were dubbed *momios* or mummies and ridiculed as archaic relics of the past.

will not serve as a basis for socialism, and it is necessary to destroy it.' This was a clear declaration of class war and President Allende took up the theme with enthusiasm in his first 'State of the Nation' address on 21 May 1971, when he said: 'The People's Government is inspired in its policy by a premise that is artificially denied by some – the existence of classes and social sectors with antagonistic and opposing interests.' The Chilean road to socialism would be a revolution such as the world had never known, a 'journey without maps'. They would walk a new road, 'without benefit of a guide, our only compass our faithfulness to the humanism of the ages, and particularly Marxist humanism'.

This exalted and visionary talk was bound to terrify the former ruling élites – the *momios* and the middle classes. They were right to be scared, and it soon emerged that UP threats to the 'bourgeois state' were not mere words. The first and overriding objective was clearly to break its opponents' capacity to resist by undermining their economic strength before they could recover from the shock of electoral defeat. The influence of the big landowners would be finally destroyed by the agrarian reform law, which was to be much more rigorously applied than under the Frei administration. The new Minister of Agriculture, Jacques Chonchol, formerly a left-wing Christian Democrat who had headed the drive for land reform in the 1960s, announced that all farms which were due for expropriation under the Frei government's *Ley de Reforma Agraria* would be taken over by the end of 1971.

At the end of the Frei government, 40 per cent of the economy was already state-owned, 30 per cent depended on state funding and only about 30 per cent was entirely in private hands. The UP quickly announced that it would nationalise another 120 major firms which had 'strategic' roles in the national economy including the banks and, above all, the copper companies. The latter had few defenders inside Chile and were obvious prime targets for the UP since they were still basically run by US managers (although part-owned by the state as a result of 'Chileanisation'). Within twelve months the government had effectively nationalised all of the *gran minería*, all banks, insurance and financial companies and most important manufacturing concerns. Not 120 but 190 large companies had been taken over. By June 1972 the total had risen to 270.

In view of the Nixon administration's obvious hostility, the nationalisation of copper involved special difficulty for the UP. The United States had never opposed other governments' right to nationalise foreign enterprises within their jurisdiction, provided full compensation was promptly paid. In this case the dispute centred on that issue. Anaconda and Kennecott, the two largest US corporations still holding minority interests in copper mines, were faced with a presidential decree which deprived them of any right to compensation on the grounds that they had already taken out excess profits which were estimated at more than the book value of their investment. In short, the companies ought to compensate the Chilean state for being expropriated, and both companies received claims to repay the difference. They responded by urging the US government to retaliate with a range of economic sanctions against Chile and by legal actions around the world to embargo the proceeds of copper sales from 'their mines'. These proposals were considered at length in Washington; and ITT joined in powerfully in support of strong action against Chile, particularly after its subsidiary, the Chilean Telephone Company, was taken over in August 1971. However, other US companies with interests in Chile, particularly banks with outstanding debts, opposed the extreme measures proposed by ITT, and Washington's eventual response was relatively restrained. Export-Import Bank credits were withheld and a number of proposed loans by international institutions were blocked; but the reaction was much less savage than Nixon's original threat 'to make the Chilean economy scream'.

When it turned its attention to banks, the UP decided to proceed without new legislation (which would certainly have been opposed) by buying up the stock of Chilean banks in the market, or negotiating directly with the owners of foreign banks. Most of the latter found no effective way of resisting these take-overs, but Allende's policy was another example of ideology triumphing over common sense. On the one hand, it was very costly to nationalise banks in this way and, on the other, foreign banks whose Chilean subsidiaries had been expropriated obviously had no particular interest in providing short-term finance or lines of credit for Chile's international trade. Allende argued that the squeeze on Chile's financial lifeline was organised deliberately by the United States for purely political reasons. Whatever the intentions of the CIA or of Chile's declared enemies such as ITT, it was, at the least, improbable that the Chilean government could expropriate foreign banks and still rely on them for credit as if nothing had changed.

Nationalisation of other major manufacturing companies was pressed forward equally fast. In some cases this was achieved by the same simple method as applied to the banks. CORFO, the state development corporation, simply bought shares in the market to attain control of major shipping lines, ceramics, food-processing, glass, sugar, petro-chemicals, electricity companies etc. None of this was authorised by law, and Congress had not approved the expenditure. Many other firms were brought under state control by the technical device of 'requisition' or 'intervention', often using an emergency decree passed in 1932 during the brief Socialist Republic led by the pioneer of Chilean Socialism, Marmaduke Grove (Don Marma). This process was frequently sparked off by a workers' strike (sometimes contrived by left-wing elements) or the forcible occupation of a factory by the workers. The closure of the business could then be used as a pretext to justify it being 'requisitioned'.

Requisition or intervention did not involve the transfer of ownership and was therefore a cheaper means to the same immediate end; but in the long run it was expensive and inefficient. Under the power-sharing convention within the UP,[5] the government 'interventors' who were then chosen to run businesses on behalf of the state were often party officials with minimal qualifications and the companies therefore accumulated even bigger financial losses. What was probably even more damaging was that the fear of being taken over by these arbitrary means made all other businessmen, whether or not their companies were considered 'strategic', completely unwilling to invest. There was almost no private investment during the Allende regime. His defenders have argued that this shows that the private sector deliberately sabotaged the elected government; but who would invest in an enterprise knowing it was likely to be subject to intervention the next day, and confiscated as soon as possible?

[5] This was in fact a well-established Chilean tradition. Coalitions always involved a share-out of government jobs among the various parties, the *cuoteo*.

Agrarian reform

The government's drive for land reform was put in train just as vigorously. The UP could not enact a completely new law but it drastically accelerated the rate at which the *latifundia* were expropriated under the 1967 law. It also quietly abandoned the Christian Democrats' declared objective of transferring expropriated land to *campesinos* individually, in favour of retaining it permanently in collective or state farms. In future agricultural production in Chile was to be organized on the same lines as in the Soviet Union under Stalin. *Centros de Reforma Agraria* would be established to give training to the workers, replacing the *asentamientos* of the Frei land reform and being themselves replaced in time by cooperatives which the *campesinos* would work on a collective basis. In the case of very large-scale operations, such as the vast sheep-raising ranches of Patagonia, state farms were to be established. Ignoring the experience of the Soviet Union and Cuba, this pressure for total collectivisation ran contrary to the *campesinos'* intense desire to own land themselves and was a striking example of the way the UP alienated even its natural supporters. At the same time efforts were made to establish state-controlled bodies as the sole buyers of agricultural produce. This predictably led to flourishing black markets and a calamitous decline in food production for normal distribution. The fall in farm production caused a sharp increase in imports of food in a country which could normally grow nearly all it needed. In 1970, $217 million was spent on food imports. This figure rose to $295 million in 1971 and $400 million in 1972.

Under the pressure of the UP's drive for quick results, the pace of land expropriation increased fast. The Frei administration had taken over some 1,300 farms covering a total of 3,585,553 hectares in six years. Jacques Chonchol, the Minister of Agriculture, working with ideologically like-minded officials in CORA (and his own former organisation INDAP), took over 3,500 farms covering about 5,000,000 hectares in only two years. They and their supporters wanted to change the previous policy so that only 20 hectares of land could be retained by the original owner of a farm. Although they could not make this a legal requirement, they nevertheless took over farms on various pretexts regardless of physical size, quality of management or any other established criteria. An even more drastic method adopted was the illegal seizure of land, the *toma.* According to one observer, there were some 2,000 *tomas* during the first two years of Allende's regime.[6] Most of these were in poorer parts of the country and they often involved the forcible occupation of land by local workers or outsiders brought in by the *Movimiento de Campesinos Revolucionarios* (MCR), the rural arm of the MIR, sometimes with the connivance of CORA officials and members of the Socialist Party or MAPU.

Chonchol left no doubt about the true purpose of his policy:

> 'In an under-developed society, with limited resources – whether in a revolutionary situation or a non-revolutionary situation where people are trying to bring about basic changes – it is a political error to aim for social improvement and economic growth at the same time.'

The agrarian reforms of 1970–3 had no discernible economic benefits and in fact contributed substantially to the fiscal and balance of payments crisis which built up over the period. 'Basic changes' certainly took place, but the 'social improvement' which was supposed to be achieved by them is difficult to identify. Landowners were dispossessed and lost whatever political influence they still had. That can be counted as a political benefit to the UP and perhaps other interests, but hardly as a social improvement. The *campesino,* in whose interests land reform had been initiated in the 1960s, usually found that, far from being enabled to work land of his own, he had merely exchanged a private landowner for the state. All the *campesino* organisations and rural unions were apparently opposed to the UP's policy of imposing Soviet-style collectives or state farms instead of dividing the land. If some individuals preferred their new situation it must often have been because they felt freer than before, not because they were better-off.

It is astonishing that Chonchol and his collaborators, who must have been aware of the disastrous consequences of forced collectivisation in other countries, should nevertheless have persisted in trying to force this policy through in Chile. It was already known to be inefficient in terms of producing food, and no one with any understanding of peasant farmers could have thought that it would be popular with them. The hard truth was that

[6] Figure quoted by Robert Moss in *Chile's Marxist Experiment* (Exeter, 1973).

land reforms, combined with efficient production, could only be achieved at a heavy cost which would have fallen primarily on town dwellers who were quite unwilling to pay it. The apparent folly of pushing the policy through is only explained if the true purpose was neither to provide food for Chile's urban population nor to bring justice to the *campesinos,* but to create a rural power base to support the political revolution which the UP hoped to accomplish.

The truth of Jacques Chonchol's words was evident to observers such as the British historian Alistair Horne, who was in Chile in the summer of 1971 and found the MIR and the MCR already in control of large tracts of the country in southern Chile. He has given a vivid personal account of that time in his book *Small Earthquake in Chile,* and the chapters dealing with land reform in the south of the country are particularly revealing. Horne discovered that Chonchol and other ministers of the Allende government, and officials of CORA, were in touch personally with the MIR leadership and fully aware of what was happening in the countryside. He met a wide range of Chileans involved in the turmoil, and visited and talked at length to one of the young MIR leaders operating in the south. Comandante Pepe, a Che Guevara figure to the Chilean press, had organised the seizure of a number of farms around Liquiñe in the Andes foothills near Lake Panguipulli. Pepe, with his pretty young lieutenant Valentina and a group of ten others, were young activists of the MIR from its birthplace, the University of Concepción. This group, working with whatever local help they could find, organised the *tomas* and then set about teaching all the workers to run the farms as co-operatives and educating them in 'revolutionary correctness'. These *tomas,* Pepe claimed, had already given the MIR control of land amounting to about 400,000 hectares, which would be one of the nuclei on which the new socialist state would be built. Their idol, Che Guevara, had failed to create this in Bolivia. Pepe and his group thought they were succeeding in Chile.

Both in Pepe's fiefdom near the Argentine border and in other parts of southern Chile where the MIR and the MCR were most active, large numbers of Mapuche Indians led a wretched existence on the fringes of small towns or crowded into the *reducciones* (reservations), which was all the land that remained to them. The Mapuche's suppressed hunger for land had long caused friction between them and those who were farming what had formerly been their land. This tension was particularly acute in the provinces of Cautín, Malleco and Ñuble. In 1971 the MIR and MCR, often claiming to operate on behalf of the Mapuche, were responsible for as many as 400 *tomas* in Cautín and 100 in Ñuble.

For the young *Miristas* the moment for starting the real revolution seemed to have arrived. When Fidel Castro himself visited Chile[7] in November of that year, he made it completely clear to every audience he addressed, and no doubt to the President personally, that he believed that the MIR and the Altamirano faction of the Socialists were right in wanting to abandon legality in favour of revolution by every means possible. Alistair Horne records words spoken by Pepe which might have been spoken by Castro himself:

> 'Historically, there is bound to be a counter-reaction against the Government, a right wing coup. As a *Mirista*, as a Marxist, my historical view is that the longer time passes, the more difficult it will be to reverse the popular processes – therefore the right wing will have to react sooner rather than later. And if you see a man about to hit you in the face, you don't just stand there waiting for the blow, do you? Of course we will defend ourselves, *hasta la muerte*; but we must organise and we feel there is not much time. It is likely that there will be a right wing coup within the year.'[8]

Pepe's prediction was premature on timing but realistic in recognising that the MIR, however fierce in its political belief, was no more than a terrorist movement in the process of turning itself into a small-scale militia. It did, however, enjoy the tolerance of the government, and sometimes more than that. Despite protests from many quarters against its activities, President Allende almost always refused to act firmly against the MIR or other terrorist organisations. The sole exceptions were in June 1971, when a prominent Christian Democrat (Edmundo Pérez Zújovic) was

[7] Castro came for what was supposed to be a brief formal visit but stayed for almost a month. His speeches caused a sensation, but most contemporary writers doubt whether he did the revolutionary cause much good. Ironically, one of the military officers attached to the Cuban President was the future President of Chile, Augusto Pinochet. Pinochet was already a passionate (albeit discreet) anti-communist, but Allende considered him a simple military professional.

[8] Quoted by Alistair Horne in *Small Earthquake in Chile* (London, 1972).

assassinated by a terrorist group known as the People's Organised Vanguard (VOP) and a year later when a plan was discovered to attack Allende's own residence. Despite the growing contradiction between the gradualist strategy of the Communist Party and the impatience of the Altamirano faction of the Socialists, the MAPU and all those linked with the MIR, Allende saw himself above all as the unifier, holding the government coalition together. In fact, polarisation was sapping his strength month by month. By the time he finally accepted the need to break with the extremists, his authority had been almost wholly dissipated.

Boom and bust

The first year of the UP was one of the best for economic performance in Chile's history. Growth reached 7.7 per cent and both unemployment and inflation dropped – the latter from 36 per cent to 22 per cent – between December 1970 and December 1971. In accordance with the then current view that the main cause of poor economic performance in Latin America was lack of consumer demand (and the need to secure the government's popularity), an average wage increase of 35 per cent was awarded to all workers. This was accompanied by a general price freeze and led to a wave of consumption as millions of previously impoverished people found themselves better off. The UP's supporters felt that the millennium had arrived and in the municipal elections of April, 1971, its vote rose above 50 per cent – the peak of its electoral popularity.

The bonanza of course had its price. By the end of 1971, Chile's international reserves (which had been at a record high at the end of the Frei administration) were all but exhausted and the balance of payments had moved from a surplus of $114 million in 1970 to a deficit of $309 million in 1971. This was not the result of what Allende repeatedly denounced as the 'invisible blockade' of the Chilean economy organised by the US administration; the prime causes were the decline in export earnings, the flight of private capital and a rising fiscal deficit. For a time higher domestic demand had been met by taking up slack in the economy, but the planning and investment required to keep up production after the first year simply failed to take place. Instead investment collapsed, and when the government conceded a further large wage increase for 1972 in the hope of repeating the previous year's success, the result was inevitably to increase inflation. Having fallen to 22 per cent in 1971, it rocketed to 260 per cent in 1972, a figure far worse than Chile had ever experienced before, and was to reach 600 per cent in 1973.

A fall in world copper prices in 1971, combined with rises in the prices of food which Chile was now obliged to import in increasing quantity, did nothing to help Allende's economic policy. But the fundamental causes of the collapse were the huge increase in the government deficit caused mainly by higher expenditure on social services and by the folly of buying banks and other enterprises for cash and then financing their deficits by subsidies from the Central Bank. The problem of increased government expenditure was compounded by unearned wage increases for most of the work force but was considered by the UP economic team to be a short-term aberration which would be corrected, according to the prevailing 'structuralist theory', when the structural changes (agrarian reform, nationalisation, etc.) had taken effect.

By June 1972 Allende was beginning to see the dangers. He changed his economics minister and introduced austerity measures, but the government had lost control of the economy. Production dropped every month. Food imports had doubled compared to 1970, and were to double again in 1973. The total amount of subsidies to nationalised companies (met by the simple means of printing more money) rose to 55 per cent of the national budget. There were shortages of almost all consumer goods – food, clothing, tobacco, household necessities. The government fought shy of admitting the problem and refused to set up a formal rationing system. Instead the nationalised distribution company established a web of neighbourhood committees which were supposed 'to assure adequate supplies, supervise price controls and struggle against speculation in monopolies'. These committees were, of course, seen as political instruments controlled by the UP. Families that supported the regime received regular food supplies; while others were forced to turn to the black market or go without.

The opposition revived

In January 1972 the opposition received a boost by winning three by-elections in Central Valley seats. They continued to try to check the UP's excesses, such as the arbitrary nationalisation of all kinds of businesses and even small farms. However, pressure in Congress, particularly by the Christian Democrats, failed to produce any agreement with the UP about the precise definition of the 'social area' of the economy which they would bring under state control. Despite personal assurances from the President that small businesses were safe, the trucking industry, pre-eminently operated by small businessmen, came under threat later that very month when CORFO announced the intention of establishing a state monopoly of all transport in the south of the country. This was a red rag to the truckers and they were supported by many other *gremios* (trade associations).[9] The *gremios*' reply started as a transport strike in the extreme south but quickly spread to all the trucking companies and, with the backing of the Christian Democrats, to engineers, taxi drivers, bank employees and even doctors, dentists, lawyers and architects. The official trade unions, still largely controlled by UP parties, stayed on the sidelines but 100,000 peasants were said to have joined what became a nationwide protest.

Eventually Allende managed to bring the strike to an end by calling on the armed forces to support him and appointing three senior officers to his cabinet. He had always been careful to cultivate good relations with the military, to visit regiments and eat with both the officers and other ranks in their messes from time to time. After years of financial stringency and meagre pay imposed on the armed forces in the 1960s by previous governments, Allende (surprisingly to many) allowed the defence budget to rise significantly in the early 1970s. After the truckers' strike of October, 1972, he evidently saw the armed forces as a means of shoring up his government and countering the destructive internal splits developing within the UP.

General Prats, the Army Commander-in-Chief, who had always been loyal to the constitutional government, became Minister of the Interior, a key post in government. Prats now urged the

[9] These professional guilds or trade associations had grown in importance as interest and lobbying groups. There were, and are, *gremios* for all the professions, small businesses and trades of all kinds, of which the truck drivers were probably the most powerful. In the later 1970s and '80s the *gremios* were to become the base for a political movement which was developed by right-wing theorists seeking an alternative to conventional democratic organisations.

Women of the opposition protesting at shortages during the Allende administration by beating pots and pans.

Demonstration by supporters of President Allende.

armed forces to help the President to control the extremists on both Right and Left, arguing that he might ultimately reach an understanding with the Christian Democrats and thus be able to break with the extreme Left. That theory was never put into practice, but the new cabinet managed to restore some calm after the truckers' strike and to guarantee a peaceful atmosphere for the Congressional elections in March 1973. When the election took place the opposition coalition, formed by the Christian Democrat and National parties, received 55.7 per cent of the popular vote against the government's 43.9 per cent. This was a setback for the UP, but the opposition had failed to achieve the two thirds majority in both Houses which was required in order to impeach the President.[10]

The slide towards violence

Both sides hailed the election results as a success but in fact nothing had been resolved. From this point on, as inflation galloped ahead, the number of strikes increased, including an extremely expensive one lasting four months at the El Teniente copper mine in which the miners rejected their Marxist leaders, ignored the condemnation of the UP government and rallied round a Christian Democrat strike leader. This was not a strike by the *gremios,* which could be dismissed by the UP as a 'bosses' strike' like that of October 1982, but an industrial strike by the most important group of organised workers against a government claiming to be unequivocally devoted to the workers' interests. There were similar strikes at the biggest mine of all at Chuquicamata.

The government also quarrelled with the Catholic Church (and gave the middle classes yet another reason to fight them) by proposing a new national educational system which was admitted to be modelled on the East German system, imposing a rigid curriculum with strongly anti-Catholic and Marxist overtones. This was clearly intended as social engineering with a political

[10] This was not to happen since the opposition came out of the election with only 30 out of 50 seats in the Senate and 87 out of 150 in the Chamber. Some authorities quote slightly different percentages of the popular vote. Those given above are from Collier and Sater's *A History of Chile, 1808-1994* (Cambridge, 1996).

purpose and it caused the military members to resign from the cabinet at the end of March. The next three months brought deepening economic crisis, growing divisions within the UP and growing unity among their opponents. There were many violent incidents in Santiago, usually sparked by the MIR, and these were barely contained by the authorities. An extreme right-wing group, *Patria y Libertad*, was also active and had received some funds from the CIA (mostly indirectly), with which it was probably importing arms.

The military reaction eventually came in the shape of tanks and armoured cars of the Second Armoured Regiment which appeared in front of the Moneda Palace on 29 June. The pretext was to rescue one of their officers held under arrest in the Ministry of Defence (opposite the Palace) for plotting with a right-wing terrorist group. In a two-hour confrontation twenty-two people were killed and thirty-two injured before General Prats, backed by other units of the Santiago garrison, persuaded the insurgents to surrender. This bungled coup attempt (named the *tancazo*) showed the lack of unity among the military leadership[11] but also the extreme tension between the regime and the Army. Another direct result was that many more industrial centres and factories were occupied by workers affiliated to the MIR or other armed groups. Allende had called by radio for the workers to arm themselves and march to the Moneda to defend his regime. They failed to respond, but it was now obvious that there were substantial arms supplies available in the *cordones industriales* (industrial belts) around Santiago.

After the *tancazo*, the workers conspicuously failed to return the factories to their owners, either public or private. These workplaces, together with surrounding housing and commercial districts, were now controlled by local committees linked to one or other political party or the MIR. However, under a new law introduced to check the alarming inflow of illegal weapons, the armed forces now began to mount regular and vigorous efforts to search for and remove arms from the *cordones*. It was becoming

[11] It also showed the Chilean Army's lack of expertise in organising a military *coup d'état*. According to the US Ambassador of the time, the column obeyed all the traffic lights and one tank stopped to fill up at a commercial gas station. They learned from experience.

clearer each week that the country was facing only two alternatives—a military coup or civil war.

Everyone in Chile expected a decisive event but no one knew when it would come. Late in July, in response to the urging of the Archbishop of Santiago, the President made another unsuccessful effort to negotiate some kind of *modus vivendi* with the Christian Democrats. They demanded the restoration of constitutional norms and other guarantees. Allende could not agree. Even if he had, his own Socialist Party made it crystal clear that it would never accept any compromise with the opposition political parties, even with the Christian Democrats whom it described as 'the enemies of Chile and the workers'. This was probably the point of no return. The left and right of the UP were in effect splitting and Allende could no longer control his own party. He was also in direct confrontation with the opposition majorities in both Houses of Congress and with the Supreme Court and the Controller General, who were the supposed guarantors of the legality of executive decisions and ultimately of the Constitution. All had formally declared the government to be outside the Constitution.

On 25 July, even before the final attempt at negotiation with the Christian Democrats, the truck drivers had called another strike on the ground that the government had failed to carry out earlier promises. The strike escalated even more rapidly than in 1972 into almost total paralysis of commercial, professional and industrial activity throughout the country. In desperation Allende persuaded the top military leaders to rejoin his cabinet. General Prats became Minister of Defence; Admiral Montero, Minister of Finance; and Air Force General Ruiz, Minister of Transport. Getting the military into government again was Allende's last effort to find a way of preserving at least the outward form of Chile's crumbling democracy, but it also had disastrous effects on the cohesion of the armed forces. Prats and the other Commanders-in-Chief felt that they had to respond to the appeal of their elected President, but many of their colleagues were by now planning to remove the government in order (as they saw it) to save the country.

However, neither Allende and his few surviving political allies, nor any of the other political leaders, were any longer relevant. The power to decide the issue was in other hands.

Coup d'état

The last straw for the armed forces was not the imminent collapse of the national economy but the mounting evidence of arms being accumulated in the *cordones industriales* and of the organisation of private militia forces which were not even under the control of the UP but led by various factions, many of them heavily infiltrated by foreign 'military advisers'. This was a recipe for a chaotic civil war which no one would be able to control. At the same time some on the extreme Left were suspected of seeking to subvert the armed forces themselves. This culminated in late August with what seemed to be an attempt to provoke mutinies in two Chilean warships. The Navy accused Carlos Altamirano, Oscar Garretón of the MAPU and Miguel Enriquez of the MIR of conspiring with sailors and urging them to shoot their officers in order to get control of naval armaments. To the Navy this was a declaration of war on the armed forces, and the senior officers in the Cabinet were forced to resign. New Commanders-in-Chief, General Augusto Pinochet and Air Force General Gustavo Leigh, were appointed by Allende on 23 August. (Admiral José Toribio Merino replaced Admiral Montero, but was still formally second-in-command of the Navy since his predecessor's resignation had not been accepted.)

When it came, the coup was brutally conclusive. Learning from the failure of the *tancazo* in June, planning had been proceeding for some months. Knowledge of it had been limited to the smallest possible number, which of course did not include the three former Commanders-in-Chief who had accepted Cabinet appointments. The widespread view that General Pinochet was a prime mover behind the coup is not supported by the other participants although officers of the Army general staff working under Pinochet's orders certainly planned the action taken by the Army on 11 September.[12] Whether or not he was responsible for planning the coup, he

[12] In his memoirs and in his book about the coup itself, *El Día Decisivo* (Santiago, 1982), Pinochet states that from the middle of 1982 (while serving as Chief of Staff), he started to convert the Army's defensive internal security planning into a plan to take over the government. He also says that in July 1973 he discussed the preparation of detailed plans for the coup with General Herman Brady, then Director of the Army's Academia de Guerra. Pinochet's account implies that he alone authorised and co-ordinated this planning.

certainly did not commit himself to act till the very last moment. He himself claims that the coup was originally intended to take place on or near the National Day on 18 September when many troop movements could easily be explained as preparation for the traditional military parade.

Undoubtedly the first open commitment was made by the Navy independently of the Army. Admiral Merino sent a personal note to his Army and Air Force colleagues on 9 September forcing the issue:

> '*Gustavo y Augusto:*
> *Bajo mi palabra de honor el Dia D sera el dia 11 y la hora 0600.*
> *Si Vds no pueden cumplir esta fase con el total de las fuerzas que mandan en Santiago, explíquenmelo al reverso.*
> *El Almirante Huidobro esta autorizado para traer y discutir cualquier tema con Vds. Los saludo con esperanzas de comprension.*'

On the back of the note he added his final exhortation.

> '*Gustavo: Es la ultima oportunidad JT.*
> *Augusto: Si no puede con toda tu fuerza del primer momento, no viveremos para el futuro. Pepe.*'[13]

On 10 September, the Chilean fleet sailed from Valparaiso to join in a routine annual naval exercise, UNITAS, with the United States and other forces. That night the Chilean ships waited hull down at sea and sailed back the following morning. Meanwhile naval forces ashore had seized control of Valparaiso. The departure of a group of marines for Santiago was the first intimation of the coup which reached Allende early that morning.

Overnight, Army commanders received orders to take over civil government offices in all the provinces as well as in the

[13] 'Gustavo and Augusto:
On my word of honour, D-Day will be the 11th and the hour 0600.
If you cannot meet this with all your forces in Santiago, please explain why on the back (of this sheet).
Admiral Huidobro is authorised to discuss any aspect with you. I greet you hoping for your understanding.'
On the back:
'Gustavo: This is the last chance. JT.
Augusto: If you can't commit all your force initially, we shan't live to see the future. Pepe.' (Author's translation).

capital. An elaborate plan to silence the radio and television stations controlled by the government was put into effect. The *Carabineros*, numbering some 35,000 armed men, came in on the side of the plotters at the last moment under General César Mendoza. Most of the country was already in the hands of the armed forces by 8.30 a.m. Only in Santiago was there any serious resistance. The President chose to face the insurrection against him in the Moneda Palace, where he arrived about 7.30 a.m. and was joined by a group including his two daughters Beatriz and Isabel, ministers, military aides, friends and fifty or sixty of his GAP bodyguards. The Moneda was soon surrounded by army units and tanks, and an armed forces command post was established opposite to it in the Ministry of Defence.

Salvador Allende made his last public appearance on the balcony of the Moneda and broadcast his famous final message to the Chilean people on the one surviving radio station available to him:

> 'This will be the last time I shall be able to speak to you.[...] I can only say to all the workers I shall not resign. In this historic moment, I will pay with my life for the people's loyalty.[...] These are my last words and I am certain that my sacrifice will not be in vain.'

Imitating President Balmaceda's action in 1891, he had always declared that he would never surrender and would take his own life first. Allende had the same courage as Balmaceda and, later that morning, he made good his word. An ultimatum was sent to him by the military command demanding that he and his entourage leave the building before it was attacked from the ground and by rockets launched by the Air Force's Hawker Hunter aircraft. The President rejected it, and when the assault began he used a sub-machine gun presented to him by Fidel Castro to join in the counter-fire with his Cuban-trained GAP team of bodyguards. Later he sent the majority of his other companions, his mistress Miriam Conteras, and his two daughters away. Only his doctor and a handful of Ministers were in the Moneda when, sitting on a red sofa in one of the great reception rooms, Salvador Allende blew his brains out.

What lay behind the coup?

More than 1,000 books, one for every day of the Allende Presidency, have already been published about the *Unidad Popular* and the dramatic end of its leader. Many aspects of the story are still bitterly disputed – none more than the contentious question of how far the blame for the UP's failure, and the coup itself, should be attributed to outside interference, particularly from the United States.

Officially US policy towards Allende, as formulated by the National Security Council in November 1970, was supposed to be 'correct but cool'. It was planned to abandon any new economic aid programmes and EXIM Bank guarantees (except for humanitarian aid) and to run down existing aid with the important exception of military programmes. However, trade and lending to Chile by private US banks, and by international institutions to which the US belonged, would continue in the normal way. In practice Washington did not follow this policy of moderate response, but neither did it carry out Nixon's threat 'to make the economy scream'. Decisions were made case by case and not on the basis of any overall design.

In November 1971 the UP administration had to seek refinancing for Chile's soaring foreign debt. Of the total of $1.86 billion, $1.23 billion was due to US lenders. The US administration had every opportunity to turn the screw on Chile but, despite that preponderance of interest, Washington failed to persuade the 'Paris Club' of lenders to make refinancing conditional on the payment of compensation for foreign assets which Chile had nationalised. Nevertheless, new lending by international institutions had dropped almost to nothing by 1972/73, partly because of well-founded criticisms of Allende's economic policies which he would not consider changing. Whatever pressure the US may have applied privately in the IBRD, IMF or IDB, it did not actually veto any proposed loans. Chile (as Kissinger commented) was already 'doing an excellent job of destroying her own credit-worthiness' in the eyes of the bankers.

Allende naturally turned for credit to the Soviet Union and other European and Latin American sources. Argentina and Brazil, for example, supplied Chile with more than $132 million in short-term credits in 1972 alone. The Soviet Bloc provided much larger sums of long-term finance in the same period, the total reaching $471 million by the end of that year. The largest sums came, however, from Western European banks which by the middle of 1973 had provided $547 million in short-term finance.[14] Much of this credit was in soft currency, short-term and tied to purchases of specified goods from the country concerned; and it was often on tougher terms than Chile had been allowed previously. Nevertheless, the argument that it was 'an invisible blockade' by the United States which destroyed the UP's Marxist experiment in Chile in 1970-3, cannot be sustained. Most of the damage was done by the UP itself.

In the aftermath of 11 September 1973, US and other liberal opinion immediately assumed that the Nixon administration and US multinational corporations had either inspired or supported the coup by covert means. There was indeed clear evidence of this in ITT documents published in March 1972 (and evidently stolen from ITT files) by the US columnist Jack Anderson, and stories in 1974 by the *New York Times* reporter Seymour Hersh. These stories led to a series of investigations by US Congressional Committees which produced many volumes of reports on all aspects of the matter from 1974 to 1976. The best known of these was the Senate Select Committee on Intelligence Activities, known as the Church Committee (after its chairman, Democratic Senator Frank Church). These investigations were undertaken in Washington at a time of agonised self-analysis following the Vietnam War, the Watergate scandal and the disgrace of Richard Nixon. As a result the Church Committee strained every muscle and turned up every stone to try to establish the complicity of US officials.

The evidence assembled by the Church Committee did *not* support, let alone prove, charges that the United States had succeeded in effectively destabilising the Chilean regime or had actively engineered the coup. Undoubtedly the CIA was working to support opposition to the UP and make its task of taking Chile down 'the road to socialism' as difficult as possible but the Committee found no evidence that the US was directly involved in the coup. It did verify that the 'Forty Committee' of the National Security

[14] Figures from various sources quoted by Mark Falcoff, *Modern Chile, 1970-1989 – A Critical History* (New Brunswick, NJ, 1989).

Council had approved a total of nearly $7 million for 'covert action' in Chile between 1970 and 1973. Most of this (approximately $4 million) went to support opposition political parties, particularly the Christian Democratic and National parties; an unspecified amount was used for payments to trade unions and other private sector organisations; and at least $1.5 million went to the main opposition newspaper *El Mercurio*. Some of these funds may eventually have been diverted to support the critical truckers' strikes of 1972 and 1973, and had the effect of prolonging them; but the strikes obviously started because of internal circumstances, and even the most persistent efforts of the Church Committee failed to show that they were led or master-minded by the CIA – which was barely credible in any case in view of the great number of completely different Chilean organisations involved.

Nevertheless many liberals based outside Chile, as well as Allende and all his supporters in the country, were – and some still are – convinced that the United States was to some degree responsible for the promotion or planning (or both) of the coup. At least two distinguished North American historians[15] seeking reasons for this persistent view have found, coincidentally, that the only hard evidence people had was Thomas Hauser's book entitled *Missing: The Execution of Charles Horman,* later made into a successful film. It is clear that Horman, a young American journalist of leftist opinions, was indeed arrested and killed by the Chilean Army very soon after 11 September, but absolutely no evidence is produced in the book to support its contention that he was killed because he knew that US agents had direct involvement in the coup. *Missing* is a powerful example of 'faction' – the skilful blending of fact and fiction – to prove a preconceived theory. Bizarrely, it probably had a greater influence on liberal attitudes to the military coup in Chile in 1973 than all the weighty Congressional Reports which it contradicts.

There is no doubt that US policy towards Chile under Nixon and Kissinger shattered the usual rules of international behaviour; and perhaps worse than that in the case of the murder of General

15 The judgements expressed here are based on conclusions reached independently by two such historians, Paul E. Sigmund in *The United States and Democracy in Chile* and Robert Alexander in *The Tragedy of Chile.*

Schneider. The Church Committee and others in the 1970s made a strong case against these excesses. The freedom of the CIA to operate independently of democratic control and often outside the law was considerably restricted after those investigations. No such rigorous scrutiny was brought to bear, of course, on the activities of the Soviet Union and its satellites and sympathisers, particularly Cuba. During the last year and a half of the UP, not only the MIR but also the Socialists and Communists, were rapidly building up the strength of their private armies with weapons illegally imported from Cuba, Czechoslovakia and elsewhere. By then Chile was teeming with Soviet bloc, Cuban and even North Korean advisers of all kinds, and many of their activities were as far outside the law as anything done by the CIA.

Ultimately, however, it has to be agreed that the coup against President Salvador Allende was carried out by the Chilean armed forces in response to their view of their national situation and without manipulation from outside. It was the Chilean Congress and Supreme Court and Controller General which declared that the UP government had so abused the Constitution that it was no longer legitimate. The opposition in Congress and the plotters in the armed forces must have known that the US government would look favourably on a new regime in Chile. But it was there, not in Washington, that the coup was planned and carried out.

7

PINOCHET IN POWER

> 'Despite the sustained crackdown, most Chileans initially assumed that once order was restored, the Armed Forces would return to their barracks and relinquish power to civilian authorities. They did not realise that a military take-over could develop its own irreversible dynamic, they failed to grasp the resentment against political elites that had festered within the armed forces for years – and they gravely underestimated the ambitions of General Pinochet.[...]'
> 'I wasn't looking for this job. Destiny gave it to me.' (General Pinochet, 1984)
> – both quotations from Pamela Constable and Arturo Valenzuela, *Chile under Pinochet: A Nation of Enemies*

More than two decades after the violent coup which deposed Salvador Allende, a clear view of his Presidency and its bloody end is still obscured by instinctive and emotional reactions. A whole generation of Chileans is too young to remember that time of political meltdown. Many more have put painful thoughts behind them or cocooned themselves with selective memory. Others have not forgotten the turmoil of that frustrated revolution and nourish various resentments or fears that history might repeat itself. Foreign observers, whose knowledge of the following two decades of Chilean history may be vague, are often still more sharply divided since, unlike Chileans, they have not had to face up to the need to be reconciled with their fellow citizens and to live in new circumstances.

For liberals around the world and the adherents of the *Unidad Popular* in Chile, Allende was the champion of the poor and the under-privileged mass of Chileans. Notwithstanding the disasters of his Presidency, he remains the charismatic leader who had charted a new road for them and been martyred in a good cause. For the Right the UP, if not Allende himself, clearly wanted to destroy Chile's traditional political system and way of life; the left-wing ideologues of the UP were the people who had reduced the economy to ruins and the nation to the brink of civil war. A military coup offered the only way out.

Outside the country, particularly in the United States and in Western European countries which had close links with Chile since independence, news of the coup came as a brutal shock. This was the model Latin American republic which had adhered to the principles of the rule of law, constitutional government and other democratic freedoms for longer than many European countries (and with fewer interruptions). It now seemed to have slipped into a kind of barbarism. The entire country had been placed under a 'state of siege' and thousands of people were apparently being arrested, tortured and sometimes executed without trial. The media and public outcry against the coup was intense. In Britain 10,000 people marched to Trafalgar Square in protest and *The Guardian* wrote (17 September 1973): 'For Socialists of this generation, Chile is our Spain.... This is the most vicious fascism we have seen in generations.' In France, Italy and elsewhere in Western Europe the uproar was even greater. In New York a massive demonstration was organised outside the UN Headquarters. Liberal and socialist activists in North America and Europe formed pressure groups and 'Chile Solidarity Committees' to campaign against the military regime and in defence of the UP secure in the belief that its leadership had simply been striving to establish a socialist society in Chile by constitutional and democratic means. Outside Chile few observers recognised that the UP had acted far outside the law and that many of the factions and parties within it were seeking to create their own totalitarian state.

The initial reactions of most Chileans were rather different. The coup was welcomed unconditionally by all the opposition political leaders. Not only the National Party but also the Christian Democrats immediately declared their support. On 12 September the National Committee of the PDC announced its position unequivocally:

> The events which Chile is experiencing are the consequence of the economic disaster, institutional chaos, armed violence and moral crisis to which the deposed government brought the country, dragging the Chilean people into anguish and despair.[...] The Armed forces and Carabineros did not seek power. Their

Bombardment of the Moneda palace, Santiago, 11 September 1973.

The ruling military junta, 1973: (*from left*) Gen. César Mendoza, Admiral Jose Toribio Merino, Gen. Augusto Pinochet, Gen. Gustavo Leigh.

President Pinochet greeting a peasant in Aisen.

> institutional traditions and the republican history of our country inspire confidence that just as soon as they have fulfilled the tasks which they have undertaken to save the Chilean nation from the grave dangers of destruction and totalitarianism which threatened, they will turn over power to the sovereign people.

The political parties which had opposed President Allende and the UP with growing unanimity in the Congress, had passed formal resolutions condemning their actions and would have impeached Allende with enthusiasm if they had been able to muster a sufficient majority to do so, could hardly have failed to welcome the coup.[1] The Supreme Court sent a message of congratulation to the military leadership and Catholic Bishops offered prayers of thanks for the deliverance of the country from communism.

It was not only Chile's establishment and the political and social élites which approved of the coup. There is plentiful evidence that the great majority of the middle class and large numbers of the working class – and particularly women at all social levels – were in favour of it. It was indeed the women of Santiago who had protested most loudly in the weeks and months before September 1973. Some of them had publicly taunted the military as cowards by throwing chicken feed at their feet in the street. However, within a few days people realised that the military were not confining themselves to measures necessary to restore internal order and normal conditions of everyday life. Instead the new Junta embarked on what seemed more like a crusade for national liberation from communism. In his first 'state of the nation' message as President of the Junta, General Pinochet spoke dramatically of the need 'to extirpate the root of evil from Chile' and to bring about a moral cleansing of the nation (*limpieza*).

Armed resistance to the coup took place only in Santiago, and there largely in the *cordones industriales* where the MIR and other extremists were strongest. The military had expected far more serious opposition, and some of their spokesmen seemed to exaggerate the level of resistance which actually occurred as justification for taking ruthless action against not only the armed

[1] Former President Eduardo Frei also wrote on 8 November 1973 to the Italian President Mariano Rumor of the World Christian Demociatic Union explaining in detail the reasons why the coup had been necessary.

guerrilla fighters but anyone identified as a UP supporter. More than 7,000 civilians were arrested within days and herded into the National Stadium in Santiago. The majority were released after a screening process, but many were brutally interrogated there and some summarily executed or 'disappeared'. There were round-ups of people considered to be UP supporters in all the other main cities. Around the country 45,000 people were detained in the first month. In Valparaiso some were held on warships, while elsewhere army barracks and civilian buildings as well as police stations were used as temporary prisons.

The armed forces were empowered to establish war tribunals to try all kinds of offences, in place of the normal judicial machinery. These tribunals sometimes passed sentences of death which were carried out immediately with little or no opportunity for appeals. At the outset of the 'crusade' to free the country of 'Marxist subversives', some suspects did not even get the nominal protection of trial by a war tribunal but were executed out of hand. There is no evidence that members of the Junta or other senior commanders in the armed forces ordered, or intended, suspects to be killed without any legal process at all, but they can have made little attempt to control or punish such atrocities and some may indeed have contributed to the atmosphere of hatred which motivated the crusade against vaguely defined enemies. Years afterwards it was established beyond doubt that in early October 1973 one of the main leaders of the coup, the Commander of the Santiago garrison, General Sergio Arellano, was despatched by General Pinochet on a whirlwind helicopter tour of military bases in the north of the country to make certain that the policy of rooting out UP supporters was carried out ruthlessly, e.g. by obliging the war tribunals to impose more sentences of death and having them carried out on the spot.[2]

The Chilean Army was led by an inward-looking caste of officers, largely of middle-class origin, whose contacts with civil society were limited because units spent years on end in garrison duty in remote parts of the country. It was proud of its traditions of obedience, efficiency and toughness and, like all conventional

[2] See Patricia Verdugo, *Los Zarpazos del Puma* (Santiago, 1989). The worst charges against General Arellano have subsequently been denied by his son in another book.

forces, was trained to act with determination (with little regard for political subtlety). Only rarely had it been involved in the military coups and *pronunciamentos* which happened so often in other parts of Latin America. Chilean officers considered themselves to be entirely professional and most were therefore lacking in experience of how to conduct a *coup d'état* when the time came. However, with other Latin Americans, Chilean officers had been sent for advanced training in US military establishments in Panama and elsewhere in the 1950s and '60s and had studied the threat of communist insurgency. They were therefore well-versed in counter-insurgency theory and US military ideas about national security developed during the Cold War.

The origins of General Pinochet

Augusto Pinochet Ugarte was the son of a customs officer in Valparaiso. He had joined the Military Academy in 1932 at sixteen and after graduating as a second-lieutenant of infantry in 1936, he rose steadily through the ranks in a conventional career by assiduous attention to his professional duty. Contemporaries considered him to have no more than average ability but he was loyal to the institution and his superiors, and noticeably careful to avoid any kind of political commitment. He shared the traditional view that the Army's role was to serve unquestioningly any President elected under the Constitution, a policy which had been carefully maintained since the exceptional military interventions in politics in the 1920s. General René Schneider met his death in 1970 as a result of upholding this tradition but his successor, General Carlos Prats, firmly continued it. Until September 1973, General Augusto Pinochet had shown no outward sign of diverging from it, but according to his own memoirs he had in fact been deeply impressed with the subversive threat posed by left-wing politicians and trade unionists in Chile. He had personal experience of their activities among the coalminers of Concepción when serving there on two occasions and also in the northern copper mines – where he first met Salvador Allende and was introduced to Marx's *Communist Manifesto*. As a result of these contacts, Pinochet writes that he saw communism as representing a deep and sinister threat to Chile, but apparently he never shared his thoughts or fears with brother officers. To them and above all to his eventual

Commander-in-Chief, General Prats, he remained the loyal, disciplined and circumspect military careerist. Rather than concerning himself with the political or economic problems facing the country (which was not the accepted way to promote a military career) he had become a specialist in military history and geo-politics (and written well-regarded books on these subjects).

By the end of Eduardo Frei's Presidency the Chilean armed forces had been reduced in size. Expenditure on both equipment and pay had been progressively squeezed and the strength of the Army was down to 20,000. Morale dropped still further when Salvador Allende was elected. Pinochet has recorded that at this moment (and so far as we know for the first time) he warned the officers under his command that Chile had embarked on the path towards communism and that it would be for them to save the country from that fate. He was then in command of a division at Iquique in the extreme north but in 1971 he was called back to Santiago to command the garrison there and shortly afterwards was appointed Chief of Staff of the Army.[3] In that capacity he acted as deputy to General Prats, and convinced both Prats and Allende of his loyalty so that, when Prats resigned, Allende chose Pinochet to succeed him on 23 August 1973.

The President's first orders to the new Commander-in-Chief were to restore the tradition of loyalty to the elected government and the integrity of the normal chain of command by getting rid of a number of senior officers whom he suspected (with good reason) of plotting a coup. Pinochet himself explains that he found it impossible to force the resignations of all these generals immediately, and from that moment, less than three weeks before the eventual date of the coup, he moved quickly to place himself at the head of the plotters. He claimed subsequently that he had in fact been planning for, or considering the possibility of, a coup for many months (see page 108) but, whatever his private thoughts, Pinochet apparently refused to commit himself to other Army and Air Force Generals who were already involved in preparing

[3] The main autobiographical sources for General Pinochet's career are *El Día Decisivo* and his (3-volume) memoirs *Camino Recorrido. Memorias de un Soldado.* Independent sources are listed in the bibliography. In 1973, when other members of the UP questioned Pinochet's loyalty to the President, Allende is said to have declared that he was just an old soldier 'not even capable of deceiving his wife'.

the coup. One of them, Sergio Arellano, records that, even as late as 8 September when the two met face to face he failed to get Pinochet to declare his support.

While Pinochet carefully sat on the fence, there was little opportunity for him to prepare for the second phase, namely what would have to be done immediately the military found themselves in control of the government. Neither Pinochet nor the other members of the Junta seemed to have clear ideas about many important questions which required immediate decision. They knew that there were enemies to be 'sought and destroyed' but their approach to problems beyond that was improvised from day to day. In this process Pinochet's was not the dominant voice, but he proved a fast and determined learner.

The end of the Unidad Popular

Although the initial action against the rank and file of the UP was brutal, the subsequent treatment of Ministers and high-ranking officials was more circumspect. More than fifty of the most prominent leaders were arrested and taken to Dawson Island, an isolated naval base in bleak Tierra del Fuego, and held there for up to a year in harsh conditions as 'prisoners of war'. Some twenty-five other leaders were fortunate enough to gain asylum in foreign embassies among the hundreds of more humble refugees who flooded into them. Most of the leading figures in the UP government were eventually allowed to leave the country and go into prolonged exile abroad. Some went to neighbouring Latin American countries or to the United States, many to jobs in universities or international organisations. Some established themselves in friendly Western European countries, notably Spain, France, Italy and Scandinavia. The most prominent of all, figures such as the Communist Luis Corvalán and the Socialists Carlos Altamirano and Clodomiro Almeyda went to Soviet bloc capitals where they continued to try to fight the Chilean political battle from exile.

Much larger numbers of Chileans of all political persuasions (or none) who felt themselves to be at risk left the country as refugees and sought to establish new lives wherever they found doors open to them abroad. They were usually the people who had some resources and contacts to draw upon outside the country.

The groups who suffered most were inevitably the poorest and most defenceless of Allende's supporters, the small-town organisers and workers' leaders or the *campesinos* who had been named as responsible for the UP's actions in rural areas, particularly the illegal *tomas* of farms. They had nowhere to hide after the coup and many 'disappeared' from their homes up and down the country. Some of these crimes were settling old scores, some the result of over-zealous actions by local officials. Chile seemed to resemble an occupied country, and the resulting fears and hatreds permeated the life of many small towns and villages as well as the cities for years afterwards.

One of the first actions of the Junta immediately after the coup was to publish a decree stating that a 'state of internal war' existed. This was a pre-condition for the suspension of civil rights and allowed the government to exercise draconian powers.[4] Decrees quickly followed dissolving the Congress and all the political parties which had formed the UP, putting others into 'recess', abolishing the trade union confederation and replacing university rectors with military nominees. To give further justification for the crisis atmosphere, a document known as the *White Book* was produced and widely distributed abroad, particularly in the United States. This described 'Plan Z', an alleged plot by Allende and the extreme Left to assassinate senior military officers and other leaders and establish an alternative armed force to seize power in Chile. This plot seems to have been largely a fabrication (some of it probably based on material supplied by the CIA) although it contained some elements of truth. However, at the time it was taken as genuine by most of the Chileans who were already inclined to support the coup and it probably achieved the Junta's purpose in publishing it – at least for the first and critical phase.

Foreign opinion was largely unconvinced and, except for a handful of right-wing cold warriors in the United States, very few believed in 'Plan Z'. On the other hand, Western commentators were ready to accept almost any allegation about the extent of repression and human rights abuses by the Chilean armed forces.

[4] The various 'states of exception' incorporated in the Chilean Constitution of 1980 and its predecessors included the 'state of war', the 'state of siege' and the 'state of emergency'. Under each the executive was authorised to assume specified exceptional powers. The Pinochet regime continued to make use of powers available under one or other of these for most of the time until 1988.

For example, the World Council of Churches believed that more than 10,000 people were killed between September and December 1973, while in France estimates of 10,000 people killed were being published within a month of the coup (*Paris Match*, October 1973). At the end of September, the US magazine *Newsweek* calculated that the rate of killing of civilians by the armed forces was 200 per day in Santiago alone. Dispute about the facts continued for the next sixteen years and many international and private organisations came to different conclusions. Probably the most reliable international monitor was the Inter-American Commission on Human Rights but the UN, and the European Community also studied it closely over the years.

By far the best source available to us now is the Report of the Rettig Commission on Truth and Reconciliation established in 1990 by President Patricio Aylwin to investigate the whole history of human rights violations between 1973 and 1990. This Commission analysed every case known or reported up to that time and concluded that 2,115 victims had died or 'disappeared' as a result of actions by agents of the state and another 164 had been victims of political violence by others. There were 641 outstanding cases on which the Commission had not reached any conclusion. (Subsequent investigation of the outstanding cases and others which came to light after 1990 increased the total of deaths and disappearances to 3,197.)

With the publication of these precise findings we know the truth – or as much as is ever likely to be known with any certainty–about the abuses for which the Chilean armed forces, including Pinochet himself, must accept responsibility. Much that was written about this before 1991 was hugely exaggerated although that does not excuse anything that was done. It must be said also that some exaggeration was inevitable because of the secrecy and fear created by the military themselves with their suppression of all freedom of communication. In such a situation rumours are bound to be accepted as fact. Indeed nobody knew the whole truth and it was impossible for outsiders or even well-informed insiders to form an accurate picture of the whole situation. Reporters could thus hardly avoid reporting rumours as fact in the Chile of 1973 and 1974.

The defence of human rights

Once the freedom of the media to criticise the actions of authority had been suppressed, the only bodies able to exercise any sort of oversight of the human rights situation were the churches. The Archbishop of Santiago, Cardinal Raúl Silva Henríquez, took the lead in organising the *Comité de Co-operación para la Paz* along with the Protestant and Jewish leaders. This committee was established to help the families of the prisoners and victims of the coup and so far as possible to protect prisoners themselves, but in time it naturally acquired a great deal of information about those it helped and became involved in various ways in the defence of accused people. In addition to clerical and lay volunteers, it was able to draw on the services of many lawyers and independent professionals which greatly increased its effectiveness. In November 1975 Pinochet demanded that the committee be dissolved on the ground that it was being used by Marxists and other extremists to create trouble, and the committee as such was dissolved. However, the Archbishop soon found other means to continue the work, and established the *Vicaría de la Solidaridad*, a purely Catholic organisation which depended directly on the Archbishopric. The new organisation was subjected to considerable harassment by the government but it grew in effectiveness. Step by step, the *Vicaría* became the best, indeed the only, body able to offer any protection to suspects, and the most objective source of information on human rights violations and many other aspects of the lives of ordinary people under the military regime.

For a variety of reasons the Roman Catholic church in Chile has lost much ground in the past half-century to Evangelical and Protestant churches, but from 1973 onwards it proved uniquely valuable as the only effective defender of individuals against the military regime. With the demise of all political parties, trade unions and other independent social organisations, only the churches, and above all the Catholic Church, could protest effectively against arbitrary actions by the secret police force, the *Dirección de Inteligencia Nacional* (DINA). The judiciary should have been able to fulfil this role, but when put to the test it failed to do so. A graphic illustration of this is the record of the Chilean courts in responding to *recursos de amparo* (writs of *habeas corpus*), where individual citizens had been arrested and not brought to trial, or had simply disappeared. Between 1973 and 1983 the Supreme Court rejected all but ten of 5,400 such petitions[5] which effectively meant that the judges refused to challenge the actions of the DINA or even to insist on proper investigation of such cases.

From September 1973 the Supreme Court accepted without challenge the assertion of the Junta that a 'state of war' existed in the country. This was considered to justify the indefinite application of a wide range of emergency powers including the use of military courts and oppressive measures such as detention of people without trial in secret prisons. Under this system many were arrested and detained and some disappeared permanently; 6,000 were actually tried by military courts in the first three years of military rule and about 200 were executed without any right of appeal to the normal civil courts. By never challenging the basic premise that there was a 'state of war' in the country the judges allowed the operation of military courts to continue unchecked for many years after there was any real emergency, let alone a state of war.

The DINA

The worst period of the 'dirty war' in Chile coincided with the existence of the notorious DINA. When first created in the aftermath of the coup, it was supposed to have the role of co-ordinating the work of the totally separate intelligence departments of the three armed services and the *Carabineros.* However it grew rapidly into an all-powerful secret police force with exclusive and virtually unlimited powers. From June 1974 it was established by a decree of the Junta and operated with full autonomy for the next three years. It was staffed originally by members of all four armed forces, taking over all their security functions, under an Army Colonel, later promoted to General, Manuel Contreras, and, despite efforts by other members of the Junta to insist on joint control over the DINA, Contreras reported only to General Pinochet. Under these arrangements, it therefore became a uniquely powerful instrument of repression, as well as a source of intelligence, answerable

[5] Figures quoted in *Report on the Situation of Human Rights in Chile* (OEA, 1985) by the Inter-American Commission on Human Rights.

only to Pinochet and giving him a position of personal power comparable in the non-communist world only to that of General Franco – whose achievements Pinochet greatly admired and on whose methods he modelled some of his own.

Contreras became the most powerful and deeply hated figure in the regime and his influence was greater than that of any other besides Pinochet. Under his sole control, the DINA was in a position to use torture and murder with virtually no restraint, and there is overwhelming evidence of the reign of terror which followed. How far the details of all the DINA's operations were known to Pinochet personally remains largely a matter for speculation but their primary targets were certainly approved by him. In the early days of the military regime, the whole of the Junta were no doubt behind the DINA, but this unanimity disappeared as Contreras' abuse of power increased.

The targets were, first, the MIR and similar terrorist groups, and then the Communist Party. All of them went underground after September 1973, but they were progressively tracked down, infiltrated and destroyed by the DINA to the point where the MIR at least no longer represented a serious threat. A degree of ruthlessness against an organisation engaged in guerrilla war and financing its activities by armed robbery, murder and any other means at all could perhaps be understood, but Contreras soon showed that he had no scruples about using the same methods against any so-called enemies of the regime he chose to target. Before long the DINA's activities reached far beyond terrorist or opposition groups opposed to the regime and were so pervasive that even senior members of the armed forces (including the Army) increasingly distrusted it.

They did so with some reason, because several of the generals who had taken leading parts in the planning and execution of the coup were soon removed from positions from which they could pose any kind of threat to Pinochet. Both General Bonilla, who had become Minister of Interior after the coup, and General Arellano, commander of the Santiago garrison, found themselves moved into less important posts. Another of the original leaders similarly treated was General Augusto Lutz. Both he and Bonilla died in questionable circumstances within a few months of being sidelined by their Commander-in-Chief. A rather different case was that of the former Commander-in-Chief, General Prats. He had left Chile after the coup and was living in retirement in Argentina but still enjoying some loyalty and respect from traditionally-minded members of the officer corps. In September 1974 Prats and his wife were killed by a car bomb outside their apartment in Buenos Aires. Prats might have become a figure of stature around whom latent opposition to the Junta or to Pinochet personally could have developed. The same might also have been thought of one of the leaders of the Christian Democrats, Bernardo Leighton, who was living in exile in Rome and was shot and all but fatally wounded there a year after Prats' assassination.

The case of Orlando Letelier

Chileans and many others saw only one feasible explanation for these events, namely that the DINA was involved in them, but there was no hard evidence. In September 1976 even more suspicions were aroused when a former minister in the Allende government, Orlando Letelier, was assassinated by a car bomb in Washington, DC. Letelier had been imprisoned for a year after the coup and when released had fled to Washington where he became one of the loudest critics of the Pinochet regime abroad. As such he was an obvious candidate for the attentions of the DINA. Suspicion that they were responsible for his murder and that of his young American assistant Ronni Moffitt, could not immediately be proved but the US authorities, outraged by the crime, pursued their investigations doggedly until they had a convincing case to bring to court. The prosecution touched the DINA at the highest levels, in the shape of Colonel Pedro Espinoza, Director of Operations, and General Contreras. According to a more junior DINA officer Captain Armando Fernández, who eventually gave himself up to the US courts and was tried and convicted for his part in preparing the assassination, General Pinochet himself was said to have been aware of the plot in advance. Fernández stated in court that Contreras had told him that 'the Chief' – in other words the President – had actually ordered the assassination.

This direct allegation of Pinochet's complicity did not emerge until ten years after the event. However, in 1978 proceedings were brought against an American citizen and former CIA employee, Michael Townley, whom the DINA had hired as an explosives expert while he was resident in Chile. Townley was duly convicted by the US Federal Court, along with three Cubans recruited by him for their various parts in the murder of Letelier and Ronni Moffitt. His evidence directly implicated Contreras and other senior DINA officers,[6] and the US government demanded their extradition to stand trial, but this was repeatedly blocked by the Chilean Supreme Court.

One result of the Letelier case was the complete withdrawal of naval and Air Force officers from the DINA. The backlash was so serious that General Pinochet was obliged to dissolve the DINA and dismiss Contreras – who was able to survive as a shadowy but powerful presence in the background, protected against all demands that he be brought to book for as long as Pinochet remained in power. The official dissolution of the DINA as an organisation was less of an improvement than it at first seemed because it was succeeded by a new body, the *Central Nacional de Informaciones* (CNI) which took over most of its functions. Under new and slightly more moderate heads, General Mena and later General Gordon, the CNI continued to exercise untrammelled powers of arbitrary arrest and detention. Its activities, including the use of torture in some of its detention centres (which has been thoroughly documented),[7] were not subject to any external control during the Pinochet regime. However, the DINA's most blatant operations abroad such as the assassinations of Letelier and Moffitt were not repeated and co-operation with like-minded security organisations in Brazil and Argentina became more circumscribed. Another clear improvement which followed the replacement of the DINA by the CNI was that the permanent 'disappearance' of people came to an end.

US policy

The election of Jimmy Carter as United States President in November 1976 also had a considerable bearing on the matter. Carter

[6] Contreas and Espinoza were not brought to trial for many years, but they were finally convicted by the Chilean courts in the 1990s after the restoration of democratic government and were still serving prison sentences in 1997.

[7] In addition to the reports of the Inter-American Commission on Human Rights of the OEA covering the human rights situation in 1973-85, there are many other impartial published sources, e.g. Amnesty International and UN reports.

came into office with a strong commitment to make the protection of human rights around the world a major element in US foreign policy. This change can be traced back to the Church Committee's investigations of the activities of the CIA in Chile and elsewhere during and before the Presidency of Richard Nixon. After much pressure by the Democrats in Congress, Edward Kennedy succeeded in pushing through a measure prohibiting all military aid and arms sales to Chile from June 1976. This was the culmination of a rising tide of criticism in the United States about continued human rights abuses in Chile. With Carter's arrival in power in Washington this swing in US policy became much more pronounced.

US military aid had continued, even during the Allende period, and official economic aid to Chile had been restored by the Republican administration in 1973, but from 1976 US military assistance stopped almost entirely and official economic aid and Export-Import Bank loans again dried up. As a result, the composition of Chile's international debt began to change from public sector to private sector loans. Despite efforts by Democrats in Congress to restrict all lending from the US to Chilean private borrowers, the US banking sector, awash with OPEC petro-dollars in the 1970s, lent more and more heavily to Chile in the period 1977-81, i.e. during the Carter Presidency. Thus the attempt to bring pressure on the Pinochet regime over human rights matters by means of economic sanctions achieved only limited success. In some ways the intensity of the sanctions programme imposed by Carter was greater than that imposed by Nixon against Allende. In any event, both the Allende and the Pinochet regimes were able to survive the best efforts of their super power 'big brother' to bring them to heel by this means.

The other proclaimed purpose of President Carter's policy towards Chile was to encourage or force Pinochet to accelerate the process of returning the country to democracy. This too failed to produce the desired result during Carter's Presidency. Ten more years were to pass before any normal kind of democracy began to return. However, in July 1977 Pinochet announced a programme for limited moves towards a sort of constitutional government. This scheme, known as the Chacarillas Plan, included the approval of a new Constitution by a plebiscite to take place in 1980, a lengthy transitional period lasting till 1985, and the introduction of a Congress to function from 1985-90, which would be two-thirds elected and one-third appointed and would then elect a President. This gesture towards democracy did not begin to satisfy pressure from outside Chile, which had already started some time before. From 1974 very large majorities voted annually in the UN and other international organisations against the Pinochet regime's record on human rights and in favour of return to democracy.

At the time of Jimmy Carter's attempt to build up pressure for change, criticism from within Chile tended to concentrate mainly on the fact that General Pinochet was steadily succeeding in concentrating executive power in his own hands. The Air Force Commander-in-Chief, General Gustavo Leigh, was the leading critic of this growing process. Having initially been as fervent an opponent of the *Unidad Popular* as any member of the Junta and, with Admiral Merino, playing a more forward role in 1973 than Pinochet, Leigh had been seen as probably the strongest and certainly the most articulate member of the Junta. But he, and indeed all other members of the leadership, found themselves outmanoeuvred. Although Pinochet himself said, on 11 September, that the Presidency of the Junta would rotate among its four members, in the immediate aftermath of the coup he soon contrived to be designated as the 'first President' of the Junta. After only nine months he moved a step further and successfully persuaded the Junta to approve a Decree Law which confirmed their legislative powers but declared roundly that 'executive power is exercised by the President of the Junta who is the Supreme Chief of the Nation'. Five months later Pinochet advanced another step through Decree Law no. 806 of 17 December 1974, which changed his title to 'President of the Republic' on the grounds that the existing legislation establishing the executive powers of the government usually referred to the President of the Republic so that someone had to bear that title.

The fall of General Leigh

It was by such legal devices – many of them drafted by his cousin Monica Madariaga, who acted as his personal legal adviser – that Pinochet's position became ever more secure in a technical sense. His fundamental power-base in the Army, heavily reinforced by his control of the DINA, was thus clothed in the trappings of legality which Chileans both look for and respect. At the same time, while Pinochet was replacing the executive authority of the Junta with another structure centred on himself alone, he was also separating the armed forces as institutions from the executive arm of government. He made use of many Army officers and some from other services in ministerial or official jobs of all kinds, but was careful to maintain a distinction between the armed forces and the government by retiring or seconding such officers from active service while they were in government jobs. Thus Army and government came together only at the top in the person of Pinochet himself, and his power did not depend exclusively – or even directly – on the Army.

Leigh, and to a lesser extent Merino, became more and more frustrated by Pinochet's progressive gathering of power into his own hands. It was Leigh, however, who took the lead in advocating that the regime should begin to soften its repressive policies and plan for the return to democracy; this was at the same time as, and perhaps because, Pinochet was developing an almost messianic belief in his mission to govern Chile himself. From early in 1976 Leigh argued within the Junta that it should move back towards democracy (and in particular that Contreras should be replaced as head of the DINA). Although Merino supported Leigh, Pinochet (though now sole head of the executive) was still a member of the Junta and thus always able to veto such proposals. The conflict between them increased month by month and reached a crisis in late 1977. When the United Nations produced a unanimous vote of condemnation of Chile, an infuriated Pinochet wanted to call a snap referendum appealing to nationalist feeling in Chile as a means of defying the UN resolution. The wording called on Chileans 'to endorse President Pinochet in his defence of the dignity of Chile, and reaffirm the legitimacy of the Government of the Republic....' Naturally enough, Leigh and Merino saw this playing of the nationalist card as an attempt by Pinochet to bolster his own authority. There was a tense confrontation behind the scenes, but Pinochet managed to force his proposal through and, after a massive publicity campaign, achieved a large majority in the referendum.

Leigh now found himself alone in the Junta in resisting Pinochet. In May 1978, he sent Pinochet a formal memorandum calling for much greater involvement of civilians in policy making immediately, for an end to the military government within five years, and for various other changes to restrict Pinochet's powers meanwhile. When Leigh made these proposals public in an interview with an Italian newspaper, Pinochet seized the opportunity to discredit him and persuaded Merino to take the same line (General Mendoza, director of the *Carabineros*, always fell in behind Pinochet in any case). The rest of the Junta were therefore united in demanding that Leigh 'retire' and Pinochet left no doubt that he was willing to use force to this end.

To find a replacement, Pinochet had to pass over no less than nineteen other Air Force Generals before General Fernando Matthei, already serving as Minister of Health, accepted appointment as Leigh's successor. Pinochet had proved that he would risk splitting the Junta, and possibly go even further, to consolidate his personal authority. With Leigh's departure he could turn to the task of creating a new constitutional base for the continuation of what was now *his* regime in all but name. Only Merino now retained any real capacity to restrain him.

The 1980 Constitution

Pinochet had spoken at Chacarillas the year before about moving back towards a form of democracy. At the time the influence of the *blandos,* or soft-liners, was relatively strong, and the Chacarillas speech was the result of a debate between *blandos* and *duros* within the regime in which the former had slightly the best of it. After Leigh's removal, however, Pinochet was able to revert to his real preference, namely a much longer period of authoritarian government. In November 1977 he had sent proposals for a new constitution to the long-established Constitutional Commission (supposedly at work since 1973 but never producing final proposals). After passing through the Commission, they were embodied in a document put forward to the Council of State, a body originally created to confer extra legitimacy to the regime by including two former Presidents, Jorge Alessandri and Gabriel González Videla.[8]

[8] Eduardo Frei, the other surviving President, had refused to join the Council of State and he and the Christian Democrats were by now in complete opposition to the regime.

Under the chairmanship of Alessandri, the Council of State modified the draft substantially. The revised version, which it produced in June 1980, would considerably reduce the influence of the armed forces, and made other changes to restore the normal powers of a future Chilean President and Congress when the new Constitution came fully into effect. However, the principal change proposed by the Council was to introduce a fixed timetable for the transition to civilian rule: this would have limited the period during which Pinochet could continue to rule with exceptional powers to five years ending in 1985.

Faced with this, the President referred the draft to yet another committee, this time consisting entirely of his personal advisers, which duly amended the Council of State's proposals reversing most of the changes it had introduced and re-introducing other undemocratic features. The most astonishing was to allow Pinochet an automatic transitional term of eight more years, to end in 1989. Thereafter it envisaged a further eight-year term for a candidate selected by the Commanders-in-Chief of the armed forces (one of whom would be Pinochet). This candidate would only need to be confirmed by a national plebiscite, and there would be no alternative name. In other words, Pinochet would be likely to remain President until 1997 without ever having to submit to a free election.

Other changes proposed were equally objectionable. The full constitution would not come into effect till 1989, and the transitional articles allowed the President complete freedom to impose at will states of emergency, and thus drastic curbs on personal liberties, without any appeal to the courts for the whole of the transitional period. By this means the right of *habeas corpus* or *recurso de amparo* could be kept in suspense indefinitely and other personal powers of the President would continue unchanged till 1989, but even then, despite the Constitution having technically become effective, the armed forces would still be able to intervene in political affairs through having a powerful role on the National Security Council and a Constitutional Tribunal. The executive was greatly strengthened *vis-à-vis* the legislature; and the Commanders-in-Chief were protected from any risk of removal from office by the President. Finally the Constitution was to be made effectively permanent since amendment would be difficult if not impossible without the approval of the executive.

This end-product, despite its many deficiencies as a democratic instrument, was still an important step on the path back to a form of constitutional government. For the first time it provided an institutional structure for the armed forces' regime, which had hitherto operated on the uncertain basis of the 1925 Constitution, overridden by the stream of unco-ordinated decrees the Junta had produced in its first seven years. The armed forces were now committed to a political charter incorporating their own ideas about the shape of a new Chile. The document also committed General Pinochet to a precise timetable for the return to civilian rule, which he had publicly accepted and could not easily evade. Although hedged with reservations, it contained the long-term promise of democratic government and constitutional guarantees of some individual freedoms. Needless to say, it was condemned by independent constitutional experts and political leaders opposed to the Pinochet regime as a deeply flawed and illegitimate document, but most eventually came to accept that it was better than having that regime continue unfettered by any basic commitments at all.[9]

In August 1980 the government mounted a new publicity campaign to get the constitution approved in another national referendum. Opposition voices were fatally handicapped in making their case against it by lack of access to the means of communication, by disagreements over details, and by lack of any alternative proposals to offer the people. Despite the opposition's views, many Chileans thought that any constitution was better than none. As with the 1977 plebiscite, there were no proper electoral registers or guarantees to prevent interference with the integrity of the voting process, but the plebiscite was so heavily weighted in favour of approval, that there was little need for manipulation of the figures. In the end the constitution was ratified with a majority of 67 per cent of the votes cast. This enabled Pinochet to rebut his critics in the United States by saying, however disingenuously, that Chile's Constitution of 1980 had been clearly approved by the Chilean people while the US Constitution had in effect been

[9] Former President Jorge Alessandri (by no means an instinctive liberal) resigned from the Council of State in protest against the emasculation or reversal of the changes which he had proposed. Although he refused to give his reasons publicly, it was well known that he objected fundamentally to the 1980 Constitution as it was ultimately promulgated.

imposed on the American people by the élites who governed them in the eighteenth century!

A constitutional President

In March 1981 President Pinochet, just elected for a further eight years by popular vote of a kind, and with the prospect of a further term of equal length after that, moved his office and staff back into the Moneda Palace. It had been carefully restored after the bomb damage inflicted in 1973 and was once more the elegant but modest *palacio* from which Chilean Presidents traditionally governed the country. This was the high-point in Pinochet's startling rise from a conventional Army career to a position of personal power which had never been achieved by any previous Chilean leader. Gradually and with remarkable political cunning he had built up his personal ascendancy over the rest of the Junta and disposed of every possible challenge, until this had brought him to the peak of power.

Pinochet could also claim credit for having presided over the slow but seemingly successful recovery of the economy from the chaos left by Allende. In 1973 inflation was officially accepted as being over 600 per cent and still rising. Production was declining in nearly all sectors and overall GDP was 4.3 per cent lower than the previous year. The government deficit amounted to a quarter of GDP and was likely to increase further since the nationalised industries were losing $500 million per year. The country was defaulting on its international debt and currency reserves had all but disappeared.

By 1980, however, GDP had been rising by more than 5 per cent per annum for three years; inflation was down to 31 per cent and falling; the fiscal deficit had entirely disappeared and the balance of payments was in the black. Chile's international debt was manageable at $10 billion and the reserves amounted to $4 billion based on a large inflow of foreign investment and loans. Whatever reservations the US and European governments felt about giving aid and comfort to a military dictator, their bankers and economists in international financial institutions found that the people now managing the Chilean economy and finances were men of the same kind as themselves – technocrats who had often studied for their higher degrees at the same North American universities or business schools. The state of the economy in macro-economic terms was probably the only part of the Pinochet regime's record which attracted any approval abroad.

In Chile business and commercial leaders and the middle classes in general, who mostly supported the government, were enjoying the benefits of restored economic stability and a boom largely fuelled by foreign borrowing and a massive sell-off of state enterprises to the private sector. But the striking improvement of the economy as a whole, which was already being described as an 'economic miracle' by some incautious enthusiasts, had not brought prosperity to the majority of the people. Unemployment was still high and real wages were below their 1970 level for those who had jobs. The improvements, which were supposed to benefit the whole country by the 'trickle-down' effect of dynamic economic growth, were hardly noticeable. For the poorer Chileans, and not only those whom the regime still treated as actual or potential enemies, the boom of the late 1970s and 1980 brought little comfort. They had survived economic shocks of all sorts in the first seven years of the military regime, but most were still no better off and the government's repressive machinery added to the suffering of any who stepped out of line.

Nevertheless, President Pinochet and his inner circle must have felt secure and confident of the future as they moved back into the Moneda Palace in March 1981. None of them can have guessed that another crisis was about to sweep over them.

8

THE CHICAGO BOYS

> 'The Chicago Boys now came fully into their own. [...] They took full advantage of their alliance with Pinochet, master-minding the most dramatic reconstruction yet seen in twentieth-century Chile. Their aims were Utopian and all-embracing. They wanted to reverse the entire state-interventionist trend that had developed in Chile since the 1920s.' – Simon Collier and William F. Sater, *A History of Chile, 1808-1994*

One of the better features of United States' aid to Chile in the 1960s was a Point IV exchange programme under which Chilean students could take higher degrees at US universities. Through this scheme a large number of able Chilean economists, many from the Universidad Católica, received fellowships to study at the University of Chicago, where they absorbed the monetarist theory of economics from its high priests Milton Friedman, Arnold Harberger and their colleagues and duly returned to Chile to pass on their faith to others. Many were converted to the view that the application of free market forces combined with tight control of the money supply were the keys not only to good economic policy but also to many, and perhaps all, aspects of social affairs. This was fundamentally at odds with much of the economic theory which had ruled in Chile and elsewhere in the 1960s and '70s and, in particular, with the view that state intervention was essential to counteract market forces. The Chicago view has been summed up by a Chilean economic historian, Patricio Meller, as follows:

> State intervention in the economy leads to distortion and inefficiency; the extreme reached during the UP government allows this phenomenon, which dragged on for several decades, to be clearly seen. Furthermore, this action by the state has been justified by the need to overcome poverty and unequal incomes;

but the result has been the opposite. In synthesis, the state is the problem and not the solution; its transformation into a subsidiary state will be the basis of economic growth.[1]

As the Allende regime weakened, some of the 'Chicago Boys', as they were called, led by Sergio de Castro, Dean of the Catholic University's Economics Faculty, went to work to produce a detailed plan for rebuilding the economy on the free market model.[2] With the support of Agustín Edwards' *El Mercurio* group (and former naval officers like Roberto Kelly and Hernán Cubillos, who were yachting friends of Edwards) this document, known as *el ladrillo* (the brick) because of its size, was circulated widely within the armed forces immediately after the coup. None of the military leaders knew much about economics. Their only strong common opinion was that, for reasons of national security, economic assets and therefore economic policy ought to be controlled by a national authority rather than by businessmen mainly concerned with profit. However this was little more than an instinctive attitude and far from being the basis of any sort of plan for rescuing the economy they had inherited. As the Air Force Commander, General Leigh, despairingly commented when the armed forces took over the economy, they had 'no programme, no plans, nothing'. Some of them began to cast about for new ideas.

Admiral Merino, the Junta member responsible for economic policy, called in Kelly to take over as head of ODEPLAN, the central economic planning office. Since they had produced *el ladrillo,* de Castro and other young monetarists came in to the Finance and Economics ministries as advisers to military and naval ministers. Some of the Chicago Boys were now in government posts but they did not get their own hands on the levers of power for another year and a half; the first ministers appointed by the Junta to take charge of the economy tended to have more contacts with Christian Democrat economists or with businessmen who wanted to preserve a strong element of state intervention and

1 Patricio Meller, *Un Siglo de Economía Políticia Chilena (1890-1990)* (Santiago, 1996).

2 'Chicago Boys' was a vague but convenient label for a large number of economists who were not all trained in Chicago and held widely varying views. The term is used in this chapter to describe the group who closely followed the Friedman and Harberger school of monetarists.

direct management of the economy. Few of these people were strongly committed to the Chicago free market economic philosophy. The Junta listened to arguments of all kinds – including those of de Castro, by which they were not immediately convinced despite his brilliant advocacy. A substantial devaluation announced three weeks after the coup led to an explosion of domestic prices which caused great alarm in the Junta. Merino, who feared that they would be accused of killing ordinary people with hunger, reacted violently, with the immediate result that Fernando Leniz, a pragmatist who understood the market economy but was no academic theorist, was appointed as Economics Minister.

Economic reconstruction

Throughout 1974 the process of economic reconstruction continued by gradual stages. Government spending was cut and the fiscal deficit reduced to 11 per cent. Price controls were abolished on a vast number of goods (a total of 3,600 items with controlled prices was pruned to sixty in a few weeks) so that a free market was established for most goods and services available in Chile. However, it was becoming obvious that the inevitable social and economic costs of creating a free market economy would fall on the poorest section of the population and price increases hit working-class Chileans especially hard. Inflation was actually higher in 1974 than in 1972 and did not fall substantially till 1976. Real wages had fallen sharply and much industrial and agricultural production was also affected. The reduction of tariffs on imported goods in the name of efficiency and the principle of 'comparative advantage' was another article of faith for the Chicago Boys. However the effect of tariff cuts was to exaggerate still further the problems facing Chilean industries which had been built up to supply domestic markets. Some were soon driven to the wall by foreign competition, and by mid-1975 even government figures showed the rate of unemployment in Greater Santiago as 16 per cent.[3] A government minimum employment plan (PEM) introduced at the end of 1975 gave a minimal income of about US$65

[3] Other sources, e.g. independent economists at the University of Chile, estimated the true rate at about 25 per cent, not including the large amount of hidden employment.

per month to up to 206,000 of the unemployed. Despite this palliative, part of the working-class population of Chile had no visible source of income whatever. Even those who were employed or drew a wage under the PEM had drastically reduced incomes which, if they were lucky, provided them and their families with barely enough to eat.

The shock of 1975

In March 1975 Milton Friedman made a highly publicised personal visit to Santiago. In his public and private contacts, including an interview with Pinochet, he argued for a yet stronger dose of the shock treatment which had so far been rather mildly applied, and boosted the case which his followers, led by de Castro, had been advocating. Thereafter Pinochet was persuaded to order the introduction of another emergency plan. Fernando Leniz was replaced as Minister of Economy by Sergio de Castro, and a former Christian Democrat economist, Jorge Cauas, who had returned from the World Bank to become Finance Minister the previous December, was given broad authority over economic policy. In April, Cauas announced an emergency plan to halt inflation and shock the economy into growth. Public spending was to be cut by another 27 per cent that year and drastic monetary controls were introduced. To stimulate private sector investment, regulations controlling the banking system were drastically cut away, import tariffs were further reduced, and foreign investment was encouraged with radical changes and incentives.[4]

When Cauas announced the new shock treatment, the economy was already much weakened both by the milder dose of free-market medicine administered in 1974 and by the general world recession which had followed the oil price explosion of 1973. These stronger measures caused even more pain. In 1975, GDP fell by nearly 13 per cent, unemployment rose further and the rate of price inflation for the year was 343 per cent, one of the highest in Latin America. However this was what Cauas and de Castro had

[4] The policy of actively encouraging foreign investment was given full expression in Decree Law 600 of 1977 and led indirectly to Chile's break with the Andean Bloc countries which were trying to create an Andean Common Market embracing Venezuela, Colombia, Ecuador, Peru, Bolivia and Chile.

expected and warned would happen. De Castro, the principal intellectual author of the plan, had persuaded Pinochet that only drastic measures had a real chance of saving the economy from indefinite decline and recession.[5] His tough mind and the total assurance with which he argued his case against both military and civilian critics made a deep impression on others in Pinochet's inner circle and in the Junta. The principal exception was General Leigh, but his influence within the Junta was already declining.

The grip which de Castro and his supporters came to hold over economic policy depended crucially, however, on Pinochet's ability to insulate them from political criticism. Without his backing, it is debatable whether shock treatment as painful as theirs could have been maintained for longer than a few months. For nearly seven years they had Pinochet's almost unconditional support: despite his cautious and pragmatic attitude to most problems, he seems to have been intrigued and captivated by the fervour with which these Chicago Boys confidently promised to transform the economy and open the way to a complete national renewal for Chile. They flatly declared that application of their ideas would not only transform the economy but would also serve to bring about fundamental reforms in almost all national institutions and make Marxism an irrelevant anachronism. They did not seem to have the taint of self-interest which the military suspected to be the motivation of many members of the commercial and industrial élites.

The Chicago Boys in power

At the end of 1976 Pinochet replaced Jorge Cauas by Sergio de Castro as Minister of Finance. It was the end of the period of emergency shock treatment and the beginning of recuperation. De Castro was supported in government by Pablo Baraona as Minister of Economy, Alvaro Bardón as President of the Central Bank and Miguel Kast, a young and intensely Catholic economist, as Roberto Kelly's chief collaborator in ODEPLAN. Almost more

[5] During one meeting General Pinochet sought to bring discussion to an end by saying 'After all we are the ones who have got the saucepan by its handle', to which de Castro replied, 'Yes, General, but you could find yourself left holding nothing more than the handle.'

than de Castro, Kast, who was to die of cancer aged only thirty-five in 1983, came to be seen as the prototype Chicago Boy combining the intellectual force of a first-class mind with great moral zeal. He and others recruited a new generation of disciples among the young economists emerging from the universities and finishing their preparation for the 'priesthood' not in Rome but in Chicago.

Their mission was to reverse what they saw as half a century of state intervention in the economy and the misguided manipulation of tariffs and subsidies, wage and price controls and the shackling of private initiative intended to reduce dependence on foreign imports or investment. In the view of de Castro and his team, this had produced only limited and stagnant growth at a very high cost and an inefficient, overprotected private sector based on import substitution rather than the exploitation of comparative advantage. In de Castro's words, Chile's past experience proved that kind of economic policy was 'the way to stay poor for ever'.

One undeniable benefit of adopting free market principles was the enthusiasm with which foreign lenders, who shared the same economic views, were again happy to lend to Chile. Having inherited a catastrophic balance of payments in 1973 with almost no foreign reserves and heavy repayments of foreign debt due in the mid-1970s, the government was able to reschedule the foreign debt without great difficulty in 1974. By 1975, however, some of the governments concerned, including the British, were not prepared to renegotiate with what was now obviously an exceptionally repressive regime. In 1976, as already mentioned, the US Congress banned all official economic aid to Chile, except for strictly humanitarian purposes, following a campaign waged by Edward Kennedy and Thomas Harkin since the coup. However, the flow of loans from the World Bank and the Inter-American Development Bank increased steadily;[6] notwithstanding pressures exerted by the Carter administration within those institutions, there was usually a clear majority in favour of all loan projects which were economically sound. The anti-Pinochet pressure groups in the United States and Western European countries were never

[6] Between 1976 and 1986 the total value of loans by these institutions to Chile reached $3.1 billion. Figures quoted by Pamela Constable and Arturo Valenzuela, *Chile under Pinochet: A Nation of Enemies* (New York, 1991).

able to get the international bankers to introduce politics into their decision-making.

At the same time the flow of private bank lending to Chile increased year by year and was greatly stimulated both by the favourable new decree law on private foreign investment, which put foreign investors on an equal footing with Chileans, and the surge of opportunities released by privatisation. The government set about selling off more than 400 of the 620 state-owned businesses, including nearly all of those expropriated or intervened by Allende and a great many of the public corporations and enterprises established and built up by CORFO (the government development body) since 1939. Where the companies concerned had been expropriated or otherwise taken over under Allende, they were offered back to their original owners. In other cases they were offered for sale to entrepreneurs, often at excessively low prices.

In the case of agriculture, the policy of privatisation or denationalisation involved returning to its former owners the land expropriated under the Frei and Allende regimes. The agrarian policy announced immediately after the coup was intended to encourage the extension of land ownership, the transformation of peasants into small farmers by granting plots of land to individuals and reducing the role of agrarian co-operatives, and the like. However, the granting of land titles alone was never likely to create viable farms, and the government became less and less willing to provide small farms with the credit and technical assistance which they would inevitably need in order to survive for long. One of the results of this was that a large number of the small farms established during the process of agrarian reform in the 1960s and early '70s were unable to survive and their owners were forced to sell off their land. Thus the concentration of land in the hands of relatively few owners, which had been weakened to some degree under Frei's *Ley de Reforma Agraria* and much more drastically by the all-out attack under Allende, was slowly and unevenly reversed under Pinochet. This was not so much the result of deliberate policy as of the application of free market theory: for example the government refused to give credits to small farmers either because they preferred to cut back state expenditure or because of their theoretical dislike of 'discriminatory' subsidies. The result, of course, was the same.

Agriculture was also badly hit by the economic shock treatment. Output of some crops increased but in the critical case of wheat production in 1976 was only 706,000 tons (according to the Instituto Nacional de Estadisticas), substantially below the 1973 level. The government admitted that more than 600,000 tons of wheat had to be imported to meet demand in that year and the farming industry's spokesman referred to a 'vertical decline in wheat production'. Overall the farming economy was still depressed three years after the coup, largely due to the lack of agricultural credit at affordable cost and withdrawal of technical support for small farmers.

The manufacturing, service and commercial sectors of the economy were also fundamentally affected by the upheavals of this period including the privatisation of state-owned enterprises. In October 1976 CORFO announced that it had received a total of $355 million for the firms sold to the private sector or co-operatives by that time. It was never entirely clear exactly which CORFO-controlled companies had been sold and to whom but it emerged in time that the majority of the larger enterprises passing into the private sector were acquired by a small number of conglomerates or *grupos*. Some of these were long-established commercial empires such as the Edwards group, with banking, newspaper and publishing interests dating back to the 19th century, and the Matte group. Others were newer ones such as those developed by Javier Vial from its original base in the BHC bank, and the Cruzat-Larraín group. Each of these, and others such as the Luksíc, Yarur and Angellini conglomerates, sought to have 'a slice of the action' in most of the main profitable areas of the economy (fishing, mining, banking, agro-industry, consumer durables). In effect the policy of privatisation transferred control of large parts of the economy from public ownership into the hands of a somewhat limited number of private entrepreneurs.

Although some of the Chicago Boys had links with one or other of the *grupos* (or joined them at a later stage), it was certainly not the intention of the military regime to allow public assets to accumulate in so few hands. Like much else that happened at the time in Chile, some of the consequences of their actions were not foreseen. When asked why these policies benefited only the rich, de Castro and his colleagues replied that all they had done was remove privileges and protection from the world of business. If one company or individual was doing better than another, it was simply because they were more efficient and productive. The free market model necessarily involved allowing some to grow richer than others and this was essential to the creation of a more prosperous economy. The theory which the Chicago Boys offered their critics, and perhaps truly believed, was that of *chorreo*, i.e. that the wealth created by economic success would eventually 'trickle down' to those at the bottom of the pile. It was the same theory as was propounded by free market economists in the 1980s in both Ronald Reagan's United States and Margaret Thatcher's Britain.

An economic miracle?

The macro-economic indicators in the accompanying table show the overall transformation achieved after eight years of the military regime.[7]

	1973	*1980*	*1981*
Annual inflation rate (%) (Consumer Price Index)	606.1	31.2	9.5
Growth rate (%) (Gross National Product)	–4.3	7.8	5.5
Exports (US$ million)			
Total	1,309	4,705	3,836
Non-traditional	104	1,821	1,411
Reserves (US$ million)	167	4,074	3,775
Fiscal deficit (%)	21.0	–5.5	–2.9
Annual increase in real salaries (%)	–25.3	8.6	9.0

True believers called it an economic miracle. The fiscal deficit had become a surplus; the growth rate since 1977 had been substantial, and inflation was down from over 600 per cent in 1973 to 31 per cent in 1980. The policy of promoting export-driven growth was beginning to produce results. Fishing products, timber, wood pulp and paper, and fruit were being produced and exported

7 Figures quoted by Patricio Meller, *Un Siglo de Economía Política Chilena (1890-1990)* (Santiago, 1996), cuadro 3-4, p. 196.

in such quantities that Chile's dangerous over-reliance on exports of copper and other metals was being much reduced. Although the supposed trickle-down effect of economic success was not evident in the *poblaciones* of Santiago and other cities – and certainly not in the countryside – the beneficiaries of the consumer boom were convinced that prosperity was back at last. De Castro and his economic team were so sure of the firmness and stability of Chile's recovery that (on 29 June 1979) the Central Bank fixed the value of the Chilean peso at 39 to the US dollar.

The Chicago medicine seemed to have got the economy back on its feet and the time was ripe to move forward to a second phase of recuperation beyond monetarism and free market reforms: namely a wider programme of structural change. This process would involve the modernisation of health care, social security and even labour relations, all of which had long been areas exclusively dominated by the state or by unions organised on party lines. By introducing free market (now more attractively described as 'social market') principles into these areas of Chile's national life, the Chicago Boys offered the prospect of fundamental changes in Chile's socio-economic structure which would create national prosperity immunised against political ideologies and pressure groups. They and most of the leaders of the armed forces saw eye to eye on the need to free Chile once and for all from distorting, and ultimately destructive, political forces which both saw as having brought the country to the brink of ruin by 1973.

Labour relations

The first important step in this programme of regeneration was in the area of labour relations. Organised labour had been one of the hardest-hit sectors of Chilean society in the years of repression. Initially the Junta had promised that trades union members and leaders who had not been active supporters of the *Unidad Popular* would not be victimised, but this promise was easily broken. Trade unions' ability to defend workers' interests was soon cut back and the government put its own nominees into the key positions. The first civilian Minister of Labour was a right-wing lawyer from Punta Arenas, Sergio Fernández, a strong believer in the free market (except in relation to labour affairs) who seemed to regard strikes as little more than pretexts for class struggle.

Union membership was at a low ebb when the *Organización Regional Inter-Americana de Trabajadores*, acting on a motion by the US AFL/CIO delegation, decided on a boycott (with effect from January 1979) throughout the American continent on cargoes from Chile, Cuba and Nicaragua. This was loudly denounced in Santiago as a plot against Chile by North American labour leaders in cahoots with the Carter administration. Protests apart, the situation was serious enough for Pinochet to send his Minister of Finance, Sergio de Castro, to Washington to try to negotiate a way round the boycott.

Following de Castro's talks with the influential President of the AFL/CIO, George Meany, Pinochet appointed an unknown young technocrat, José Piñera, as Minister of Labour with a brief to offer labour law reforms. Piñera was from a well-known Christian Democrat family and in fact a product of Harvard, not Chicago. Although not yet thirty years old when he joined the Cabinet, he was a brilliant and politically sensitive economist who had already expounded to the Junta a beguiling vision of structural reforms including a new deal in the labour field. Piñera's Labour Code was a skilful blend of liberal and restrictive provisions. Workers would again be free to organise in pursuit of their own interests, to elect their leaders without government interference, and to strike without inevitably coming into conflict with the law; but on the other hand employers would be free to take on new manpower to replace those on strike after only thirty days; and after sixty days strikers would be deemed to have quit their jobs permanently. Furthermore collective bargaining could only cover wage demands, and was restricted to factory or plant level only so that much of the strength which organised labour could muster in the past in Chile and in free societies generally was in effect undermined.

The outline of Piñera's plan had been judiciously presented to the AFL/CIO who were persuaded that the inclusion of free elections and the right to strike, however circumscribed, represented a big step forward. They protested for form's sake but in effect accepted that the new code was sufficiently liberal to pass muster. As it worked in practice, however, the trade unions found that their negotiating power was extremely limited. In 2,574 new contracts negotiated in the first year of the Code, the average pay increase was only 8 per cent which was meagre when compared with a rate of inflation still over 30 per cent. Moreover, a series of restrictive amendments to the new law soon removed many of its original concessions to the workers' interests. Labour courts were abolished and employers were allowed to offer new contracts less favourable than those previously negotiated and to cut many long-established benefits. These changes were justified by the Minister of Labour as necessary to allow greater flexibility for employers. So they did; but invariably at the expense of the workers.

Modernisation Chicago-style

In September 1979, in a speech celebrating the sixth anniversary of the coup, General Pinochet publicly espoused the idea of reconstructing Chilean society on free market lines. This speech was largely the work of Piñera and another young Turk, the former *gremialista* and lawyer Jaime Guzmán, who had been one of Pinochet's inner circle of advisers from the early 1970s and subsequently became converted to free market ideas. It set out the objective of building a truly 'free society' in Chile by creating prosperity, making people 'free' economically rather than returning to what they and the regime's leaders considered the false freedom offered by old-style political democracy. To this end Pinochet announced the 'seven modernisations' to be undertaken: labour, social security, education, health, justice, agriculture and regional government. It was ironic (and the subject of much hilarity at the time) that this slogan was taken from Maoist China.

This vast agenda would inevitably take many years to achieve. The Chicago Boys (a group which now included several technocrats who had never studied in Chicago) were the ideal instruments from Pinochet's point of view. They did not (at least at this stage) represent any of the business interests which for so long had been dominant in Chile. At the same time, de Castro and company were an effective counterweight to the *duros* in the government who wished to preserve a strong role for the state in controlling key elements of the economy and distrusted the economic groups which were taking over so many former CORFO enterprises. The *duros* and the Chicago Boys coincided, however, in wanting the military regime to continue at least for long enough to allow their modernisations to take root. To de Castro and most of his co-religionists, authoritarian government was a necessary precondition for their kind of revolution – not desirable in itself perhaps, but essential for the achievement of their economic and social goals.

They moved quickly after the 'seven modernisations' speech in 1979. Piñera himself became Minister of Mines and undertook the recasting of the law governing mining and mining investment. Others, including Hernán Büchi who was to be an outstanding Minister of Finance after 1985 and later a presidential candidate, designed new health and social security systems allowing citizens the choice between a range of privately-run health insurance (ISAPREs) and pension plans (AFPs). At CORFO the process of selling off state assets continued and some monopolies regarded as strategic were divided into smaller, self-financing corporations so that they could at least be better managed and less of a burden on the state treasury than when they were huge bureaucratic monsters.

Some of these reforms have conclusively proved their value and almost all survived into the 1990s after the disappearance of the authoritarian regime which created them. The health and pension systems, in particular, are now accepted as permanent improvements – at least for the generation of Chileans who became wage or salary earners after the social market reformers had done their work. Older and unemployed people had no choice but to continue relying on the former inadequate state-controlled welfare system which could not provide pensions based on invested savings. Similarly the poorer sections of the community will probably never be able to afford the substantial cost of contributing to health insurance schemes and must continue to rely on the public hospitals and basic medical services provided by the state. Notwithstanding these gaps in social welfare, it is noteworthy that many other countries, in Latin America and elsewhere, have followed Chile's example in pursuing these modernisations.

The Labour Code was, and remains, much more controversial. Unquestionably employers benefited from it but almost none of the trade union leaders, and few of the workers themselves, have been persuaded that it truly serves their interests. It has only survived to the time of writing because no fundamental revision has so far got past the barrier imposed by the built-in right-wing majority in the Senate. However, the success of the Chilean economy since the mid-1980s must be attributed at least in part to the way in which wage levels and other labour costs have been kept down under the 1979 Labour Code.

The cost of free markets

From the moment the Chicago Boys were able to put their ideas into practice, a variety of criticisms were aimed at them. The most telling was that the inflexible application of their doctrine had a terrible cost in terms of the destruction of the earning capacity and standard of living of the poor. By the end of 1975 when the worst effects of the shock treatment were hitting everyone in the working classes, even those in jobs were desperately poor and those without were destitute. At the end of the decade the boom was apparently making many well-placed Chileans richer, but the 'trickle-down' effect had barely touched the poorest half of the population. In 1975 ODEPLAN itself estimated that as many as 21 per cent of Chileans were living in conditions of extreme poverty (in effect destitution, since a family was excluded from this category if it had even as little as 2,000 pesos, the cost of a transistor radio). The government and its advisers were not without social conscience, particularly in relation to the obvious needs of the poorest families, and a serious effort was made to improve their lot after the 1975 study. Preventive health care for mothers and children and measures to improve sanitation and nutrition in the poorest areas sharply reduced the number living in extreme poverty and the rate of infant mortality, but there remained as many indicators of persistent poverty as of improvements.

The terrible condition of the poor in the Santiago *poblaciones* was still obvious to many independent observers (not only the government's critics) in the 1980s. For example, improvements in health care for the very young had been due to deliberate targeting and achieved at the cost of neglecting the old and chronically ill who depended on public hospitals. The ODEPLAN estimate in 1975 that 21 per cent were living in extreme poverty was followed by a similar study in 1982 which found that this figure had fallen to 14.2 per cent. On the face of it this was a good result but other studies showed that – even in 1985 – 45 per cent of all Chileans were still poor and that 25 per cent of those were indigent.[8]

One result of the poverty, overcrowding and squalor of the *poblaciones* was the growth of new community groups. Frequently the primary aim of these groups was simply to break out of their hopeless living circumstances and organise new *tomas* of land on which to settle. Tents and makeshift shacks sprung up overnight on vacant sites in the outskirts of the city as families decamped in crudely organised migrations. In their physical conditions these new communities were often no better than the old ones, but they were fiercely independent in spirit. Sometimes the leaders were former Socialist or Communist activists or Christian Democrats. Often local parish priests or church organisations took the lead. In the eyes of the authorities all were left-wing subversives, and the priests, often of foreign nationality, became objects of particular suspicion to the local authorities and the security forces. Another grassroots change which became evident was the growth of the Evangelical churches, particularly in poor city districts: hundreds of thousands of poor Chileans who had hitherto considered themselves Catholics but were now disillusioned with their original Church's ambiguous relationship with the state, turned to the Evangelical movement or to other even newer sects. To some degree the left-wing or 'libertarian' tendency among the Catholic priesthood was also a response to the failure of the Catholic hierarchy as a whole to offer leadership and a voice to the *pobladores* and the poor.

However there were undoubtedly real improvements for many in Chile in the late 1970s. From then till 1982 the underlying deprivation of the poorest was, to some extent, submerged by the economic success of the country as a whole. There was an extravagant consumer boom, much of it based on imports. Piñera claimed that in ten more years Chile would be a developed country, and de Castro predicted that annual *per capita* income would reach $3,500 by 1990.[9] Encouraged by the enthusiastic approval of the International Monetary Fund and the World Bank, they and their

[8] Figures quoted in an article by Aristedes Torche entitled 'Distribuir el ingreso para satisfacer las necesidades basicas', published in *Desarrollo Economico en Democrácia* (1987).

[9] In fact it did not reach this level till 1994.

political masters were ready to believe that they had indeed produced an economic miracle. Early in 1981, as Pinochet assumed office in the role of constitutional President, Ronald Reagan succeeded Jimmy Carter and United States policy towards Chile took on a softer tone. Even if there was still widespread poverty and deprivation, Chile's prospects for the next decade were much brighter.

Collapse of the miracle

Predictably, the boom of the late 1970s and 1980/81 proved as vulnerable to external factors as others had done before it. First came the steep rise in world oil prices (the second 'oil shock' within a single decade), and then interest rates soared. Large parts of Chilean industry, now controlled by a few powerful groups, began to come under intense pressure from internal as well as external causes. In particular the fixed and increasingly unrealistic exchange rate between the peso and the dollar compounded the problem. Many of these groups were not financing their dizzy growth from profits but, to a dangerous degree, by foreign loans usually denominated in dollars and often with variable interest rates. Since the Chicago Boys in government had failed to appreciate the need for close supervision of this borrowing, the groups (particularly those headed by Vial and Cruzat-Larraín) were able to juggle funds between the various companies they controlled and thus give a false picture of their true viability. Overseas borrowing – principally by the private sector – had increased by more than 100 per cent between 1978, when it was $7 billion, and 1981 when it had risen to $15.6 billion. Over the same period the value of imports surged from $3.2 to $7.3 billion, while exports fell to $3.8 billion, thus producing a frightening trade gap. According to the Chicago theory this was not the crisis it seemed to be; the books could be balanced simply by borrowing more from abroad and a process of 'automatic adjustment' would bring down wages (as if they were not already low) and production costs, and would also make imports more expensive.

The first outward sign of the coming storm was the bankruptcy of the largest sugar-refining group, CRAV, in May 1981. Other bankruptices followed and by 1982 the number had risen to 810 – more than three times the rate for 1975-81. Sergio de Castro, still Minister of Finance, insisted that this was only a passing aberration. He was adamant that the peso/dollar rate at 39 should be maintained and the only remedies he would consider were to reduce wage levels and cut the military budget – both unacceptable politically. For the next ten months Pinochet continued to support de Castro, but increasingly the business establishment and the President's military advisers argued that it was essential to devalue the peso. The world economy was apparently moving into a recession which was bound to hit Chile hard because of its heavy dependence on foreign trade. Interest rates continued upwards and, to make matters worse, copper prices were falling and oil prices rising – creating a deadly squeeze on the balance of payments.

In November 1981 four relatively small banks and four finance companies had to be declared insolvent and taken over by the Central Bank. The government felt that the risk of a financial panic and possibly the collapse of the whole private banking system could only be countered by taking over the debts of these private institutions. In accordance with the pure doctrine of free market economics, these privately-owned banks and *financieras* should simply have been allowed to fail, but when it came to the point even a government with dictatorial powers, which hardly needed to concern itself with public opinion or the arguments of any organised opposition, could not face the practical consequences of the Chicago philosophy. From the moment the Central Bank took over the debts of these private banks it was assumed by all concerned that the Central Bank would not in the last resort allow any Chilean bank to become bankrupt.

It had become very clear that in order to rein back the mounting trade deficit and stabilise the balance of payments the government would either have to devalue the peso or act to reduce wages and government expenditure. De Castro still would not contemplate devaluation, and the gulf between him and the most convinced of the Chicago faithful (such as Miguel Kast) on the one hand and the majority of the Cabinet and Pinochet's other advisers on the other became wider week by week. In April 1982 the President finally changed course and fired de Castro.

It was perhaps the most dramatic reversal of political fortune in the history of the regime. De Castro had been the architect and manager of an economic policy, indeed a new economic deal, which had achieved notable successes since the low point of 1975. His influence had spread well beyond the economy and his reputation in international financial circles had been a huge asset to Chile in a period when the reputation of the President and his regime was in every other respect abysmal. By 1982 his usefulness was all in the past and without him Pinochet would be free to change policy again. It remained to be seen if he would alter course by a few degrees or turn tail.

Chicago survives

Pinochet's immediate decision was to bring into his cabinet two of his most experienced military advisers, Generals Danús and Frez. Both believed in the value of a free market economy in principle but were far more pragmatic than the Chicago Boys. One result of their arrival was to put a stop to plans to sell off or split up remaining state corporations and in particular to kill off the Chicago Boys' hope of privatising the copper giant CODELCO and other 'strategic' industries. The debate on whether to devalue or to reduce wages was hard fought over the next few weeks. The new Minister of Finance, Sergio de la Cuadra, supported by Miguel Kast (now Chairman of the Central Bank), continued to resist devaluation, which they feared might spell the end of all the free market reforms. They insisted instead on the need to reduce salaries and short-term interest rates, but others – particularly the Generals – now had a stronger case to make. Reserves continued to fall, interest rates stayed high, and the peso/dollar parity came under still greater pressure. Finally, on 14 June 1982, Pinochet cut the knot and decided on a devaluation of 18 per cent, which he ordered General Danús, a known proponent of devaluation, to announce on television that night. It came as a bolt from the blue.[10]

A few days later the government also moved to break the link between wages and the cost of living index which had been established in 1979. The debate on which means to use to meet the crisis was resolved by using both, but unfortunately the crisis was still not solved. The government had moved away from the 'neo-liberal' or free market economic model as constructed by

[10] Miguel Kast, who was in Germany seeking to persuade bankers there that the peso would continue to be held at 39 to the dollar, only heard of its devaluation to 46 after the event.

de Castro and his allies. It devalued the peso, re-introduced a preferential exchange rate for the dollar to help large debtors to meet their commitments, and opened the way for wage reductions. Many critics felt that this was the death-knell for monetarism and the Chicago ideology, but the crisis had farther to run before the shape of a new economic policy would become clear. For the moment, however, one important pillar of the model remained solid: the government refused to resort to the usual counter-cyclical measures – increasing the money supply and fiscal deficit financing–despite the increasingly agonised demands of those businessmen who were fighting bankruptcy.

After the emergency intervention of November 1981, apologists for Chile's version of the free market argued that state intervention to save the banks was a vital measure in order to preserve the system but that others should not expect the same protection. No one really believed it, and we see in a later chapter what followed when much larger banks, some at the centre of the major economic groups, met the same fate at the beginning of 1983 and how much of the Chicago 'model' survived the financial crisis of 1982/3. In the middle of 1982, however, Chicago was far from being the fashionable flavour. The strangest feature of this precipitate fall from grace was that the issue which seemed to have been central – the peso/dollar parity – should not in theory have been a problem at all. The monetarist view was that currencies should float freely against each other. However de Castro had judged that, while this might work in a massive economy such as the United States, Chile's was far too small, and now far too open, to run the risk of speculation on the dollar.

To the ordinary people who had to live with the practical consequences of his policy it seemed obvious that the free market model which might work perfectly as a mechanism in the abstract had to be adapted carefully and sometimes quite drastically, if it was not to grind living men and women into dust. A perfect working model producing automatic balance was no substitute for a real economy with a fair proportion of contented workers and consumers. In the Chile of 1981/2 there were not enough of either.

9

FRIENDS, FOES AND FOREIGN QUARRELS

> 'Be it thy course to busy giddy minds with foreign quarrels; that action, hence borne out, may waste the memory of the former days.'
>
> – Shakespeare, 2 Henry IV, V

Since the end of the nineteenth century, all Chilean governments have had one consistent foreign policy objective. Bluntly stated, this is to preserve the territorial gains achieved by their military success in the War of the Pacific. The war increased the national territory by about a third and, more important, it transferred into Chilean control the vast nitrate deposits which were to provide almost half of all the government's revenue for the next forty years. The fact that most of the companies which mined and exploited this resource were controlled by foreign capital till the 1960s and yielded large profits for the shareholders until the nitrate industry collapsed in 1930, does not diminish the crucial importance of nitrates to Chile throughout the period.[1] To a large extent the same considerations applied to copper when it became the dominant element in the national economy.

Having won control over the Norte Grande and its mineral resources by war, Chile was well-placed to secure its gains by treaty and revert to the tradition of respect for international law which it had normally followed. Definitive peace treaties were eventually concluded with Bolivia in 1904 and with Peru in 1883 and 1929. Since then Chile has pursued its foreign policy objectives

[1] British entrepreneurs, notably John T. North and his British and Chilean associates, were the principal beneficiaries during the boom years. From the 1920s they were replaced by Guggenheim & Sons of New York, who controlled the industry until it was nationalized under President Eduardo Frei in 1967.

by a shrewd combination of deterrent armed force; the international prestige of a country with a long record of stable and constitutional government; and careful diplomacy based on international law and the resolution of disputes by peaceful means. However, the emergence of an authoritarian military government in September 1973 destroyed the second and third of these props almost instantaneously. Chile's main objectives in international affairs remained the same as ever but the means available to achieve them were now much more limited. The country was in the hands of a government which relied on force alone; it could thus make no persuasive claim to democratic or constitutional legitimacy, and would soon become almost a pariah in the eyes of many other states.

Conditioned reflexes and diplomatic manoeuvres

Naturally all the countries of the Communist bloc (Cuba being among the first), broke off diplomatic relations, and if they did not move out quickly their missions in Chile were expelled with minimum ceremony. According to contemporary press reports (e.g. *Revista Ercilla*, 26 September 1973), there were possibly 13,000 people from communist countries in Santiago at the time who could have been mobilised in defence of the regime. Some were supposed to be agents of governments as remote as North Korea and North Vietnam. Nearly all of them left at once, leaving behind a large quantity of property and equipment of all sorts, including illegal arms and explosives imported under diplomatic cover. Among the communist states represented in Chile, only the People's Republic of China maintained diplomatic relations after the change of government. Having been recognised by Chile during the Frei regime and before any other American country had done so, Beijing seized the opportunity to steal a march on Moscow and was one of the first governments to accept the new regime in Santiago, thereby achieving in Chilean eyes a peculiar esteem. Several Western European countries, particularly Italy and Sweden where the ruling parties had been particularly close to elements in the UP, granted asylum to many political refugees and deliberately downgraded their presence in Santiago in token of their disapproval of the military regime. Latin American countries such as Brazil, Argentina, Uruguay, Paraguay and Peru, where the military were also in power, maintained correct relations, but in 1974 Mexico broke with Chile completely and the democratic governments in Venezuela and Colombia found their relations strained.

In 1975 a British doctor, Sheila Cassidy, who had been living in Chile for nearly four years, working in hospitals and clinics in Santiago, was arrested by the DINA because she had treated a fleeing MIR leader (Nelson Gutiérrez) who had been wounded in a shoot-out with the security forces. Sheila Cassidy was held incommunicado for ten days in a DINA interrogation centre and tortured with electric shocks to get her to reveal the identity and whereabouts of other MIR leaders. When she was released two months later and allowed to leave the country, the government in London under James Callaghan recalled the British Ambassador indefinitely and kept contacts with Chile at a junior level for the next five years. The relationship between the two countries had not been so strained in all the 150 years since the first exchange of representatives initiated by George Canning in 1823. The London government had compelling grounds for removing its Ambassador and backed up this gesture by imposing a total ban on sales of arms to Chile and refusing export credit guarantees even for non-military goods. However, business went on as usual with France and Germany whose governments disapproved of the new Chilean regime as strongly as Britain's but who still found it possible to carry on normal relations (including authorising some arms sales) despite the contrary pressures from Chilean exiles and human rights organisations.

The case of Sheila Cassidy illustrates one of the more difficult choices which have to be made by governments in foreign affairs.[2] To express the disgust and anger which British people felt, a strong message of condemnation had to be conveyed both to the Chilean regime and to the world at large. For many the action taken was by no means strong enough but, as the United States was to discover in the Letelier case a year later, the Chilean government could not be forced to put a stop to the repression,

[2] Sheila Cassidy has published a moving account of her life in Chile during the UP regime in 1971-3 and her increasing involvement in Chilean affairs, culminating in her ordeal in 1975 at the hands of the DINA. Some Chileans regarded her book *Audacity to Believe* (London, 1977) as tendentious, but it had an important influence on British opinion at the time – and subsequently.

torture and killing practised in its name. In short, the British reaction to the Cassidy case was a necessary gesture but had little, if any, practical effect. At best it may have obliged some of the more far-sighted members of the Chilean government and its moderate supporters to think harder about the long-term damage their country would suffer if it were condemned by the great majority of world opinion and became totally isolated. It had no discernible effect at the time on the DINA's appalling methods.

Other European governments, notably France, were prepared to condemn human rights abuses in Chile in the strongest terms. President François Mitterrand took a close personal interest in the subject, and the French Marxist Régis Debray, who had been so prominent in supporting Salvador Allende during his lifetime, kept Mitterrand's attention engaged, as did Allende's widow who was often in Paris and had long been on friendly terms with the French President. But the French government was never persuaded to break or downgrade relations with Santiago. The European Community also focussed collectively on the Chilean situation and made frequent joint statements about it. This gave some satisfaction to the pressure groups which had formed throughout Europe to mobilise opposition to the military government and, above all, to Pinochet personally. However, it cannot be claimed that joint Western European efforts to make the government in Santiago change its ways had any greater effect than the British gesture. There was only one country which had any real capacity to influence the Chilean government.

The many shifts in United States' policy towards Chile after 1973 have been described in earlier chapters. From 1973 to 1976, with Republican Presidents, Richard Nixon and then Gerald Ford, in the White House, there was a considerable degree of tolerance, even warmth, towards the new Chilean administration – although this did not extend to the Democrats in Congress. For the Republicans Pinochet was unquestionably preferable to Allende in his total opposition to communism; and in promising to re-establish some sort of stability – not democratic, but at least orderly–in a country that had seemed on the verge of anarchy in 1973. The repression of all forms of opposition, the disappearances and the illegal killings taking place in Chile were atrocious, but on a far smaller scale than what was happening in neighbouring

Argentina where four or five times as many people were believed to have been killed or disappeared in the same period.[3]

Jimmy Carter's election to the Presidency in 1976 marked a fundamental change in US policy towards Chile. Earlier in that year the sustained efforts of the Democratic Senator Edward Kennedy and others had finally produced a congressional ban on military aid and sales of equipment to Chile – the 'Kennedy Amendment'. This was accompanied by the imposition of a $27.5 million ceiling on economic aid; and both limits were to remain in force until the President certified that there had been substantial improvement in the human rights record in the country. The 'Kennedy Amendment' was the first significant practical step taken by the United States to demonstrate popular condemnation of what was seen to be happening in Chile. (Earlier congressional moves to restrict CIA operations which followed from Jack Anderson's ITT revelations and the Church Committee's investigations were closely connected with Chile but not aimed at Pinochet in particular.) Carter's election confirmed that questions of human rights would henceforth be a major factor in the shaping of US foreign policy. The *realpolitik* of Henry Kissinger was replaced in Washington by a spirit of naive if well-intended idealism, which had been little in evidence since the days of Woodrow Wilson. To Chileans, threatened by a more powerful military dictatorship in Buenos Aires, Washington seemed to be applying double standards with a vengeance.

Chile and the Southern Cone

Before the coup in September 1973, Chilean military planners feared that Peru and possibly Bolivia might take advantage of an internal crisis in Chile to exert some kind of pressure in the north. They thought that Peru, then governed by a military Junta headed by General Velasco Alvarado, was preparing to deploy a force of 500 tanks recently acquired from Russia to reoccupy

[3] Estimates of the total number of deaths and disappearances in Argentina during the 'dirty war' range from 11,370 to about 30,000. In 1984, the official *Comisión Nacional sobre la Desaparición de Personas* put the number of disappearances at 9,800. To this must be added a figure of at least 1,570 known deaths reported in the Argentine press. These are minimum estimates.

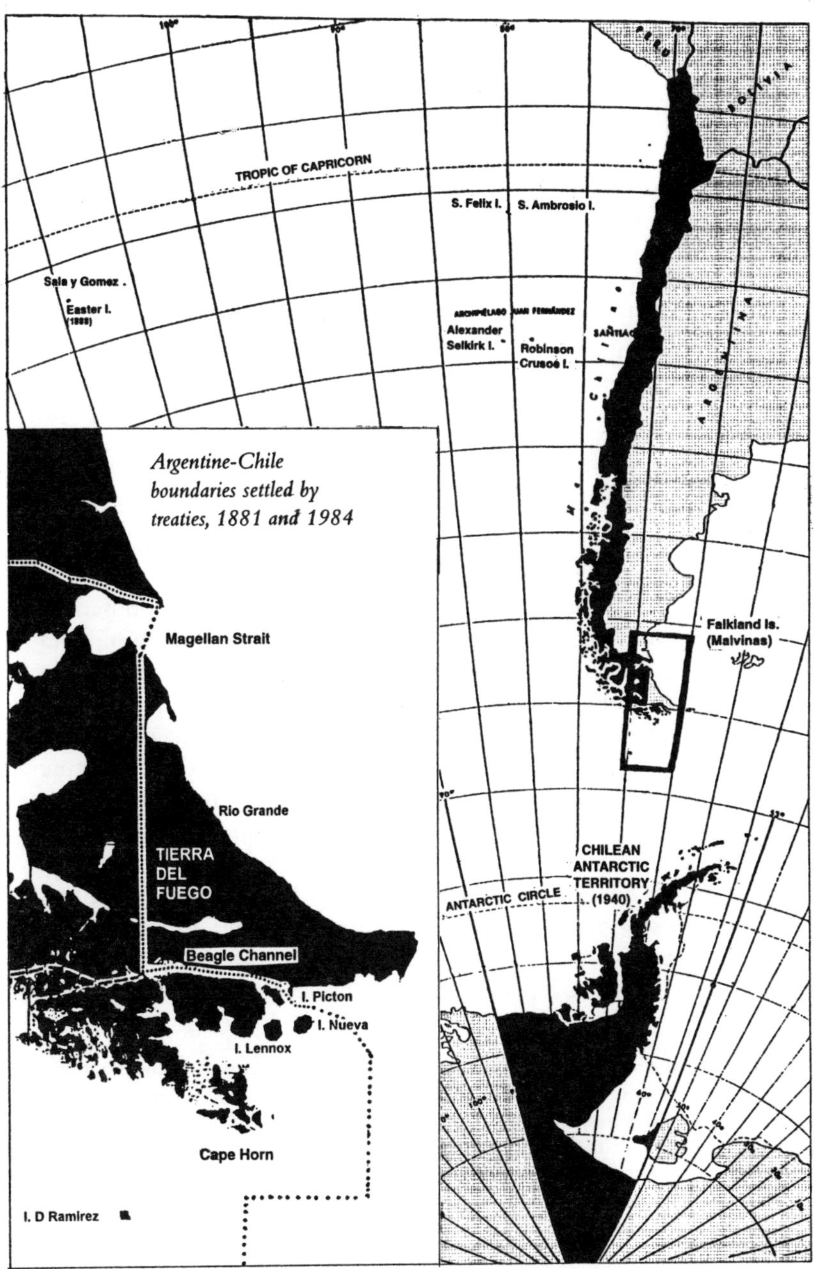

Southern Chile and Antarctica.

Arica and other parts of the territory lost to Chile in 1880. To counter this the Chileans looked to the military regime in Brazil for support. Informal contacts were established even before the coup but it was fortunate for Chile that the Peruvian threat weakened and eventually petered out when Velasco had a heart attack and was superseded in Lima. However, the Chileans were threatened even more seriously in the far south where Argentina maintained its old claim to three small islands at the eastern end of the Beagle Channel, south of the Magellan Strait and Tierra del Fuego. In this case Chile had no obvious source of international support. With the military in unchallenged control in both Buenos Aires and Santiago, there was an obvious risk of armed clashes, particularly at sea. There was also a greater military capacity to pursue them – at least on the Argentine side.[4]

The Beagle Channel dispute

The origins of the dispute about the islands of Picton, Lennox and Nueva in the Beagle Channel went back as far as 1881, when a Treaty between Argentina and Chile was supposed to have settled all their disputes over territory but left some boundaries to be demarcated by later agreement, including that in the extreme south of the continent. This boundary, not considered particularly important at the time, was simply defined as the 'Beagle Channel east of 68°34" (the north/south meridian dividing the Argentine and Chilean sectors of Tierra del Fuego). The Treaty stated that all islands south of the Beagle, as far as and including Cape Horn, belonged to Chile, while the Isla de los Estados and others east of Tierra del Fuego and Patagonia belonged to Argentina. Argentina nevertheless argued that Picton, Lennox and Nueva, though clearly shown on most maps to be to the south of the Beagle Channel (and thus Chilean according to the Treaty), were in fact in the

[4] One of the inevitable results of the military taking power in the Southern Cone was, of course, an increase in expenditure on armaments. Chile's spending on defence rose from $177 million in 1972 to $984 million in 1980, and the total personnel of the armed forces almost doubled in the same period from a total of 47,000 to 92,000. Self-interest apart, there was strategic justification for some of this increase based on the theoretical threat in the north and the very real one posed by Argentina along the entire length of their 2,500 mile common frontier.

Atlantic Ocean and therefore Argentinian. From 1904 till 1967 this issue rumbled on but in the latter year Chile decided to submit it to arbitration by Britain in accordance with an agreement reached in 1902. Argentina agreed to arbitration, and in 1977 the international tribunal of jurists established by the British Crown for the purpose came down unanimously in favour of Chile's claim. The Argentine government's reaction, announced in January 1978, was to declare the arbitration 'null and void', implying that the question would now be settled by force if necessary – regardless of international law.

Whatever others thought, Argentina and Chile both considered that the ownership of these three uninhabited islands would give Chile the ability to assert control over navigation through the Beagle Channel, the only inland passage between the Atlantic and Pacific Oceans apart from the Magellan Straits. As long as the Panama Canal remained open to all shipping, this might not be very important, but the future of the Canal was uncertain and to strategists and students of geo-politics in Argentina and Chile it was much more than an academic issue. With these thoughts in mind, Argentina had developed a strategic theory, the so-called 'bi-oceanic principle', to support its claim. This theory asserts that Chile is a Pacific power and should therefore have maritime jurisdiction and interests only in the waters west of Cape Horn; while Argentina is an Atlantic power with jurisdiction east of Cape Horn.

The 'bi-oceanic principle' also had a bearing on another long-standing dispute between the two countries about the division of territorial waters at the eastern mouth of the Magellan Straits. But its most far-reaching implications (not considered by the arbitration tribunal) related to the territorial waters and the sea and sea-bed south of Tierra del Fuego and stretching south towards the Antarctic. The ownership of the Beagle Channel islands would have quite a significant effect (under normal international rules) on the size of the Argentine and Chilean economic zones in those waters, and some day these zones could, with advances in technology, provide valuable oil and mineral assets.

After the failure of the British-sponsored arbitration award, Chile sought to keep up pressure for a peaceful solution by engaging Argentina in further bilateral talks. The two Presidents met at Mendoza in April 1978, and further meetings followed up to

October between the countries' Foreign Ministers and experts. When there seemed no more hope of progress by that route the Chileans turned their minds to the alternative idea of mediation, and began to try to involve the Pope as the mediator (this was complicated by the death of both Paul VI and John Paul I in quick succession in that year). As late as 12 December, Hernán Cubillos, the Chilean Foreign Minister, thought he had reached agreement with his Argentine opposite number (Washington Pastór) whereby the two countries would accept the mediation of the newly-elected Pope John Paul II. At the last moment, however, the Argentine Foreign Minister, despite having the support of the President, General Videla, was prevented from signing this agreement because the Argentine armed forces council (which had the final word) refused to agree. It seemed that an armed clash in the south, and perhaps at other points along the common frontier, was now all but inevitable. On 20 December the Chileans again proposed mediation by the Vatican but Argentina rejected it the next day in terms which seemed final.

By this time Argentine and Chilean troops and armour were deployed and on full alert at many points along the frontier, and an Argentine naval force was moving towards the islands. The Chileans moved to intercept the naval threat in the South Atlantic and put contingents of marines on the Beagle islands themselves. Argentine helicopters were said to be about to land their own troops on the islands, but providentially the operation was delayed by bad weather.

It was the new Pope who, with an eleventh-hour intervention, saved the two countries from what would certainly have been a disastrous war. John Paul II, responding to repeated urging by both the Argentine and Chilean bishops, informed President Videla at noon on 22 December that he was ready to offer mediation to prevent war between two Catholic countries. Videla accepted, although a formal declaration of war was reported to be on his desk at the time. The mediator chosen by the Pope was Cardinal Antonio Samoré, who knew Latin America better than anyone else in the Vatican and, despite his seventy-two years, plunged immediately into his task with determination and energy. After two weeks of intense shuttle diplomacy by Samoré the immediate risk of military confrontation was averted by agreements signed at Montevideo on 8 January 1979.

Cardinal Samoré engaged in a prolonged series of discussions with both sides for the next two years and finally produced a proposed settlement, slightly more favourable to Argentina than any which had previously been on the table. Even that, however, was rejected by the Argentine Junta and it was not till 1984 that an agreement was reached confirming Chile's ownership of the Beagle Channel islands and resolving the related question of maritime rights and jurisdiction to the south. The 1984 Treaty of Peace and Friendship between the two countries ended a saga of intermittent hostility, often bitter and more than once threatening to explode into war, which had continued for more than a century. The treaty has already lasted longer than the more sceptical observers expected and has certainly helped to produce a new mood of constructive co-operation between Argentina and Chile. It is one of the many political achievements attributable to the personal influence of Pope John Paul II.

Chile, Britain and the Falklands War

For the handful of military planners and diplomats concerned with such remote areas, the linkage between the Beagle Channel and the Falklands disputes is obvious. Until 1982 few other people even knew exactly where these places were, but their problems briefly engaged the attention of much of the world for three months in that year. With hindsight, it is hard not to conclude that the spark which finally lit the fuse leading to the Falklands war was the determination of the high command of the Argentine armed forces to fight a 'clean' patriotic war somewhere abroad –to counter criticism about the 'dirty war' they had waged at home. Once the crisis between Chile and Argentina had passed in 1979, the attention of the Junta in Buenos Aires, and in particular of the Commander-in-Chief of the Argentine Navy, Admiral Anaya, turned to the Falklands. This was the third of the three international problems they had set themselves to solve. Persuaded that they were making progress over the Beagle Channel through the Papal mediation and that their relationship with Brazil was tolerable, they began to believe that they might·be able to seize control of the Falkland Islands through a bloodless *coup de main* without fighting a real war.

This idea evidently appealed greatly to Argentine military planners;

and the British government, by a series of unconnected decisions and actions, contrived – quite unintentionally – to encourage it. Negotiations had been dragging on for years with no success in finding a compromise between British and Argentine claims to the Falklands. One of the few remaining hopes which remained in play in 1980 was the idea of a lease-back arrangement to defuse the sovereignty issue, put forward by Nicholas Ridley, then a Minister of State in the British Conservative government. Under this scheme sovereignty would be ceded in theory to Argentina but the islands would be leased back to Britain for a fixed period. Ridley's proposal was debated in the House of Commons at the end of 1980 but almost unanimously and contemptuously rejected, which effectively snuffed out the last hope of a solution which would have had any appeal for Argentina.

In 1981, quite independently of the outstanding problem in the Falklands, the Conservatives carried out a major defence review largely based on the assumption that Britain no longer needed (nor could afford) to maintain a global defence capacity. They assumed that Britain would never again have to fight a distant war outside the NATO area or deal with a post-colonial crisis in any other part of the world. The government therefore decided to sell one of the Royal Navy's three remaining aircraft-carriers, *Invincible*, and pay off the ageing ice patrol vessel *Endurance*, which for years had been the only regular British naval presence in the South Atlantic. Misguidedly the Argentines took these to be calculated decisions by the British not to attempt to defend the Falklands. In fact Margaret Thatcher and her government were moved by no more than a determination to save money and were ready to seize on any convenient method of doing so. When they thought about them at all, most British people saw the remote Falkland Islands and the 1,800 islanders as no more than a relic of empire.

In the last week of March 1982, the Argentine Junta finally decided to invade the Falklands, their invasion fleet sailed and on 2 April a force occupied Port Stanley, overwhelming the token garrison of Royal Marines. The next day the United Nations Security Council passed a British-sponsored resolution calling on Argentina to withdraw unconditionally. Simultaneously the British government announced its decision to send a Task Force as soon as possible to retake the islands. In Britain people realised slowly that there would be a real war in the islands if Argentina could not be persuaded to withdraw her occupying forces. To the Argentine Junta and to many other governments, including the United States and most of Britain's closest allies, it seemed hardly possible that any country in the latter part of the twentieth century should undertake such a campaign at a range of 8,000 miles and with almost every factor weighing against success.

The present writer was preparing at that precise moment to go to Chile to take over as British Ambassador and on the morning of 2 April was due to make a courtesy call on the Chilean Ambassador in London. By sheer coincidence this was the day, and almost the hour, of the Argentine landing in Port Stanley. What would normally have been a formal call devoted to polite platitudes and little more, turned into a tense and lengthy conversation. The Chilean was Miguel Schweitzer, an Anglophile lawyer who had been picked by President Pinochet to go to London in 1980 when full diplomatic relations were resumed. Neither of us wasted much time on diplomatic niceties but plunged straight into speculation about the crisis. All I knew was the little I had gleaned the previous day from a few rushed words with frantic officials in the Foreign and Commonwealth Office. However, I had no idea exactly what the Argentines were attempting or whether any deterrent naval movements had been made by the British in the weeks when the likelihood of some form of Argentine military action was being openly discussed throughout the Southern Cone.[5]

Miguel Schweitzer knew little more than I did (perhaps less) but had heard that the press in Buenos Aires was already reporting the invasion as a *fait accompli*. He asked whether the British would surrender or resist a direct Argentine landing. I said that one could not expect a handful of marines, however determined, to stand out for long against a serious invading force, but that I felt sure that the British government would not quietly accept an Argentine take-over, abandon the islanders or back away from a

5 The first threat of confrontation on the ground occurred on 18/19 March when a party of some fifty Argentine workers landed without permission not in the Falklands themselves but in South Georgia, to salvage scrap metal from old whaling stations there. This was in pursuit of a commercial contract, but the vessel which brought them was an Argentine naval transport and a group of Argentine marines was among the party. The purpose was evidently to establish an Argentine presence surreptitiously in a dependency of the Falkland Islands.

confrontation. That was my own instinctive reaction recorded at the time. I had no other authority for saying so but was reassured by the debate in the House of Commons the following day when speaker after speaker said much the same. Few of us realised at the time how hard it would be to make that promise good. Schweitzer maintained that the Chilean reaction to the threat from the Argentines in 1978 had been the same – it was, he said, crucial to stand up to them and be prepared to fight. To my relief he did not refer to the possibility of co-operation between Britain and Chile in the face of a common threat – a thought which must have been in both our minds but which we left unsaid. I was also well aware that there might be a price tag on any facilities or other help which we sought from Chile.

My predecessor as Ambassador in Santiago, John Heath, had been *en poste*, like Miguel Schweitzer, since 1980 and both had worked hard to rebuild a working relationship. While the Pinochet regime continued in power it was not possible for the old friendship to be renewed, but a strictly circumscribed range of contacts existed. They did *not* include military or naval co-operation in Santiago, and there was no defence attaché on Heath's small staff until shortly before April 1982. Now, under the pressure of extreme necessity, political reservations could no longer be allowed to prevent the British Task Force from obtaining any help the Chileans were willing to provide.

The first and vital requirement was intelligence. The British had practically none. The Secret Intelligence Service (SIS), under sustained financial pressure imposed by both Labour and Conservative governments for years past, had closed all its stations on the continent except for a single officer (Mark Heathcote) operating alone in Buenos Aires, who had now been forced to leave. The military and naval attachés there had also left, and in any case, neither had the means to monitor Argentine preparations for the invasion; knowledge of the Argentine order of battle, particularly in the air, was hopelessly out of date. Past British decisions to give almost no priority to the defence of the Falklands meant relying on bluff. When it was called, the Chiefs of Staff, the Foreign and Commonwealth Office and the Cabinet were groping in the dark.

There was no way of filling the gap except by seeking outside help wherever it could be found, and the only possible sources were the CIA and Chilean intelligence organisations. The CIA provided the SIS with an up-to-date assessment of the state of the Argentine armed forces and the British intelligence machine, under the central direction of the Joint Intelligence Committee (JIC), was able to elaborate this into a fairly accurate and detailed order of battle. How much detailed intelligence about Argentina's mobilisation for the Falklands invasion was available to the CIA, or was passed to the British as soon as it became known, is still a matter for speculation. The most urgent requirement was, of course, for tactical information about the deployment of the Argentine naval and air forces which the Task Force would face as soon as it reached the South Atlantic. Some was available from satellite surveillance provided by the US National Security Agency which had covert intercept bases in both Chile and Argentina. The British equivalent, GCHQ, no longer had any surveillance capacity targeted on South America and the only other help available through normal intelligence liaison contacts came from their counterparts in New Zealand, who were able to offer some assistance. The British therefore had to look to Chile, the country which had most reason to keep Argentina and its armed forces under close scrutiny.

After the Falklands campaign many of the war correspondents and 'investigative' journalists who reported on it for the insatiable appetites of the world's media rushed into print with their books on the war. Some were a calculated mixture of fact and speculation, some were more scrupulous, but in what they wrote about the secret struggle for intelligence all were inevitably trying to make bricks without much straw. After fifteen years the flood of books about the Falklands war has subsided and, in so far as it is possible to put together a true picture without access to official records, there is a better chance of making well-informed guesses which are likely to be somewhere near the truth. Even now, however, hard facts are few.

One well-known exponent of what might be called the 'intelligence documentary' is the novelist and military historian who writes under the name of Nigel West – a *nom de plume* for the former Conservative Member of Parliament, Rupert Allason. His book *The Secret War for the Falklands* (Little, Brown, 1997) is based on a mass of material from other published sources and as much official information as is likely to be revealed until the official records (or at least some of them) are opened after thirty years. This book also deals more fully and carefully than any earlier account with the question of Chilean assistance to Britain in 1982. Much of Nigel West's information is inevitably in the nature of intelligent deduction by an experienced investigator rather than verifiable fact, but it is more accurate and written with more detachment than the earlier account by Duncan Campbell published by the *New Statesman* in January 1985 under the heading 'The Chile Connection'.

The invasion of the Falklands was naturally seen by the Chileans as just another engagement in the long-running campaign being conducted by Argentina to achieve a dominant position in the South Atlantic and south of Cape Horn. Any possible doubts about this were removed by General Galtieri in a broadcast immediately after the landing at Port Stanley when he spoke of it as 'the first step in recovering Argentina's territory'. The Chileans were convinced that if Britain lost the Falklands, they themselves would once again come under attack. It was thus clearly in their national interest to do what they could to help Britain regain the islands. The Chilean government was in a political dilemma here because in the past it had consistently expressed support for the Argentine claim to sovereignty at the United Nations, but it was also deeply concerned that the Falklands, which provided the best natural harbour south of Bahia Blanca, should not fall into Argentina's hands.

The Chileans had built up an elaborate system of communications and electronic surveillance along the frontier with Argentina and from offshore facilities.[6] Their capacity to monitor Argentine air activity and communications was potentially critical because of the frightening vulnerability of the Task Force to attack from the air – and, most dangerous of all, by the air-launched version (AM-39) of the French Exocet missile. On the morning of 4 May 1982 one of these missiles, launched by an Argentine Navy Super

[6] According to Nigel West's account, the Royal Air Force lent the Chilean Air Force both Canberra and Hercules aircraft equipped for these purposes. He also records that these three Canberra PR9s together with a total of nine Hawker Hunters (an aircraft already in service in Chile) and thirty spare engines were officially 'sold' to Chile after the war; and speculates that this may have been a gesture of thanks by the British.

Etendard flying from the Rio Grande air base on the coast of Tierra del Fuego, hit and sunk the British destroyer, the *Sheffield.*

The strange case of the Sea King

By that time the threat from surface ships of the Argentine Navy had been checked by the sinking of its cruiser, the *General Belgrano.* The Argentine fleet stayed in port thereafter and the risk of attack by sea-borne Exocets was less serious. But the threat from the remaining air-borne Exocets was critical, since they alone could enable Argentina to win the battle for the Falklands in an hour or so. If the Argentines were able to hit, incapacitate or even sink either of the British aircraft-carriers, the prospect of a successful attempt to reoccupy the Falklands would become almost hopeless since there would be virtually no air cover for the landing or later operations. According to the French government, Argentina had only received five (of a total order of fifteen) of the AM-39 Exocets and ten of the Super Etendards which were to be used to deliver them. However, no-one could be certain, that Argentina had not acquired some from other sources since Aerospatiale had already sold a large number to other countries (including Saddam Hussein in Iraq). It was this acute concern about the Exocets at Rio Grande which led to the episode of the Sea King helicopter of the Royal Navy's 846 Squadron, which landed in Chile near Punta Arenas on the night of 17/18 May – an event which hit the headlines around the world and caused embarrassment to both governments.

Predictably, and with due solemnity, the Foreign Minister in Santiago made a formal protest to the British Ambassador about this invasion of Chilean air space and insisted that the three-man crew should be presented at a press conference there to show that Chile had no secrets to hide. The pilot, Lieutenant Hutchings, told the world's media by way of explanation: 'We were on sea patrol when we experienced engine failure due to adverse weather. It was not possible to return to our ship. We therefore took refuge in the nearest neutral country.' This was true as far as it went, but did not explain what the Sea King was doing at the time or why it should have had to land out of fuel in a remote spot on the shore of the Magellan Strait or why its crew should have set fire to it although they were in a friendly country.

According to Nigel West's book, the Sea King's mission had been to infiltrate a Special Air Service (SAS) team into the area of the Rio Grande airfield either to reconnoitre for an attack on the remaining Exocets and the Super Etendards or, if possible, to destroy them at once. The book describes vividly and with circumstantial detail (but, for understandable reasons, without much supporting evidence) how it became necessary for the reconnaissance mission to be aborted because it had been detected by radar before reaching Rio Grande; how the SAS team of nine led by 'Captain Andrew M.' was dropped off somewhere in Chilean Tierra del Fuego by the Sea King before it flew on towards Punta Arenas; and how the team eventually made contact, apparently by pure luck, with an SAS colleague who had come to retrieve them and lead them to discreet hides until they could fly back to Britain.

Had this part of the story become known in May 1982, the Chileans would have suffered even greater political embarrassment than they did. In fact, of course, everyone involved in Santiago, London and Buenos Aires knew very well from the outbreak of hostilities that it was perfectly feasible for a SAS operation to be mounted against airfields on the mainland, and the Argentine commanders naturally made their defensive dispositions on the assumption that they might be attacked.[7] One issue raised by this operation which could have had more far-reaching ramifications was the wisdom (indeed the legality) of extending offensive operations to mainland Argentina if the SAS had been successful in destroying the Exocet missiles and Super Etendards on mainland Argentina.

If this version of the Sea King helicopter story is basically correct, it conflicts with the one widely believed at the time, namely that it was involved in some kind of Anglo-Chilean operation against Argentina. Whatever information may have been supplied which helped Britain to evict Argentine forces from the Falklands,

[7] According to Nigel West's account, the Commander of the unit of the 1st Marine Brigade deployed to defend the naval airfield at Rio Grande, Manuel Pita, had actually been to England years before to attend a training course on clandestine operations run by the SAS, which included Argentine and other officers from foreign countries. The counter-measures he organised at Rio Grande succeeded in frustrating his former teachers, and indeed he may have learned them in England.

there is no evidence whatever that Chile took part in the campaign in any direct way or allowed the British to use its airfields or other defence facilities, or any part of its territory, to mount warlike operations against Argentina. Equally there is no sense in which the Chilean Navy can be said to have been deployed purely to help the British Task Force; it has a long and very close relationship with the Royal Navy but it is inconceivable that it would subordinate Chile's interests to those of any other country. If the deployment or movements of Chilean naval units (e.g. submarines), or indeed of Chilean land forces, during April, May and June 1982 was helpful to the British, this was an incidental result and not their principal purpose.

Collusion?

It was also alleged against the British government, particularly by critics of Margaret Thatcher, that after the Falklands war it tried to temper the weight of international disapproval of the Pinochet regime in gratitude for help given by Chile at a time of great difficulty. Having arrived in Santiago to take up the post of British Ambassador at the end of the Falklands campaign, the present writer knows very well how relieved and pleased most Chileans were that Argentina's attack on the Falklands had been punished. They hoped that their powerful and unpredictable neighbours would have learned the lesson that aggression does not pay and that this would restrain them in the future. But Chilean satisfaction at the outcome did not, as I soon discovered, mean that they were ready to support Britain in circumstances where there was no perceptible advantage to Chile herself.

One of the first problems which the British forces faced after the Argentine surrender was how to look after, shelter and feed tens of thousands of Argentine prisoners. It was vital for everyone, not least the prisoners themselves, to repatriate them to Argentina as quickly as possible. They could not be sent back directly, and the Argentines had at first also refused to accept them through Uruguay. Would Chile be willing to accept them at Punta Arenas, the nearest mainland port capable of receiving them? Our request was flatly refused, apparently because the Chileans did not want to be perceived as the guardians of a defeated Argentine Army, and still less as helping the British. We realised that Chile would not be providing us with any practical help in the clearing-up process after the war. As soon as the war ended, we were 'back to square one'.

Chile also quickly reverted to its traditional diplomatic position on the disputed question of sovereignty over the Falklands/Malvinas ('Malvinas' now came back into general use). Chile had previously accepted Argentina's claim to the islands on the ground that it was the legitimate successor to Spain in that part of the former colonial empire (including the islands), but the government in Santiago had opposed the use of force by Argentina in invading them in April 1982 (and voted with Europe, the United States and most of the Commonwealth rather than with the rest of Latin America at the United Nations). After the crisis was over, Santiago saw no reason to stay out of line with the rest of the Latin American group and reverted to its former 'politically correct' position on the Falklands issue[8] seeking, so far as possible, to soften Argentine anger and accusations of betrayal levelled against its policy and actions during the conflict.

The indirect contribution which Chile made in influencing the outcome of the conflict can best be explained by the old saying: 'My enemy's enemy is my friend'. Crude as political analysis but true enough of the calculated view taken by the Chilean armed forces, and the instinctive reactions of Chileans in the street. People spotted as being British in Chile in 1982 were liable to find themselves unusually popular. It was a happy, if not necessarily long-lasting, revival of an old friendship and Chile re-emerged into Britain's consciousness as something more than a far distant country producing a lot of copper, good fruit and wine but governed by a military dictator at the head of a jack-booted army with a bad reputation. But, in Britain as in Santiago, there were few political leaders prepared to acknowledge publicly the bond of mutual interest which had recently been so clear. Almost the only public statement on the matter after the middle of 1982

[8] A year or so after the conflict, I had the opportunity, during an informal talk, to ask President Pinochet for his personal opinion on the matter. He said that the islanders should certainly have the right of self-determination, that is to say they should decide whether to accept British or Argentine sovereignty–or indeed be independent. Within hours the Foreign Minister telephoned to inform me that I should not understand this to mean that sovereignty did not belong to Argentina in international law.

was a passing remark by the then Foreign Secretary, Francis Pym that it should not be forgotten that 'Chile had been helpful to us during the war'. When the British Minister for Trade, Peter Rees, visited Santiago and ventured to say that the successful revival of the Chilean economy made Chile, led by Pinochet, an example of good economic management and a source of stability in the Southern Cone, he was vehemently attacked in Parliament for 'singing the praises of a hated dictator'.[9]

According to Chile's fiercest critics, in Parliament and outside, the Thatcher government (as a *quid pro quo*) was not opposing the Pinochet regime strongly enough. In particular they insisted that we were wrong when we occasionally refused to join the majority in the UN in outright and unqualified condemnation of its human rights record. It is true that in 1982 and 1983 British spokesmen argued that Chile's human rights performance, though still poor, had improved to the point that the UN was no longer justified in singling it out and sending a Special Rapporteur to investigate and report on its record, while leaving other countries with worse records to go their own way unchecked. By 1984, however, we judged that the situation had deteriorated again and therefore voted for the re-appointment of the Rapporteur, joining strongly with the rest of the European Community and the United States to try to force Pinochet into a change of heart. Conspiracy theorists such as Duncan Campbell decided that this meant that 'the Foreign Office's remit to present Pinochet's case to the world had, evidently, expired'.

In fact there never was any understanding, tacit or explicit, between Britain and the Pinochet government. All votes in international organisations are decided after a careful assessment of each issue and taking all the relevant circumstances into account. It is naive to suppose that a general disposition in favour of this country or that will not have some weight in the final decision, but the overall balance will be struck only after looking at the specific issue objectively. The truth is that the human rights picture in Chile had improved in 1982 and 1983, and was by then much

[9] When I expressed somewhat similar opinions to Ministers in the Foreign and Commonwealth Office on various occasions, I met the same sort of reaction. At one meeting the Minister replied that I was no better than the British visitors to Italy in the 1930s who praised Mussolini because he had made Italian trains run on time.

better than in the 1970s; but it did deteriorate again in 1984. There were therefore reasonable grounds for the British to vote differently from year to year. Those who were committed always and without reserve to oppose Pinochet were the ones who failed to look at the facts.

The approach to Antarctica

As already recorded, the Treaty of Peace and Friendship of 1984 between Argentina and Chile not only embodied a compromise solution to the Beagle question and the division of zones of economic interest in the seas south of Cape Horn (the Drake Passage and the so-called '*Mar Chileno*') but also established mechanisms for the settlement of other disputes arising in future and for developing cross-border economic co-operation to the benefit of both countries. The success of the mediation by Cardinal Samoré owed much to his skill and that of both the Chilean and Argentine negotiators who travelled again and again to Rome for five years while the process edged towards its conclusion. Never stated but alive in every mind throughout was the fact that the Argentine military Junta, which had set out to impose its territorial demands by force first on Chile and then on a distant and supposedly indifferent Britain, had failed on both occasions. The result had been its disgrace and removal from power and the trial and imprisonment of the military leaders who had served their country so badly. The civilian governments which succeeded them in Buenos Aires, first under Raúl Alfonsín and then under Carlos Menem, had no wish to repeat these disastrous errors. They would never renounce the Argentine claim to the Falklands, but were ready to compromise with Chile and saw benefit in doing so.

The immediate result of the 1984 Treaty was the relaxation of tension in the Beagle Channel and the waters east and south of the disputed islands where naval and air patrols had so often been involved in confrontations. With the dispute settled on paper, both sides could afford to stand further back in the sensitive area. The little ports of Ushuaia on the Argentine side of the Channel and Puerto Williams on the Chilean side began to attract tourists instead of warships and to seem more like commercial centres than naval bases with civilians attached. Another important result of the improved atmosphere was to encourage both countries to strengthen their support for the Antarctic Treaty.

This Treaty, concluded in 1959 as a result of the International Geophysical Year, preserves the Antarctic continent indefinitely for peaceful scientific purposes, prohibiting the introduction of any arms or military installations and, most important of all, freezing all existing territorial claims. As the Treaty's consultative machinery developed, the signatories were able to make subsidiary agreements protecting Antarctica (at least to some degree) from creeping environmental damage due to the impact of a growing number of national scientific research stations which have been established there. Up to the time of writing the continent has also been saved by international agreement from the risk of the much more serious damage which would result from any attempt to explore for oil, minerals and other natural resources. The attempt to preserve Antarctica from environmental disaster has succeeded hitherto, but it will need to continue and to become yet more effective as pressures to exploit the last untouched continent inevitably grow. It is a common interest of the entire world to resist this threat, and a co-operative and enlightened commitment by Chile and Argentina, two of the original signatories both with long-standing territorial claims themselves, should make a major contribution to keeping the Treaty in force and effective.

The Argentine–Chilean Treaty of Peace and Friendship, though not specifically intended to cover Antarctica, may prove to have a critical impact there also, because it provides two countries with overlapping claims with the best of motives for resisting any temptation to revive them. We must fervently hope that at the end of the twentieth century national claims to parts of the territory of an uninhabited continent (where human life can only be supported in the same way as in a space station) could again become active political issues. If the Antarctic Treaty were to lapse or be allowed to fail for any reason, Argentina, Chile and Britain would all be faced with an old-fashioned problem. All three have formally established claims to segments of Antarctica which end at the South Pole. (All three segments, however, overlap with others and there is one segment which is claimed by all three.) The resolution of that conflict would make the Beagle Channel and Falklands disputes seem simple. However, if the lesson of history is learnt and remembered in all three countries, good care will be taken that Antarctica remains internationalised and that these anachronistic claims never emerge from the academic shadows. The Southern Cone of South America has already suffered enough from geo-political thinking and thinkers.

10

THE LONG WAY BACK

> 'A state without the means of some change is without the means of its conservation.[...] In all forms of Government, the People is the true legislator.'
>
> – Edmund Burke, *Reflections on the Revolution in France*

Chile was not the only Latin American country to be hit by an overwhelming financial and economic crisis in 1982/3. It began with another sharp increase in the price of oil – the 'second oil shock' of 1979. Automatically the world slid into recession and demand for the exports on which the smaller economies depended was sharply reduced. Acute balance of payments problems quickly followed. The storm broke first and most dramatically in Mexico in August when the government suspended all payments on foreign debt, and from there the shocks spread throughout the continent.

In Chile's case the peso was seriously overvalued and the problem was badly exacerbated by the level of foreign borrowing by the private sector, often for speculative and non-productive purposes. De Castro and his team were directly to blame for the exchange rate and indirectly responsible for other aspects of the problem since it was their lifting of restrictions on foreign borrowing and general deregulation of the banking system that allowed the explosion of debt. Furthermore the balance of payments pressure which made some such borrowing necessary was the direct result of the growth of imports which their policies had stimulated. They could claim that the fall in commodity prices (particularly of copper) and rises of both oil prices and interest rates were beyond their control and undoubtedly made the crisis worse, but the root cause lay in their own policies.

With the fall of Sergio de Castro, the Chicago Boys were out of favour. Pinochet and his other advisers had to spread the blame for the crisis if it was not to be left on their shoulders alone.

The groups which had benefited most from the boom, and indeed had been the enthusiastic collaborators of the Chicago Boys, were naturally held responsible for the crash. As the crisis deepened, Pinochet followed the well-tried policy of turning a poacher into a gamekeeper by selecting one of the chief figures in the biggest of all the economic conglomerates, Rolf Lüders of the Vial group, to take charge of both the Finance and the Economic Ministries. Lüders found, as he already suspected, that the entire banking system was in danger of collapse. Almost half the external loans flowing into the system had been received by these economic groups and been used largely to finance on-lending to enterprises which they themselves controlled; domestic interest rates had reached 35 per cent per annum or more, and bankruptcies threatened to engulf a large part of the country's productive industry and agriculture.

In January 1983, Lüders decided that the only way to avert the disaster was to take over or dissolve ten of the major banks and financial institutions, including the principal cornerstones of the Vial and Cruzat-Larrain groups. According to a mid-1983 study by Alejandro Foxley (later to be Finance Minister under President Patricio Aylwin):

> The macro-economic policy applied between 1973 and 1982 ended in a resounding failure. The economy did not grow, the rate of investment dropped sharply, the external sector reached an acute crisis, unemployment more than tripled past levels, real salaries and pensions decreased and government spending for social programmes declined.[1]

This sweeping broadside hits a number of its targets but ignores some of the better features, and would of course be disputed by defenders of monetarism. However, it is undeniable that 1982 saw the worst economic collapse in Chile since the Depression of the 1930s. The state was once again forced to take over about 80 per cent of the formerly privatised financial system and a substantial number of industries owned by the major economic groups. The well-justified joke was that this was 'the Chicago

[1] Article republished in J. Samuel Valenzuela and Arturo Valenzuela (eds), *Military Rule in Chile: Dictatorships and Oppositions*, (Baltimore: Johns Hopkins University Press, 1986).

road to socialism'. It was a paradox which would have been comic had it not brought such tragic consequences.

By the end of 1982 GDP had fallen by 14.1 per cent, the peso by 40 per cent and industrial production by 21 per cent. The balance of payments was negative by $1.2 billion, having been positive by the same amount in 1980. These were the sort of macro-economic indicators which mattered to the monetarists. As for those which more directly affected the ordinary citizen, 810 companies went bankrupt, and GDP per capita was lower in 1982 than in 1970. Unemployment rose to nearly 20 per cent (more than 26 per cent if the minimum employment schemes launched by the government are ignored) and these official figures certainly underestimate both total unemployment and its (much higher) levels in the most depressed areas.

The people protest

As the crash hit standards of living, a wave of anger ignited an outburst of street protest not only by the principal victims but also by many middle class people who were not so badly affected but still reacted to the problems of the poorest. In a way which had almost been forgotten after nearly ten years of military rule, Chileans took to the streets to reject economic policies which had imposed unfairness and hardship on them all for the sake of an ideology developed by academic economists living in another world. Another result of the economic crisis was that the associations representing industrialists, mining companies, farmers and many other sectors which had been ignored or brushed aside by the Chicago Boys began to regain influence. The organisation which united the whole range of industry and commerce in Chile, the *Confederación de la Producción y del Comercio* (CPC), produced its own blueprint for economic recovery, which included several important departures from Chicago orthodoxy and in particular some reflation and deficit financing and export incentives.

This was the moment of greatest crisis for General Pinochet. In European countries a fall of even 1 per cent per annum in GDP is considered a disaster, but in Chile it had fallen by more than 14 per cent. Over the next five years the President proved himself once more to be a tough autocrat but also – and this was less obvious from his record before 1982 – a resourceful political operator. Alternating between menace and warmth, he might act either as the *patrón* of the estate, the authoritarian boss, or as a politician, sensing and manipulating the instinctive reactions of the people. Pinochet often expressed his admiration for Spain's longest-lasting dictator, General Franco, and just as Franco became extraordinarily skilful in playing off his various supporters (the Church, the Army and the Falange) against each other, so Pinochet used those tactics with similar skill, alternately bringing into play the Chicago Boys, traditional business interests, the Army, the Junta and a battery of civilian advisors – discarding or sidelining each when they had served their purpose.[2]

The first popular protest against the government erupted on 11 May 1983. Similar events followed every month, but although they continued for almost three years, the nature of their support and even their purpose changed in 1984 and 1985. The greatest effect was probably felt on the very first of these days of protest. This massive public demonstration by a population which seemed to have been cowed by ten years of repression was a revelation of the intense frustration felt by the majority of Chileans at the failures of the military regime. Although seen by some observers abroad as simply an outburst against Pinochet and in favour of a return to the democratic ways of the past, its roots were much more complex and not primarily political. For most of those who boycotted factories, offices and schools and protested noisily with car horns in the street or by banging pots and pans at home, it was primarily a demonstration against the condition of the country, the bankruptcy engulfing so many small people and the grinding poverty of life in the *poblaciones*.

Initially the copper workers' trade union, the *Confederación de Trabajadores del Cobre* (CTC), sought to make the protest a general strike, but the shrewder political figures involved, particularly the President of the Christian Democrats, Gabriel Valdés, persuaded the CTC that the time was not yet ripe. The immediate effect of the protest movement was to provide a new opening for the

[2] While serving in Spain in the 1960s, the present writer saw Franco's skill in manipulating the political controls of his regime. The two men were similar in many ways, not only in both being life-long professional soldiers who had taken to politics like ducks to water. However, Pinochet, after finally achieving dominant personal power, developed an earthy authority which was more impressive than Franco's somewhat cold and colourless personality.

old political parties and leaders. Having been banned for almost ten years, they now seized the opportunity to reorganise and reassert their presence as legitimate actors in the affairs of the nation. The Christian Democrats did this more effectively than any and took the leading role from the beginning. The Radical, Liberal and Social Democratic parties also began to stir, and individual members of the National Party returned to public prominence. But neither the political right nor the Socialist Party, many of whose leaders were still in exile, succeeded in re-establishing themselves as effective organisations for several years. The government, though still determined to suppress the Communist Party and others on the extreme left, turned a blind eye to the increasingly open activities of non-Marxist parties.

The Democratic Alliance

It was thus the Christian Democrats who took the lead in creating a coalition of democratic parties called the *Alianza Democrática*, to articulate and press political demands on the government. Their manifesto called for the immediate resignation of President Pinochet, the establishment of a provisional government, and the election of a constituent assembly to prepare a new constitution. Pinochet himself recognised by the middle of 1983 that the protest movement was not going to peter out, and reacted by appointing a right-wing politician and former leader of the National Party, Sergio Onofre Jarpa, as Minister of the Interior, with a brief to manage some kind of political *apertura* (opening) to counter the impact of the protests. If Jarpa was supposed to offer a velvet glove, Pinochet was also prepared to use the Army as well as the *Carabineros* to suppress street demonstrations. In August, on the very day that Jarpa took office, troops as well as the police were deployed in Santiago but the change in tactics did not prevent people taking to the streets, particular in the shanty towns. This use of the iron fist led to twenty-six deaths, mostly from indiscriminate gunfire.

Barely ten days later, the Army General who held the key appointment of *Intendente* (governor) of Santiago was assassinated by MIR terrorists as his car waited at a traffic light on a city street. The threat of a new surge of violent repression alternating with terrorist attacks gave greater urgency to Jarpa's efforts to create a political dialogue with the opposition. One of his first conversations was with the new Archbishop of Santiago, Juan Francisco Fresno, who had succeeded Cardinal Raül Silva Henríquez. Fresno was far more acceptable to the regime, and under his auspices a series of meetings took place between the Minister and the Democratic Alliance.

Jarpa's objective was to get agreement with the opposition on a quicker return to democracy than previously envisaged, starting with the election of a Congress but not including election of a new President before the end of Pinochet's term. However it was never clear that Pinochet was prepared to approve any concessions at all. Whatever hopes Jarpa himself nourished were quickly snuffed out by the politicians' sustained but unrealistic demand for Pinochet's resignation. By October the attempt at political dialogue had failed and Jarpa turned his attention to the economy in the hope of finding other ways to buy off opposition.

The Finance Minister who had succeeded Rolf Lüders was a respected conservative economist from Valparaiso, Carlos Cáceres, who had successfully renegotiated Chile's agreements with the International Monetary Fund in July 1983 but in the process had been obliged to give a state guarantee for all the external debts of the private sector. The harsh deal imposed by the IMF and the creditor banks left insufficient scope for the government to reflate the economy as it wished and to meet demands which were being pressed strongly by the CPC and all the private sector business associations. In March 1984, the President therefore decided that Cáceres had outlived his usefulness and demanded his resignation, along with that of the latest Minister of the Economy, and appointed replacements, Luis Escobar and Modesto Collados, who were much more acceptable to the private sector (and to Jarpa). Each of them had already put forward ideas of their own to reactivate the economy by direct means and thus to get it moving as quickly as possible in order to defuse opposition and enable the regime to continue in power.

With these appointments, the free market model came under real threat. For the next twelve months industry and agriculture were boosted by higher tariffs, export incentives and a mild reflation, but belief in the market economy had taken root so strongly in the business community that as soon as Escobar and Collados had given the economy a few months respite, fears of a return to the old statist economic system, which could easily be manipulated by politicians, surfaced once more. The Chicago Boys' ideas had not been entirely rejected by Pinochet and his inner circle, and their influence began to revive little by little. As the recession passed its low point in 1984/5, Pinochet once more jettisoned a Finance Minister who had served his purpose, turning this time to a young technocrat educated in the United States – but in New York rather than in Chicago and as an engineer and not an economist. Hernán Büchi looked like an eccentric young musician or artist but was in fact a shrewd economic manager who worked out an effective blend of neo-liberal economic principles combined with willingness to intervene in the markets for limited purposes. He was prepared, for example, to use tariff and price support measures to protect traditional agricultural producers from unfair foreign competition and the wilder fluctuations of markets. At the same time he reassured the IMF and the bankers that Chile would continue to meet its debt obligations, and was notably successful in managing monetary and fiscal problems. While accepting the free market model generally, he was above all a pragmatist and a problem solver.

Büchi's success in nursing the economy back to health and simultaneously managing the foreign debt problem to the satisfaction of the IMF was the more remarkable because it was achieved at a time when the internal political situation was bad and getting worse and international pressure on the regime was growing. By October 1984, in the wake of another day of protest which led to nine deaths and 250 arrests, Pinochet was saying defiantly that there would be no changes in the timetable for implementing the 1980 Constitution, nor any further dialogue with the politicians. He also threatened to reimpose the most extreme measure of internal security, the state of siege, if terrorist incidents such as assaults on the police and police stations continued. Finding his position thus undermined Jarpa tried to resign early in November but was persuaded to stay on for three months till February 1995. Meanwhile Pinochet turned again to the *mano dura* and on 7 December declared a state of siege. One hundred and forty people were sent into internal exile, six opposition publications were suppressed and three leading figures in the Democratic Alliance were arrested.

Washington changes course

On 10 December 1984, President Ronald Reagan, who till then had generally refrained from criticising the Chilean military regime, came out with a strong condemnation of Pinochet's action in imposing this state of siege: 'The lack of progress towards democracy in Chile and Paraguay is an affront to human consciences.' Pinochet's reaction to Reagan's remarks was even more outspoken. In a meeting with three US Congressmen visiting Santiago on 13 December, he roundly declared:

> 'Why should I believe anything the US says or stands for? The US won World War II but lost half of Europe. You lost half of Korea. You lost Vietnam. You lost Cuba. You lost Nicaragua and you will lose El Salvador if you are not careful. What kind of allies are you? You are not dependable.'[3]

The unhappy Chilean ministers who, despite their President's complaints, had to preserve some kind of working relationship with the US government, were driven to despair. Until Pinochet made brutally clear that he would change nothing, and declared a new state of siege into the bargain, this was one of very few governments which consistently voted in favour of official international loans to Chile. However, in January 1985 the United States abstained on a $430 million loan proposed by the Inter-American Development Bank. This shift in policy was confirmed in April when Secretary of State George Schulz announced the replacement of the US Ambassador in Santiago, James Theberge, a specialist on communism in Latin America who was also a strong proponent of the view that foreign economic pressure overtly applied would not move Pinochet. His successor was a more activist career diplomat, Harry Barnes, who felt that the United States should not hesitate to use pressure of all kinds to accelerate the end of the Pinochet regime.

The switch of policy in Washington was most evident in June 1985, when Chile, whose finances were now in the hands of

[3] Quoted in Carlos Portales' article 'Democracia y Relaciones Estados Unidos – Chile: Discurso y Realidad', *Cono Sur*, no. 4 (April-June 1985). Pinochet may have realised that the toughening of Washington's line on Chile was partly due to its need to avoid charges of having double standards when the United States was striving simultaneously to upset the Sandinista regime in Nicaragua.

Hernán Büchi, needed nearly $2 billion in new loans from private foreign banks to finance vital development plans, and the bankers insisted that these loans would only be forthcoming if guaranteed by the World Bank. The US Treasury discreetly indicated that it would only support this provided certain conditions were met. The most important of these was the ending of the state of siege, which was in due course lifted. The United States then gave its support to the required loans and guarantees.

In this case at least, with US leverage being applied through the international financing mechanism, Pinochet's hand was forced in a way which had not happened in Carter's time. However, the climb-down was only achieved because, following the debt crisis of 1982/3, it was the Chilean government itself and not the private sector which had to borrow in international markets to meet obligations it had taken over from the private sector. The June 1985 situation might not often recur, but whatever methods might be used it was clear that the US attitude to the Pinochet regime had once again been reversed. Except on the extreme right, represented by the rabid anti-communist Senator Jesse Helms, there was now broad agreement in the US Congress in favour of building up pressure for a much quicker return to democracy. The largely passive approach favoured by Ronald Reagan in his first term went little further than the sort of private exhortation advocated by exponents of 'quiet diplomacy' such as Theberge and General Vernon Walters, an old acquaintance of Pinochet and frequent visitor to Chile on Reagan's behalf. With Barnes as its spokesman in Chile, the United States now began to express its views more openly and on some occasions with stronger sanctions to back them.

The National Accord

Despite the failure of Jarpa's attempt to contrive a political *apertura* and Pinochet's renewed intransigence, the Chilean political parties were definitely still in business and Archbishop Fresno took a new initiative to support them by inviting three prominent individuals to act as moderators with the political parties. These were José Zabala, head of the Christian Employers Union; Sergio Molina, formerly Finance Minister under Eduardo Frei; and Fernando Leniz, businessman and Economy Minister after the 1973 coup. After several months in which the politicians edged closer to each other, two new parties of the Right, the *Union Nacional* and the *Partido Nacional* and one on the Left, *Izquierda Cristiana*, joined the group which had originally formed the *Alianza Democrática*. The only parties not included were the Independent Democratic Union (UDI), a pro-government, *gremialist* party recently formed by Pinochet's civilian collaborators such as Jaime Guzmán and Sergio Fernández, and the Communist Party and the MIR on the Left.

The agreement which finally emerged was the *Acuerdo Nacional*, or National Accord for the Transition to Full Democracy, signed under the aegis of the Archbishop, now a Cardinal, on 25 August 1985. It called for re-establishment of civil and political liberties; the election of a Congress and President; constitutional guarantees of private property; policies to overcome poverty by increasing growth and employment; and other agreed social objectives. The immediate steps required included the end of states of siege and emergency and both internal and external exile; the establishment of electoral registers and an electoral law; and a plebiscite to approve all these measures. Apart from the very broad range of support for the *Acuerdo Nacional*, the most striking changes embodied in it were the acceptance of most of the 1980 Constitution and particularly the provisions outlawing groups opposed to the principles of democracy (e.g. the Communist Party) and the guarantee of private property rights. This showed how far the democratic Left was prepared to move to achieve a broad alliance for democratic change. The support it received from two parties of the Right showed their disillusion and frustration with the impasse created by Pinochet's stubborn refusal to move. For a moment there seemed to be a broad consensus building up in favour of early change which even found some support within the government.

The *Acuerdo Nacional* was also warmly welcomed by the US administration and the European Community countries which were co-operating closely in order to maximise pressure on Pinochet. However, he continued stubbornly to maintain that Chile's stability and slowly returning prosperity were threatened by Marxist conspiracies, and to accuse the centrist politicians of naivety in flirting with communism. According to Pinochet only he stood between Chile and another Marxist disaster.[4]

It was true that, within the limits set by agreements with the IMF, the economic recovery was gathering momentum. Exports, especially of fruit and other non-traditional items, were increasing, imports were down, and businesses which had been renationalised as a result of the take-over of economic conglomerates in 1983 were privatised again. Devices such as debt-equity swaps were cutting down the size of the foreign debt and bringing in new investment from the United States, Europe and even Australia and New Zealand. Under Büchi's pragmatic management, agriculture was recovering and industrial and commercial enterprises which had survived the crash were again able to operate profitably. While the Vial and Cruzat-Larraín empires had been broken up, more cautiously managed enterprises such as those of the Matte, Angellini and Luksic groups went from strength to strength and smaller businesses also flourished.

As the recovery developed, the middle classes' enthusiasm for street demonstrations on days of protest began to evaporate. These had tended to become progressively more violent and less coherent from March 1984 onwards, partly because the far left – which had formed its own umbrella organisation, the *Movimiento Democrático Popular* (MDP), to join in the protest movement – actively tried to provoke confrontation with the security forces in the streets. Politicians supporting the *Acuerdo Nacional* who were anxious not to be outflanked on the Left, and believed also that only real pressure on a broad front would ever force Pinochet to negotiate, were ready to work with the MDP (effectively the Communist Party) in organising demonstrations. However, growing differences on tactics put considerable strains on the solidarity of the *Acuerdo Nacional* coalition and tended in particular to divide the Christian Democrats from the parties on the right. The young leader of the *Unión Nacional*, Andrés Allamand, who seemed to be one of the very few promising leaders of the new generation, summed it up: 'We can't accept the Christian Democrats' alliance with the

[4] The opposite view was expressed powerfully by Gabriel Valdés speaking at a mass rally in support of the *Acuerdo Nacional*: 'The people are on their feet saying: enough dictatorship, enough decay, enough repression. You, Señor Captain General Augusto Pinochet Ugarte, are the obstacle to democracy in Chile.'

Communists. Pinochet will never sit down at the table as long as the left persists in the tragic illusion that it can force him out.'

As the unity of the democratic parties began to fray, a new wave of violence broke out between the extreme Left and the various undercover security forces. One particularly horrific event was the discovery in a quiet road outside Santiago of the bodies of three well-known members of the Communist Party, all with their throats cut (*degollados*). In August 1985 the civilian investigating judge concluded that a counter-terrorist unit of the *Carabineros* had abducted and killed them and then dumped their mutilated bodies by the roadside. The judge had to declare himself without jurisdiction in the case since it involved members of the armed forces and internal security and was thus outside the scope of civilian judges. However, several *Carabinero* officers were accused of the crime and the outcry was so strong that the Director and member of the Junta, General Cesár Mendoza, was compelled to resign. Mendoza had been an unquestioning supporter of Pinochet since 1973. Although he was not charged with being personally involved in the case of the *degollados*, he must have been well aware of the existence of the undercover unit, known as DICOMCAR, operating far outside the law. His forced resignation and the damage done to the reputation of the *Carabineros* were another blow to the regime's standing.

In the latter months of 1985, Cardinal Fresno and his three collaborators strove to maintain some momentum behind the *Acuerdo National* and to persuade Pinochet at least to meet them to discuss it. Others tried to add their weight.[5] The most important source of support for the *Acuerdo* proved to be the Air Force member of the Junta, General Fernando Matthei. He seized on the fact that the greatest barrier to agreement in the process of transition was Pinochet's intention to be the only candidate for the Presidency in 1989, expecting to be elected on a simple 'yes or no' vote. There were others inside the government who agreed with Matthei's view that this travesty of a fair election would only serve to divide the country and create distrust between the armed forces and the population as a whole with potentially

[5] The present writer was one of the Ambassadors of the European Community who sought to encourage contacts between senior figures in the armed forces, in particular General Matthei, and the leaders of the *Acuerdo Nacional*.

disastrous consequences.[6] Pinochet's drive for a further eight years in office was also weakened when it emerged that the new head of the *Carabineros*, another officer of German descent, Rodolfo Stange, agreed with Matthei. Both Admiral Merino and General Benavides, the Army member, were thought to support their view, if more cautiously.

Pinochet's response was more defiant than ever. At a meeting of the Junta with the whole Cabinet present in December 1985 he asked the Secretary General of the Presidency to read out a speech made by the Argentine Admiral Massera in his own defence when brought to trial for responsibility for the 'dirty war' in Argentina. Massera had finished by saying that he was the victim of a 'trick of history' and in spite of being the victor in a 'just war' was being tried by the vanquished. As Pinochet saw it, that would be his own and his government's fate if he gave way and relinquished his grip on power. He replaced Benavides on the spot, underlining yet again that he would contemplate no change whatever in the 1980 Constitution or in the procedure for election of a new President with himself as the sole candidate.

At the beginning of 1986, the prospect of a negotiated solution seemed as remote as ever. The Christian Democrats concluded that they must distance themselves from the Communists and avoid being associated with them in organising more protests. At the same time they reinforced the *Acuerdo National* by launching a new civic movement, the Civil Assembly, which was not specifically linked to the political parties, but threatened that, if no progress were made by the middle of the year, a general strike would follow. Before this happened, however, the Communist Party abandoned 'peaceful protest' and declared that 1986 was to be the decisive year in which the Pinochet regime would be overturned by violence and sabotage culminating in a mass popular uprising. A new terrorist movement linked to the Communists emerged into prominence with a series of daring operations, including the kidnapping of members of the armed forces and bomb attacks on power lines and isolated police posts. This was the

6 Some supporters of the President also calculated that Pinochet would have a better chance of being elected if he were to stand against several other candidates, i.e. if the opposition vote were divided.

Frente Patriótico Manuel Rodríguez (FPMR)[7] whose efforts in 1986 produced the worst level of confrontation since the first national protest in 1983.

Terror and counter-terror

Violence escalated almost at once. During the attempt at a general strike on 2 July 1986, a military patrol captured two young demonstrators in an obscure suburb of Santiago and proceeded to douse them with petrol and set them alight. One, Rodrigo Rojas, died of burns; the other, Carmen Gloria Quintana, survived to become a symbol of resistance to the regime (she was publicly blessed by the Pope during his visit in 1987). The casual cruelty of this incident was very damaging to the reputation of the Army, all the more so because at first it denied responsibility, although it admitted later that the atrocity had been committed by soldiers. It was made worse by the fact that Rodrigo Rojas, though Chilean by birth, had lived in the United States.

It was not long before other sensational news rocked the country. A month after the burning of Rodrigo Rojas and Carmen Gloria Quintana, the government announced the discovery of huge quantities of arms in remote abandoned mineshafts in northern Chile and later in Santiago itself. Initially there was much scepticism about the size of these arsenals and their origin, but arms were known to have been reaching Chile through Peru in 1984 and 1985 because the security forces in both countries had intercepted some of them. It now appeared that from early in 1986 large quantities were being landed at remote coastal settlements in northern Chile from Cuban 'fishing' vessels and hidden away in old mineshafts and caves up and down that remote and sparsely inhabited coast. From there some were transported within weeks to other hiding places in and around Santiago.

In the rising tide of terrorist and counter-terrorist actions which seemed to be engulfing Chile in 1986, it was not easy to interpret

[7] It was named after a famous historical figure, Manuel Rodriguéz, who had been one of the most effective guerrilla leaders and tacticians of the patriotic forces when they were under greatest pressure from the Spanish Royalists during the struggle for independence from Spain. He had a reputation somewhat like that of the Scarlet Pimpernel but based on fact.

events. Many opponents of the government were deeply suspicious of these arms finds. Some, for example, thought that they could have been planted by the security forces in order to be 'discovered' and used to justify draconian counter-measures. With hindsight, however, it appears unlikely that massive quantities of arms were smuggled in by pure coincidence at more or less the same time as the Communists, both within and outside the country, announced a new campaign of armed action against the Pinochet regime. Their return to a policy of 'armed struggle' had been decided in principle several years previously. But, at the beginning of 1986, the new leader of the Chilean Communist Party, ex-Senator Volodia Teitelboim, declared in a Radio Moscow broadcast to Chile: '*Este será un año de combates titánicos*' (This will be a year of titanic battles). By the middle of the year it was clear that his words were not mere rhetoric: there had already been dozens of shootings and bomb attacks claimed by the FPMR, which had now clearly emerged as the leading paramilitary force opposing the regime – terrorists or freedom fighters according to viewpoint. It was certainly members of the FPMR who organised the smuggling of these massive shipments of arms.

By mid-August the quantity of armaments recovered was 3,115 M-16 rifles, 114 Soviet-made and 157 US-made rocket launchers of various types, about 2 million rounds of ammunition, 2,000 hand-grenades, heavy machine guns and quantities of other weapons and explosives. United States satellite intelligence had originally revealed the presence of Cuban vessels in Chile's northern waters, and US arms experts now identified much of the finds as former US Army material abandoned in Vietnam, and other items as Soviet war material manufactured as recently as 1983 and 1984. The total haul recovered was so much larger than could conceivably have been needed by the FPMR that it was argued (not least by the US Secretary of State) that it might have been intended to equip a guerrilla army to be used against some future civilian government after the end of the military regime. That might indeed have been part of the Communist purpose in bringing the arms in, but some must also have been intended for use in the 'titanic battles' which had been so clearly announced.

The idea that an amateur, clandestine and tiny terrorist group could actually have defeated the Chilean armed forces in a military campaign is self-evidently absurd. When the situation was far more favourable, in 1973, the 'people's army' committed to defending President Salvador Allende and his government had not been able to mount a serious counter-strike against the armed forces which were then much weaker than they later became. How could the FPMR alone expect to achieve more in 1986? In fact they very nearly did. On the evening of Sunday 7 September, a carefully planned and executed attack intended to kill President Pinochet was carried out against the motorcade in which he was returning from his country house in the Maipo Valley a few miles east of Santiago.

The road back to the capital was staked out by the FPMR group of twenty-eight men and women, which carried out this attack, code-named '*Operación Siglo XX*'. It succeeded in blocking the road behind and ahead of the convoy of cars as it reached a hill called the Cuesta Las Achupallas and the assault team opened fire at short range with automatic weapons, grenades and rocket-launchers. Five of Pinochet's bodyguards were killed and twelve others injured in the ambush and one vehicle was completely destroyed. Pinochet himself was travelling in one of two identical armour-plated Mercedes cars with his young grandson Rodrigo, a naval aide-de-camp and his driver. All of them escaped alive.

The reasons for this apparently miraculous escape were, first, the exceptionally heavy armour plating of the Mercedes limousine and, secondly, the fact that at least two of the missiles fired at it from a US LOW anti-tank weapon failed to detonate. The third factor which saved Pinochet and his aide and grandson was that his driver had the skill and nerve to reverse the Mercedes at speed out of the ambush, knocking aside the caravan which was blocking the road behind him, and getting out of range at maximum speed. Once they saw this the attackers broke away.

One of the people originally named as a leading figure in *Operación Siglo XX* was a young Chilean who had recently returned from Cuba. César Bunster was the son of a member of the *Unidad Popular* who had been Allende's Ambassador in London at the time of the coup. Bunster had returned to Chile legally at the beginning of 1986 and found a job as receptionist at the Canadian Embassy, which provided him with good cover. In time he proceeded to rent a substantial house – as an operational base near the spot selected for the ambush – and five vehicles and a caravan from different sources. Another group of FPMR members brought in the arms needed for the attack from their hiding places and stored them in a cellar at the operational base. Two women members of the group rented a room in the village of San José de Maipo through which Pinochet's motorcade had to pass, so that they could alert the assault group. The attack was meticulously carried out and sufficiently ruthless to envisage and inflict death and severe injury on many people apart from its real target. Pinochet's survival was interpreted by some of his more devout partisans as a sign that he enjoyed divine protection.[8]

The failure of this assassination plan was openly regretted by people on the extreme Left. It also had important and far-reaching effects on mainstream Chilean opinion. A significant part of the political Right had never wavered in its support for Pinochet and hoped that he would continue in power till 1997, if not longer. Now, however, a much larger number of middle-class and other Chileans, who had recently wanted an earlier return to democratic government under a freely elected civilian President, were appalled by the renewed violence from the extreme Left and driven back into supporting 'the devil they knew'. The failure of the assassination attempt thus strengthened the regime. At the same time, all the democratic centre and centre-left parties were finally persuaded of the impossibility of working with the Communists in future. In their anxiety to develop the political *apertura* which they believed was attainable through the *Acuerdo National*, many of the politicians had been equivocal in their attitude towards the Communist Party. Now they turned their backs on the Communists. Another unexpected consequence was to weaken the consensus which had developed within the Junta, and among some members of the Cabinet, that Pinochet should not be nominated as the sole candidate for the Presidency in 1988.

The immediate and all too predictable reaction to *Operación Siglo XX* took the form of revenge for the death of the five bodyguards. Four members of the Communist Party or the MIR were abducted from their homes by armed and uniformed gangs on the two succeeding nights, and their bodies were later found

[8] The Mercedes was put on show in Santiago afterwards and the superstitious claimed that the shattered glass of one of the car windows formed an image of the Virgin Mary. More cynical Chileans said that the whole affair had taken place not at Cuesta Las Achupallas but at '*Cuesta Creerlo*' – meaning 'It's hard to believe'.

with gunshot wounds in different parts of Santiago (a fifth man targeted by the death squad – a lawyer working for the *Vicaría de la Solidaridad* – gave the alarm by shouting for help to a neighbour who happened to be an Army colonel). A more protracted operation to catch the terrorists followed, and the deadly cycle of violence and retaliation was now so commonplace that there was only relief that more murders did not take place in the nights immediately after 7 September.

The government imposed a state of siege yet again and ordered the arrest of fifty or more well-known figures from the Left, including Ricardo Lagos, leader of the moderate wing of the Socialist Party. Within relatively few weeks, however, they were all released in order to lower the political temperature, at least temporarily, in advance of Pope John Paul arriving on the first papal visit in the history of Chile. This was intended by the Vatican and the Chilean Church to bring the Pope into contact with the greatest possible range of Chileans and to encourage reconciliation in all quarters. In the event, the visit was a triumphant success and most of the efforts made by the government to use the Pope's presence for the regime's own advantage were firmly resisted. It had a particular significance even for the million or so Chileans who are not Roman Catholics, not only because of Pope John Paul's great personal charisma but also because of the role he had played in mediating the territorial dispute between Chile and Argentina which had so nearly led the two countries into war in 1978.

The Pope's visit also underlined the increasing concern of the international community that Chile should soon return to democracy and that the abuses of human rights which had multiplied again since 1983 should finally cease. The specific criticisms of the Chilean government which continued to be expressed in resolutions by the UN and other organisations, with the support of the US administration and the European Community, added point and direction to the clear message which the Pope clearly intended to leave behind him. (The regime's supporters continued to react violently to any international criticism, and Pinochet himself went so far as to accuse the CIA of being involved in some way in the assassination attempt against him.)

The plebiscite of 1988

In the middle of 1987, both government and opposition in Chile began to concentrate closely on preparations for the plebiscite due before the end of 1988. A series of basic laws governing the electoral machinery, the formation of political parties etc. was slowly being put in place. With this well advanced, Pinochet turned again to his former Minister of the Interior, Sergio Fernández, his strongest civilian collaborator and the man with a proved ability to organise the campaign for a 'Yes' vote. The first resistance to Pinochet's ambition came within a few weeks when Admiral Merino and Generals Matthei and Stange all repeated in public that they felt it would be better for their nomination to go to a younger, civilian candidate than to Pinochet.[9] Fernández was equal to the situation and set to work to mobilise all the government's resources and leverage to ensure both that General Pinochet would be nominated by his fellow Commanders-in-Chief and, after that had been achieved, that more than half of the electorate would vote 'Yes'.

Working through the highly effective and centralised control system available to the Minister of the Interior and in close liaison with the Army, Fernández' team pursued this two-pronged campaign for the next fifteen months. One of the most important assets at their disposal were the *alcaldes* (mayors) throughout the country, who were all appointed by the government and thus certain to support Pinochet. The Pinochet campaign for re-election also had a near monopoly of the media, and could find many ways of inhibiting the ability of the opposition to communicate with the electorate on level terms. Finally the campaign was being conducted against a background of strong and broad-based economic recovery under the astute control of Hernan Büchi. Investment was again flowing strongly into Chile from the United States, Japan, Britain and many other countries of the European Community and the Pacific Basin.

There seemed a very real possibility that Pinochet could actually win the plebiscite. Sergio Fernández and his team certainly thought so. The opposition would need to organise well to have any

[9] Even the possibility of Pinochet resigning his Army rank and standing as a civilian candidate was considered among many other options.

chance against the formidable strength of the government and President in power. On 1 February 1988 sixteen parties which had previously formed the *Concertación de Partidos por la Democracia* with the leader of the Christian Democrats, Patricio Aylwin, as their spokesman announced the formation of the '*Comando por el No*' and a basis for a political programme for the future. The starting point, which Aylwin and most realistic politicians had long accepted, was to recognise the 1980 Constitution as a fact of life. The programme also included a range of proposals for reforming the judiciary and labour legislation and for more expenditure on health, education and housing specifically to benefit the poor. Alongside this campaigning organisation, a *Comité por Elecciones Libres* (CEL) had been formed by Sergio Molina, one of the leading promoters of the *Acuerdo National*, to encourage people to register to vote (no easy matter for poor people in remote parts of the country) and to develop independent systems for monitoring the outcome of the plebiscite so that any electoral fraud would be detected.

This effort to mobilise the 'No' vote in the plebiscite, and to nullify any risk of the government manipulating the outcome, was obviously vital. The contest could not be won unless the government's built-in strengths could in some way be countered, and a number of public and private US bodies were ready to provide funds to assist the process. The US AID programme provided $1.2 million to assist with voter registration from early in 1988; then the National Endowment for Democracy gave its support for a number of initiatives by the CEL. The Ford Foundation had been involved for some time in financing economic and political research by the think-tanks associated with opposition parties, such as FLACSO and CIEPLAN. European foundations, particularly from Germany, also provided help for various Chilean groups working towards a new democratic Chile. Some of the US foundations paid for visits by the best experts to advise on and help set up computerised systems to monitor the electoral process.

All this help could be, and was, criticised by the regime as illegitimate foreign interference in the plebiscite. This could not really be denied since it was intended to maximise the 'No' vote, but Genaro Arriagada, the director of the campaign, replied that accepting foreign funding was the only possible way of matching the infinitely greater resources available to the government. Some of the greatest problems for the opposition were, however, solved by a strictly Chilean mechanism established in accordance with the Constitution itself. This was the Constitutional Tribunal set up in 1985 with the responsibility to oversee the working of the new democratic system. It was this Tribunal which shrewdly insisted that an Electoral Tribunal be set up in time to supervise the plebiscite and modified the law on political parties to remove certain restrictions on left-wing parties. Perhaps most important of all, the Constitutional Tribunal insisted that the opposition should have equal access to radio and television during the plebiscite campaign.

As the date, 5 October 1988, approached, fears grew that the plebiscite could still somehow be hijacked by the authorities or even that disturbances would be contrived to enable the process to be cancelled. Rumours abounded as always in Santiago at tense moments. The US Ambassador complained to the Foreign Ministry about reports that the plebiscite was to be sabotaged, and the State Department called in the Chilean Ambassador to the same purpose. European countries followed suit and the Chilean government, though infuriated by the implications, knew that the eyes of the world were on them. On 5 October itself, there was a massive turnout with long but orderly queues at the polling tables from the early morning onwards. The monitoring of results by the opposition enabled the CEL and the *Comando por el No* to announce their own figures independently computed on the basis of the results reported from individual polling tables. The first figures given by the government at 7.30 p.m. gave a big majority for 'Yes' (favourable to Pinochet) but based on a minimal number of votes counted. At 10 p.m. the count, according to the government announcement, was 51 per cent 'Yes' and 46 per cent 'No'. At this point the *Comando* released their figures, which agreed closely with the final result: 44 per cent for 'Yes' and 55 per cent for 'No'.[10]

At midnight when Pinochet met the Junta and his Cabinet he was faced not only with defeat by an indisputable margin in the

[10] The turnout was very high – 97 per cent of all those registered to vote or 92 per cent of those qualified. All the many international observers present in Chile at the time agreed that the plebiscite was free and fair.

plebiscite but also with the fact that the result could not be concealed from Chileans or the hundreds of foreign observers present to monitor the process and its result. On arriving, General Fernando Matthei had confirmed the result to the waiting press: 'I am certain the 'No' has won, but we are calm.' There was no more room for resistance by the hard-liners in Pinochet's camp. As a final throw to keep the regime in full control despite losing the plebiscite, Sergio Fernández asked the Commanders-in-Chief to sign a decree giving the President new special powers. Matthei and Merino refused. Merino added quietly that all of them had sworn to uphold the Constitution and must do so. An hour later the Vice Commander-in-Chief of the Army, General Santiago Sinclair, who had been one of the 'unconditionals' for many years, reported to Pinochet that the Army stood ready at his disposal. Pinochet repeated Merino's words: '*La Constitución se cumple.*' For him it was the point of no return.

These historic events inside La Moneda only became known much later to the anxious millions still waiting to hear an official announcement of the result of the plebiscite. For them the climactic moment of release came when the two most senior political leaders of Right and Left, Sergio Onofre Jarpa and Patricio Aylwin, appeared together on the TV channel of the Catholic University soon after midnight and agreed that the 'No' vote had won. The world knew then that the long regime of Augusto Pinochet was about to end. After more than fifteen years of authoritarian government and through persuasion and peaceful campaigning, the majority of Chileans had made their decision clear beyond doubt and reasserted their democratic tradition and beliefs.

11

REBIRTH OF A DEMOCRACY

'Chilean society had evolved enormously since 1973;... the old democratic culture had strongly reasserted itself. There was a new appreciation for the values of moderation and compromise that had once been bitterly discarded – and a firm rejection of the Utopian visions that had scarred a generation.'
– Pamela Constable and Arturo Valenzuela, *Chile under Pinochet: A Nation of Enemies*

Pinochet's defeat in the plebiscite of 1988 was the end of a long withdrawal from the commanding position which he had occupied at the beginning of the decade. He had lost his battle, but for those who still supported the military regime and for many who thought it had lasted long enough but wanted its achievements to be preserved for the future the campaign was by no means over. Most foreign observers failed to appreciate that the plebiscite was by no means an overwhelming defeat for the regime or even for Pinochet personally. He had after all won the approval of 44 per cent, a strikingly high level of support in what was generally conceded to have been an honest poll (though one in which Pinochet had a strong built-in advantage). It proved that very many Chileans were not sure that they wanted to return to full democracy – even after fifteen years of dictatorship. Supporters of the regime believed that another candidate acceptable to them should be able to add enough to Pinochet's hard-core support to win an open election for the Presidency.

The elections of 1989

Pinochet, with whatever reluctance, announced that presidential and congressional elections would be held simultaneously in December 1989. The victorious *Concertación de Partidos por la*

Democrácia obviously had to transform itself quickly from being simply an instrument constructed to oppose Pinochet into a true electoral coalition with policies appealing to the whole Chilean people. The first step, somewhat irritatingly for the other members of the *Concertación*, was an internal struggle among the Christian Democrats to decide which of them should become the presidential candidate. Since the PDC was by far the largest and best organised party, it would certainly be one of their number but the choice was not at once obvious to those concerned.

Three candidates emerged as front-runners. One was the former Foreign Minister of the Frei government of the 1960s, the bearer of two aristocratic Chilean names, Gabriel Valdés Subercaseaux. He had been several times President of the party and played the leading role in bringing it back to life in the 1980s.[1] Another was the untried bearer of an even more famous political name, Eduardo Frei Ruiz-Tagle, a son of the former President, Eduardo Frei Montalva. The third was another of the elder Frei's closest collaborators, and one of the founding fathers of their party, Patricio Aylwin Azocar. Valdés, who seldom disguised his ambition to become President, saw this as probably his last chance to achieve it. Both he and Aylwin were over seventy years old but Aylwin, an avuncular rather than a patrician figure, had the important advantage that he had been the spokesman and *de facto* leader of the *Concertación* when it achieved the defeat of Pinochet. It was to a considerable extent due to his political skills that the opposition had not only succeeded in uniting to defeat Pinochet but also been able to shape a viable plan for an alternative government. In the end Valdés withdrew in favour of Aylwin, who seemed the better choice as President for a transitional period. (Frei was able to wait for another day.)

The man who eventually emerged to campaign for the Right was Hernán Büchi. His political credentials as an individual, indeed his public persona, were largely unknown and he hesitated and changed his mind for several weeks before finally allowing himself

[1] Valdés was one of many prominent Chilean politicians who had been working abroad in 1970-3 and who tried to return immediately after the coup. There is good evidence that he hoped, perhaps even expected, to be invited to assume important office – perhaps the highest of all – by the military Junta. In the event he was not approached and not even allowed to return to Chile at once. In due course he became one of the regime's chief critics.

Demonstration in favour of the 'No' option in the plebiscite of 1988.

President Patricio Aylwin (*left*) takes office, 1980; with General Pinochet (*centre*) and the Minister of Defence, Patricio Rojas (*right*).

to be drafted into the contest. Büchi was essentially a technocrat and, despite his considerable achievements in managing the revival of the Chilean economy in the second half of the 1980s, he had no consuming interest in politics and little stomach for electioneering. He was the first to realise this but his backers hoped that as the architect of economic recovery he would command support among the uncommitted section of the electorate, and that his youth and unstuffy lifestyle would appeal to young voters. The recipe never seemed likely to work, and what chance Büchi may have had was badly damaged by lack of unity on the Right. The *Renovación Nacional* (RN) adopted a moderate position, but the other main party supporting Büchi, the *Unión Democrática Independiente* (UDI), spent much of its effort campaigning against the RN for seats in Congress, giving an impression of disunity in the presidential campaign. Büchi strove to show that he was not still tarred by his association with Pinochet and the military government, but this was all but impossible because the UDI was clearly devoted to preserving Pinochet's legacy and influence. Another damaging factor was the emergence of a populist millionaire, Francisco Javier Errázuriz, who contrived (mainly by playing to the gallery) to divert almost a third of the vote which might otherwise have gone to Büchi.

The result of the election was a decisive victory for Patricio Aylwin. With 55.2 per cent he won without the need for a second round – a similar vote to that achieved by the last Christian Democrat President, Eduardo Frei Montalva, in 1964. It was virtually the same size of popular vote as in the 1988 plebiscite, a resounding endorsement of the *Concertación* and of Aylwin personally. Büchi's vote was 29.4 per cent and Errázuriz' 15.4 per cent (between them they won only about 1 per cent more than Pinochet had achieved in the two-horse race the previous year).

Screwing down the Constitution

The congressional elections produced a majority for the *Concertación* in both houses but not sufficient to allow it to put through the constitutional reforms it had always wanted. In the lower house, it had seventy-two seats and the opposition a total of forty-eight. In the Senate, the *Concertación* had twenty-two seats against sixteen for the opposition but the latter could also expect the support of the blocking group of nine 'institutional' senators designated by Pinochet precisely in order to prevent change. This mechanism was to serve its purpose very effectively throughout the Aylwin government. The only modifications to the 1980 Constitution which were actually approved before Aylwin assumed power were a relaxation of the constitutional bar on communist participation in politics; a change in the composition of the National Security Council to reduce the military element in it; and adjustments which made further amendment of the constitution slightly less difficult than before. (Originally it was all but impossible for the 1980 Constitution to be altered except by general consent of all the political parties – as in fact happened in July 1989.)

On the government side, the architect of these negotiated changes to the Constitution was the former Minister of Finance, Carlos Cáceres, whom Pinochet chose to become Minister of Interior (in effect head of the government) after losing the 1988 plebiscite. It was principally Cáceres who persuaded Pinochet to accept a certain minimum of constitutional change as a means of achieving agreement with the *Concertación* on the process of transition. However, it is arguable that other legislation pushed through in the final year of the military government clawed back more power from the new President and Congress than was conceded by the constitutional changes. A complicated 'bi-nomial' electoral system was introduced which guaranteed over-representation in Congress for the political parties which came second in numerical terms, which would normally be those of the Right. A new law governing the armed forces made it very difficult for the President to exercise any degree of control over them and prevented him from replacing the Commanders-in-Chief. A number of judges were induced to retire and replaced by younger nominees of Pinochet who could be expected to maintain conservative positions.

The opposition protested vigorously against most of these decrees, the *leyes de amarre* (hold-firm laws), which were rather obviously devised to restrict the freedom of action of future governments. However, Aylwin had decided long before that an agreed transition was preferable to a protracted struggle which would be all too likely to result in violence and possibly provide an excuse to delay the handover of power even longer, and therfore had little alternative but to strike the best deal he could. With Cáceres, a relatively co-operative and conciliatory figure at the Ministry of the Interior, the Constitution was at least made somewhat less rigid.

The most important of all the arrangements agreed between Cáceres and the *Concertación* came just before the elections in December 1989, when it was finally agreed that the first head of the independent Central Bank would be a jointly agreed personality and not another Pinochet nominee. By striking this deal the opposition tacitly accepted that the free market economic system and the main lines of the economic policy established during the military regime would continue under the incoming government with an independent Central Bank acting as guarantor. This was particularly important to the entrepreneurs who had built up the economy so successfully over the previous ten years on the basis established by de Castro and his Chicago Boys and developed by their more pragmatic successors. One of Chile's leading entrepreneurs, Andrónico Luksic, spoke for many other business leaders in stressing that it would be folly to put at risk the economic gains achieved at such high cost in the late 1970s and the 1980s by any precipitate changes of policy. Efficiency had given Chile decisive competitive advantages by the end of the 1980s and the benefits were at last trickling – if not exactly flowing – down to the workers.[2]

Chile's re-encounter with history

Patricio Aylwin and the *Concertación* took power in March 1990 with a clear mandate but with their freedom of action heavily circumscribed. Over the next four years the new President showed himself to be admirably suited to the delicate task of ruling in these circumstances. The system which he had to operate was still a presidential one with the power of initiative firmly held by the executive, but even if he had had the taste for it he could not act as a President of the traditional Chilean kind. Instead his patient and careful approach to problems, his grasp of politics as

[2] The Luksic empire was built partly on foundations provided by a famous British-built railway, the Antofagasta (Chili) and Bolivia Railway Co., and a great US copper company, Anaconda, which he had acquired in 1979 and 1986 respectively. Both were in the doldrums but within a few years their assets became major parts of a powerful mining, transport and industrial conglomerate.

the 'art of the possible' and his negotiating skills were exactly what the country needed after twenty years of turbulence. As Aylwin put it in an address to the nation, Chile was involved in a new meeting with its own history. His task, as he defined it, had four main objectives. First, there was the overriding need to develop and broaden the democratic consensus which had been constructed by the *Concertación* since October 1988, but which called for reasonably smooth relations with the military and a degree of co-operation with the political opposition. Secondly, there was the urgent need to tackle all the human rights abuses going back as far as 1973 and never admitted or addressed, let alone resolved. Thirdly, the democratic government had to show that it could maintain strong economic growth. And fourthly, it was determined to make a start in repaying the 'social debt' owed to the millions of people who had been the losers in the harsh if necessary process of creating the free market economic model. An average *per capita* income of little more than $2,000 at the end of the 1980s was not impressive for an allegedly successful economy.

The problem of broadening the 'democratic consensus' was essentially that of reconciling the military and their right-wing supporters to a reversal of roles. Since the opposition had become the government, the former rulers now had to accept a secondary and ultimately subordinate position in the nation's affairs. However, this could not simply be imposed on the armed forces. They had not been defeated. Pinochet had maintained control, allowed moderate political forces to emerge and eventually handed power over in accordance with his own plan and at a time he had himself proposed. Military rule in Chile was not the totally disastrous failure it had been elsewhere in Latin America, as in Argentina under General Galtieri. In the eyes of many Chileans it had in some ways been a success story. Moreover, the Chilean people had shown by their votes in 1988 and 1989 that they wanted moderate middle-of-the-road politics and rejected extremism of the Left as well as the Right. Aylwin responded to this by regularly consulting with the opposition in Congress and, whenever possible, agreeing on legislation before it was submitted for formal consideration. An outstanding example of this was the agreement reached at the beginning of the Aylwin government on an increase in business taxation and the value added tax to raise revenue for social purposes, and later changes to the labour laws which allowed somewhat more freedom for trade unions to function effectively. This was a reversion to the tradition of government by consensus which had often operated before.

Dealing with the past

This policy was greatly assisted by the personal authority and skill of Gabriel Valdés who became President of the Senate and a powerful supporter and representative of the new democracy. There was a noticeable reintegration of the Right into mainstream politics – although the UDI still remained closer to Pinochet and the military. However, there were raw nerve-ends over human rights. The natural demands of the victims for justice could not be denied and Aylwin moved quickly to set up the Commission on Truth and Reconciliation (*Comisión de la Verdad y de la Reconciliación*) to produce a detailed report on all the violations of human rights in the Pinochet years. The Commission was headed by a senior Radical ex-senator, Raúl Rettig,[3] with a balanced membership, and was required to report within a year. In March 1991 it produced a magisterial report documenting almost 3,000 reported cases involving assassinations, executions and disappearances (further details of the types of cases covered and conclusions about them are in Chapter 7). However, the Commission's role was limited to investigating and establishing the facts of these cases and it had no responsibility for pursuing or prosecuting offenders. Another criticism of the Rettig Report was that it did not cover cases – such as allegations of torture, or the use of exile and other forms of repression – which did not result in death. One part of the problem was therefore left uninvestigated.

In setting the Commission's task, President Aylwin said specifically that it would be to achieve justice 'within the limits of what is possible'. There were real limitations, not least that the amnesty law passed by the military regime, which protected offenders from

[3] Rettig had quarrelled with Allende in the 1950s but later became Ambassador to Brazil during Allende's Presidency and could not therefore be considered biased in either direction. Other members of the Commission included Jaime Castillo Velasco, a Christian Democrat who had been arrested and exiled several times by the military government, and Gonzalo Vial Correa, a conservative historian and ex-minister of General Pinochet.

prosecution in relation to events before 1978, could not be revoked because there was not a sufficient majority for that in the Senate. However, the Rettig Report did contain some stinging criticisms of the failure of the judiciary to act properly to curb abuses in 1973-78 as well as later. It also had the important effect of enabling the families of people illegally killed during the military regime to know the full circumstances and at least to have official recognition that their relatives had been victims of repression and not terrorists or criminals as they had previously been labelled. The Report also proposed a generous compensation scheme for the families who were victims of this repression. Over the next five years a new body, the *Comisión Nacional de Reparación y Reconciliación*, headed by Alejandro González, worked on the individual cases and awarded pensions and education grants to widows and children. This body also continued the investigatory work of the Rettig Commission and eventually reported on nearly 2,000 further cases, including many only reported after the original Rettig enquiry and others which Rettig had not been able to investigate fully.[4]

The prosecution of people accused of these crimes was normally left in the hands of the judicial authorities and of private individuals willing to pursue legal actions on behalf of relatives or friends. This was seen by some as a failure by the Aylwin government to do everything it could possibly have done in the interests of abstract justice. However, in April 1991, less than a month after the publication of the Rettig Report, this argument was weakened by the assassination in broad daylight in Santiago of the leader of the UDI, Senator Jaimé Guzmán. As we saw earlier, Guzmán had been influential as a young Roman Catholic, right-wing activist in the early 1970s, and later as a political adviser to Pinochet and one of the chief architects of the 1980 Constitution. The crime, attributed to the FPMR, was widely condemned, and it showed starkly that not all the blood which had been shed in Chile was on the hands of the military or its right-wing allies. The juxtaposition of the Rettig findings with the assassination of Guzmán proved (yet again) how violence breeds violence. Subsequently, there appeared to be a greater willingness to let old wounds heal.

[4] The González Commission concluded that 899 of these cases involved killings or disappearances, making a total of 3,197 proved cases of which 1,102 were disappearances unexplained to this day.

Perhaps the most welcome result of the Rettig and González Commissions' work was the fact that many of the military, who for so long had either denied that there ever were outrages or argued that they were justified and necessary, now tacitly accepted that the truth had been established. Truth and reconciliation were well served by this painstaking process. One member of the Rettig Commission, José Zalaquett, a prominent member of Amnesty International, wrote:

> It can be argued that in a country that has been deeply divided, repentance and forgiveness could bring about unity, and that unity, in certain circumstances, would reinforce the foundations of democracy.[...] Thus forgiveness could also be a means of prevention, if the truth has been revealed and there has been an admission of responsibilities.[5]

One case in which exemplary justice was finally achieved arose from the assassination of Orlando Letelier in Washington in 1976 (see Chapter 7, pp. 127-8). After sixteen years of pressure from the US administration, this eventually ended in 1993 with the conviction and sentencing to long terms of imprisonment of the former head of the DINA, General Manuel Contreras, and Colonel Pedro Espinosa. It was an event of symbolic importance for all who felt that some penalty needed to be paid by two of the men ultimately responsible for the terrible crimes committed by agents of the DINA and subsequently the CNI. Not all the guilty were punished but, after protracted resistance, particularly in the case of Contreras, these two were finally brought to account.

Civil-military relations

Relations with the Commanders-in-Chief of the armed forces had always seemed likely to cause difficulties for Aylwin. The greatest challenge arose, of course, with General Pinochet himself. According to the Constitution and the organic law governing the armed forces, Pinochet had the right to remain as Commander-in-Chief of the Army till 1998, and there was no way in which

[5] José Zalaquett, 'Human Rights: Truth and Responsibility in Chile', *The Ethics of Responsibility* (Washington, DC, 1991), quoted by Alan Angell in his contribution (Chapter 4) in Leslie Bethell (ed.), *Chile since Independence*, (Cambridge, 1993).

he could be obliged to resign. In 1990 the Army had returned to the barracks, but before it did so Pinochet had secured its future position (and his own) with military thoroughness. At their first formal interview after the election, Aylwin asked Pinochet to resign but did not attempt to force the issue. Pinochet refused, saying that his continued presence in command of the Army would be the best assurance the new President could have that the armed forces would cause him no problems.[6] There was no lack of deputies keen to find means to force Pinochet's resignation, and the Minister of Defence also tried on more than one occasion to make him accept civilian control.

Over the four years of Patricio Aylwin's Presidency (and indeed after it) Pinochet resisted all such attempts and occasionally underlined the fact that he had not left the stage and still had the power to intervene. When, in 1990, Congress and the press began to inquire into financial scandals involving army officers, and members of Pinochet's own family, he responded by the dramatic step of 'mobilising' all ranks at short notice to their barracks. Again, in 1993, the whole corps of generals was called to a meeting at the Ministry of Defence ostentatiously wearing full combat dress. The first of these demonstrations took place during one of the President's visits to European countries. It was therefore widely reported internationally and taken as a clear sign that the democratic government of Chile was little more than a façade behind which the old dictator still exercised the real power. However, Aylwin showed skill and a cool head in defusing these incidents, and little by little relations improved. The civilians showed that they understood that the military would not tolerate anything like a witch hunt – and the military (for the most part) learned to accept civilian authority in matters outside the armed forces' area of direct interest. Some officers may indeed have welcomed the revival of the idea of strictly professional armed forces insulated from politics, which had been eclipsed in 1973.

[6] In a sense this proved to be true. Indeed some thought that the presence of General Pinochet on the sidelines at the head of an efficient army was helpful to Aylwin in restraining the more extreme tendencies within the Concertación. On the other hand, the President was said to have told his Spanish counterpart, Prime Minister Felipe González, that having Pinochet in the wings in Chile was as problematical as having Franco in the same position would have been.

The economy: growth with equity

The problems of dealing with the past and reinforcing the new democratic system were, of course, much more tractable because the Aylwin government was working with a strong current of economic growth behind it. The *Concertación* accepted that the free market economy had brought Chile sustained growth over the previous five years and even doctrinaire socialists now agreed that private initiative could deliver desirable economic development more efficiently than state-run 'enterprises' . The economic policies of the previous government – export orientation, low and non-discriminatory tariffs, and strong guarantees for private investment–were all maintained. The lessons of the 1970s and '80s had been well learned by almost everyone in Chile.[7] Only the Communist Party still clung to its old economic panaceas, despite the final collapse of the state socialist system in the Soviet Union and Eastern Europe and the impending collapse in Cuba.

The new economic team was headed by Alejandro Foxley as Minister of Finance. Notwithstanding their previous views, Foxley and his colleagues now found themselves managing the economy in much the same way as their predecessors, fine-tuning interest rates and the money supply to correct macro-economic faults but declining to interfere with market forces in general. The only obvious change was that there were only a small number of further privatisations after 1989.

The key economic indicators for the last two years of the military regime and the first six of democratic government by the Concertación led by Patricio Aylwin (1990-4) and then by Eduardo Frei (1995-) were as shown in the table overleaf.

The fall in growth and sharp increase in inflation in 1990 were due to inflationary increases in public spending in the preceding years designed to increase Pinochet's electoral support. This was quickly corrected by Foxley, and the strength of the economy made an impressive revival from 1991 onwards. Nevertheless the *Concertación* knew that, in the words of a contemporary Argentine Finance Minister, 'no one actually lives in the macro-economy'. They did not see macro-economic performance as an end in

[7] The lesson was reinforced by the fact that the major Western economies, and many in other parts of the world, adopted similar free market policies in the 1980s – years after Chile had done so.

GDP: GROWTH, INFLATION, UNEMPLOYMENT

	GDP (% growth)	*Inflation (%)*	*Unemployment (%)*	*GDP per capita (US$)*
1988	7.3	14.7	8.3	1,890
1989	9.9	17.0	6.3	2,180
1990	3.3	26.0	5.7	2,320
1991	7.3	21.8	6.5	2,580
1992	11.0	15.4	6.2	3,160
1993	6.3	12.7	4.9	3,320
1994	4.2	11.4	6.5	3,730
1995	8.3	8.2	5.5	4,740

Source: Banco Central de Chile, *Boletin Mensuel*.

itself, merely as the means to an end; and one of their principal innovations was a new social development fund, financed largely with the additional revenue from higher taxation. Using this fund, the Aylwin administration increased spending on public services like health and education by about one-third between 1989 and 1993. These had been starved of funds for years because of the overriding priority the military regime had given to fighting inflation and controlling the huge and debilitating government deficits of the 1970s. The *Concertación* described this policy as one of promoting 'growth with equity' and deliberately directed more resources into areas which would benefit the poorest people. They can fairly claim at least to have made a start towards paying the 'social debt'.

The social debt

Poverty is relative and there are probably worse examples of it elsewhere in Latin America, and certainly in other continents, than in Chile in recent times. Nevertheless the *poblaciones* of Santiago and other cities in Chile contained widespread and extreme poverty in the 1970s and '80s. Government-financed relief programmes were aimed, with some success, at limited and specific targets such as reducing infant mortality and improving children's diet, but other individuals were left to sink or swim as best they could. Hospital services and even basic drugs were often beyond reach because of their cost. Large numbers of Chilean families lived outside the market economy because they had no jobs and the only forms of official help available were the minimum employment schemes organised in the worst recessions to provide bare subsistence for those who managed to qualify. The market economy might offer a reasonable standard of living for those who could get into it. For those who could not, there was no longer a recognisable social welfare system. The only organised safety nets were provided by charitable effort, usually based on the churches.

According to official figures, in 1989 (even after several good years) as many as 40 per cent of all Chileans – more than 5 million – were living in poverty. By 1995 the figure had dropped to about 30 per cent and by 1996 to 24 per cent.[8] Although this meant that about 3.5 million people still lived in a state officially described as 'poverty', it also meant that about 2 million had moved forward to a better life. Between 1990 and 1995 real income grew by an average of 4 per cent per year and minimum pay by about 5.5 per cent per year. Trickle-down was finally seen to be working –not fast enough for the *Concertación* but much better than in the previous decade and a half when the academic theorists believed that it should have started to make itself felt.

However, the Chicago Boys and their collaborators can claim the rate of domestic saving as a major source of economic strength for the country as a whole. The AFP private pension system set up by José Piñera, Minister of Labour and Social Security at the beginning of the 1980s, had become a powerful engine of economic growth. By 1990 it represented 16 per cent and by 1995 almost 20 per cent of total saving in Chile. In 1995 the total of private pension funds was 38 per cent of GDP and projected to rise to 50 per cent by 2003 and over 60 per cent by 2010. Over the same period the percentage of the Chilean workforce which contribute to the system has grown from 29 per cent (1982) to 55.1 per cent (1995).[9]

[8] Such statistics are notoriously tricky and open to dispute. These, which I believe to be the best available, are taken from publications of the *Consejo Nacional para la Superación de la Pobreza*, the Council for Overcoming Poverty, set up in 1994 by the Chilean Ministry of Planning (MIDEPLAN).

[9] Figures quoted in Genesis Investment Management Ltd, *The Chilean Private Pension System, 1980-2010* (London, 1996). The Chilean system has its critics but it has been imitated widely by other countries in Latin America (Peru, Argentina, Colombia and Uruguay).

Alongside the strong growth in domestic savings and investment (Chile had the highest savings rate in Latin America), the level of foreign investment remained high under the Aylwin government, dropping somewhat in 1991 but rising to a peak of nearly $4 billion in 1996. These investment flows have driven the economy forward powerfully since the mid-1980s and have transformed it, in some ways, into a developed one. It still depends heavily on exports of primary commodities, but fortunately Chile's have been in strong demand for many years and the country has also been successful in adding value to these basic commodities.

Those (like the present author) who visit Chile every year or two and compare their impressions of the new situation with what they remember from the past, cannot doubt that Chileans in the late 1990s are better fed, better clothed, better housed, and perhaps better educated. The *Concertación* claim that this is partly though admittedly not wholly due to the increase in government social expenditure since 1989. That certainly played a part but the main reason for the improvement has been more than ten years of strong economic growth with the knock-on increases in employment and in the general level of wages and other benefits. Chileans who are in reasonably well-paid jobs–about 95 per cent of the working population now have regular work of some kind – are better off in most ways than ever before. According to projections of GDP *per capita* (which seem likely to be realised), the figure ($4,740 in 1995) was scheduled to rise to about $5,500 by the end of 1997 and to $7,000 by the year 2000.

Re-entry to the international community

Another area to which President Aylwin gave high priority was foreign relations. He embarked on a series of high-profile official visits to European countries, the United States, Japan, etc. and was well received everywhere as the first truly democratic President of Chile since the time of Salvador Allende twenty years earlier.[10]

[10] Pinochet rarely travelled outside Chile as President. In 1978 an official visit to the Philippines, then under the rule of Ferdinando Marcos, had been planned in order to achieve better relations in at least one part of the world, the Pacific Basin. The visit was cancelled by Marcos at the last moment probably due to

These visits were intended to re-establish Chile as a fully-fledged and respected member of the Western democratic family to which it had belonged for longer and with fewer non-democratic aberrations than most others. Aylwin also used his journeys as occasions for promoting Chile's vital export trade and to push forward projects for integrating its economy more closely with those of its trading partners.

Having suffered for so long from intermittent boycotts by Washington and a general reluctance by Western countries to maintain more than formal relationships with Chile at government level, Aylwin was naturally interested in joining various new regional and inter-American agreements which were emerging at the end of the 1980s. Chile's previous diplomatic isolation was dramatically reversed by the attendance of all the Latin American heads of state (except for Fidel Castro) at Aylwin's inauguration in March 1990. Senior representatives from many other parts of the world also attended the ceremony, although a number of them underlined the symbolism of the occasion by contriving not to have formal contacts with the outgoing President.

Chile's main practical interest lay in the free trade agreements which were playing an increasingly important part in the development of economic co-operation in the western hemisphere. The biggest trading group which the Aylwin government hoped to join was of course the North American Free Trade Area (NAFTA), embracing the United States, Canada and Mexico. Nine months after its inauguration, President George Bush, during a brief but significant visit to Santiago, stated publicly that Chile would be Washington's first choice to be included in NAFTA. The United States then proposed either that the NAFTA agreement should be extended to include Chile or that the United States and Chile should negotiate a separate and parallel bilateral agreement. This was a resounding vote of confidence by Washington, underlining both the success achieved by the new model Chilean economy and the rebirth of democracy there. (Mexico might not be able to pass the same test of democratic purity, but it has always been

---

pressure from the United States. This humiliating episode was one of the reasons for Pinochet's subsequent visceral distrust of the US government and unwillingness to risk such treatment again.

treated as a special case by the United States because of the two countries' physical proximity, with all which that implies.)

Once the long-standing obstacle of the Letelier case was removed, the Kennedy amendment was lifted by the US Congress and the Pentagon started to rebuild links with the Chilean armed forces. However, much of the goodwill generated by this sweeping away of the debris of the past was soon dissipated by an extraordinary incident known as 'the case of the poisoned grapes',[11] which led to the suspension of all Chilean fruit exports to the US market for a brief but critical period during 1989, and caused large financial losses to Chilean producers and exporters. The angry reactions of Chileans to this affair, which has never been properly cleared up, troubled relations with the United States for a very long time afterwards.

Worse in the long term was the fact that the United States failed to make good its promise to incorporate Chile into NAFTA (or negotiate a bilateral agreement with the same effect). A long succession of visitors from Washington, including Senators and Congressmen as well as representatives of the administration, went to Santiago confirming that negotiations to this end would be undertaken by the 'fast track' procedure, and thus not subject to step-by-step haggling in Congress. Despite these undertakings the US administration of President Bill Clinton has never delivered on its promises of reasonably quick progress towards a free trade agreement.

Meanwhile, in March 1991, Brazil, Argentina, Uruguay and Paraguay signed their own free trade agreement intended to lead in time to the creation of a common market in the Southern Cone known as Mercosur. Chile's foreign trade has in recent times been roughly evenly divided between the United States, the European Union, Latin America and Asia (including Japan).

[11] The US Food and Drug Agency claimed that, on inspection in the port of Philadelphia, three grapes (in one box, among a whole shipload) had been found to be poisoned with strychnine. The *bona fides* of this discovery and of the forensic test used were repeatedly challenged by Chile, where it was believed that the grapes had been planted either by agents of their US competitors or by political opponents wishing to exert economic pressure on Pinochet (or, in an extreme version, by the CIA for some similar purpose). Whatever the truth, it is hard to believe that three poisoned grapes could have been discovered by pure chance or that it was in Chile's interest to plant them.

While still hoping for a free trade agreement with the United States, whether through NAFTA or otherwise, the government therefore began to look for similar agreements within Latin America, with the EU, and even with the whole Asia/Pacific region. Chile in effect spread its net as widely as possible, seeking to consolidate existing markets and create new ones, but being prepared to join in wider political projects where that seemed necessary. The fruits of this broad approach to international trade and commercial relations were eventually seen in 1996 with formal associate membership of Mercosur; membership of the APEC agreement, including the United States and all the principal countries of the Pacific Basin; and an association agreement with the European Union.

The problem of Chile's long-term relationship with NAFTA was to some extent finessed by the Aylwin government by concluding separate bilateral free trade agreements with Mexico, and subsequently with Canada and with Colombia. This showed that Chile could make progress in consolidating its own international relations without waiting indefinitely for the United States and above all the US Congress to decide on their overall policy towards Latin America. When President Clinton renewed his invitation to Chile to become the first country in South America to join NAFTA (notwithstanding the contradiction in terms), Chile could afford to be a little more relaxed in the knowledge that its trading interests were, so far as possible, already protected by a range of bilateral agreements. The most important of these is probably Mercosur which will provide Chile with a large market for industrial products and with a field for investment of capital and entrepreneurial skill outside her own frontiers, but more readily accessible than those of NAFTA.

All the same, the democratic government which in 1990 had received such a warm welcome from the United States and other democracies was irritated by not being admitted as a full member of any of the clubs it had applied to join. At the end of Patricio Aylwin's Presidency in March 1994, the negotiations with Mercosur and the EU were still in progress. For a country which still maintained a low external tariff, a very open attitude towards foreign participation in its markets and strong incentives to foreign investment, the practical significance of tariff reductions and other steps towards free trade was not great. The real need was to enjoy the status of belonging fully to the best clubs and not to be excluded from any potentially beneficial trading agreements.

Patricio Aylwin could show a more impressive record of success in handling relations with his immediate neighbours. As always the most critical was with Argentina, and the Treaty of Peace and Friendship signed by the military regime in 1984 was soon given greater substance by the *Concertación* government. No less than twenty-four border problems were identified in 1991 by Presidents Menem and Aylwin as requiring solutions, and of these twenty-two had been settled by negotiation by 1994.[12] (The last of all, the delimitation of the border on the southern ice-cap, Campo de Hielo Sur, is yet to be concluded.) Other advances were made towards integrating the economies of Argentina and Chile, in particular through agreements for the construction of oil and gas pipelines across the border and other joint infrastructure developments. Several large projects of this kind began in the 1990s mainly in consequence of the strong impulse given to them by Aylwin's administration. Progress was also made in easing relations with Peru and Bolivia, but no final solution was reached with either. In particular, Chile remained unwilling to make any concession of sovereignty in response to the Bolivian demand for access to the sea although Bolivia was offered various arrangements for assured routes across Chilean territory and dedicated port facilities through which it could import and export its goods freely.

Transition: fact or façade

Some observers looking at Chile from a distance in the period between Pinochet's defeat in the plebiscite of 1988 and the end of Aylwin's mandate in 1994 suggested that the new Chilean democracy was little better than a facade. They found difficulty understanding that Pinochet had only been voted out of the Presidency but not defeated by a popular revolt or anything like

[12] These problems were mostly practical ones involving the siting, adjustment or replacement of boundary markers at various points and similar matters. There was only one, the ownership of a remote slice of territory straddling the border in the extreme south, the Laguna del Desierto, which had to be referred to an arbitration tribunal. The tribunal eventually decided in Argentina's favour and Chile accepted it.

it. Few could appreciate how a military dictator could leave the office of head of state (however reluctantly) but remain Commander-in-Chief of the Army unless he still held the reins of power and was governing the country indirectly through a puppet President. At the very least, they thought that Pinochet was in some way sharing power with his successor. Many Chileans, including some prominent Christian Democrats, also thought that the transformation achieved by 1995 was at best incomplete.[13]

In his state of the nation address at the end of his Presidency, Patricio Aylwin gave his own verdict:

> 'Those who imagine, because General Pinochet is still Commander-in Chief of the Army, that Chile has a system of 'shared power' or 'cohabitation' understand nothing about what actually happened. It is quite clear that, from the very day of the first democratic government following after the dictatorship, political power resided in the constitutional organs appropriate to all democracies; the President of the Republic and the National Congress, freely elected by the people, subject to the proper powers of the judiciary and limitations which apply in any constitutional regime. The armed forces, including the Commander-in-Chief of the Army, are obedient to and subordinate to the Head of State; that is in accordance with the constitutional rules in force and that is what occurred.'

In later accounts of the process of transition up to 1995, Aylwin agreed that Chilean democracy would be less than perfect until the Constitution could be amended to eliminate what were described as the *enclaves autoritarios* in the Constitution, to which the *Concertación* had objected since its formation. However, he believed that these deficiencies did not threaten the continuation of the new democracy but merely affected its purity. He was entirely confident that Chile's reborn democracy had returned to stay.[14]

[13] Senator Andres Zaldivar, an old colleague of President Aylwin who had been Minister of Finance under Eduardo Frei in the 1960s, expounded this view in a book *La Transicion Inconclusa* arguing that the democratic system would continue to be highly vulnerable until the 1980 Constitution, and the electoral law, were made fully democratic.

[14] Conversation between the author and former President Aylwin (Santiago, 12 March 1997) and published speeches, e.g. at the Universidad de Guadalajara, Mexico, 29 November 1996.

Others have expressed different and less categorical opinions but few would question that the evident success of the transitional process was due as much to the tact and skill of the new President in handling relations with Pinochet as to the unsupported force of constitutional principle. Whatever the balance struck, it is undeniable that the transition was a great success and that the people who managed it, first and foremost President Aylwin and his closest collaborators in the *Concertación* government, have earned an honourable place in Chilean history. Even in 1987, barely three years before he took office, there were few people in Chile or outside it who predicted that the military regime, having survived all the pressures of the previous fourteen years, would hand over power peacefully in accordance with the constitution it had devised.

As leader of the *Concertación* from its original formation in February 1988, Patricio Aylwin had to speak and act as representative of a range of political opinion and not only as President of the Christian Democratic Party. He could not present himself in the traditional manner of Chilean Presidents, as a figure of authority, which in any case was not his natural style. Some Chileans had supported the authoritarian methods used by Pinochet not out of political preference but simply because they favoured decisive government (provided it was not applied to their disadvantage). They tended to be critical of Aylwin's less decisive and more subtle style. However, by the end of his Presidency in 1994 many of those critics had come to realise that he had performed the role which had fallen to him better than any of the other leaders of the *Concertación* could have done. He had achieved more to consolidate the new democracy than his critics had expected and probably as much as history will judge to have been possible.

12

END OF AN ERA

The elections of 1993

By the middle of Aylwin's term in 1992, manoeuvring for the succession had inevitably begun. Eduardo Frei Ruiz-Tagle had established himself as the Christian Democrat candidate for the leadership of the *Concertación* and was the natural front-runner because of the dominant position of his party, which had averaged 27 per cent of the popular vote in all elections in the 1990s. Perhaps even more significantly, Frei was helped by the appeal of his name. He was a businessman who had not played any notable political role during the military regime, but – when the right moment arrived in the late 1980s – took over his family's claim to the leadership of their party from his sister Carmen, who was originally thought more interested in assuming their father's mantle.

Eduardo Frei II was at first opposed for the leadership of the *Concertación* by a more experienced and charismatic political figure. This was Ricardo Lagos, a long-established and highly articulate member of the Socialist Party. Although originally a Radical, Lagos had come to prominence as a Socialist in the mid-1980s not only because of his political skill but also by virtue of having been arrested and harassed by the regime in those days. He also drew strength from having founded a new left-wing umbrella party, the *Partido por la Democrácia* (PPD) to unite left-wing opposition to the regime and contest the elections in 1989 and thereafter joined the Aylwin government as Minister of Education. However, Lagos was not a Christian Democrat and some of that party and its potential voters regarded him as too close to the extreme Left to be a candidate for the *Concertación.* He finally accepted that it was of overriding importance to preserve unity and agreed to support Eduardo Frei's candidature for the Presidency in 1993.

The Right was still in disarray, mainly due to the continued split between the RN and the UDI. Eventually they patched up their differences and agreed to support a single candidate, who was also the bearer of a great political name: Arturo Alessandri, the nephew of Jorge Alessandri, President in the 1950s and early '60s and grandson of another former President, Arturo Alessandri, the 'Lion of Tarapacá'. The fact that both the Centre-Left and the Right were led by successors of such renowned political dynasties demonstrates the ingrained habit (possibly a conscious preference) of Chileans to look for a man who is more than a party politician to elect as President.

The outcome of the presidential election in 1993 was a resounding victory for Eduardo Frei, who won with a majority of 58 per cent (the highest percentage achieved by any President since 1931). Arturo Alessandri came second with about 25 per cent. A poor third place went to another right-of-centre candidate, José Piñera, who won only 6.2 per cent of the vote – far less than the third contender had achieved in 1989.[1] The extreme Left was again left far behind.

Eduardo Frei's stunning electoral success confirmed the strength of the *Concertación* which had successfully put aside its internal strains and proved itself more solid than any of the political coalitions which had existed in Chile within living memory. This is well illustrated by the fact that in the elections of 1989 and 1993 and the intervening municipal elections in 1992, the *Concertación* consistently won more than 55 per cent of the popular vote – made up approximately of 27 per cent for the Christian Democrats and 17 per cent for the Socialist Parties. It seemed that the Chilean electorate had been at least temporarily immunised against extremist politics of both the Left and the Right. At the same time, the RN and the UDI combined were able to muster about a third of the votes – more or less the same proportion as parties of the Right have usually had in recent times.

In the aftermath of the collapse of communist governments and of communism as a political ideology in Europe, the Communist Party of Chile, for all its past popularity, completely failed

[1] This was ironic since the independent candidate in 1989 had been the millionaire businessman, 'Fra Fra' Errázuriz, who had no record of public service of any kind, while Piñera had been one of the outstanding economic reformers during the last ten years of the military regime. Apparently Piñera's impressive record counted for little with the electorate as compared with the populist appeal of Errázuriz.

to regain anything like the support it had enjoyed before 1973. The new political structure left the Communists marginalised and with little or no prospect of finding a way back into the mainstream.

The economic foundation for a stable democracy

Another even more powerful reason for the Chile's stability in the 1990s is the fact that the economy has gone from strength

SELECTED ECONOMIC INDICATORS, 1981-1996

	1981	*1982*	*1984*	*1986*	*1988*	*1990*	*1992*	*1994*	*1996*
Population (million)	11.3	11.5	11.9	12.3	12.8	13.1	13.5	14.0	14.4
GDP ($ billion)	32.6	24.3	19.2	17.7	24.2	30.4	42.7	52.2	71.9
GDP growth (%)	5.5	−14.1	6.3	5.6	7.3	3.3	11.0	4.2	7.2
GDP per head (US $)	2,880	2,110	1,610	1,440	1,890	2,320	3,160	3,730	4,990
Consumer price inflation (annual average %)	19.7	9.9	19.9	19.5	14.7	26.0	15.4	11.4	7.4
Unemployment (%)	15.6	25.5	24.7	10.8	8.3	5.7	6.2	6.7	6.5
Exports f.o.b. ($ billion)	3.8	3.7	3.7	4.2	7.1	8.4	10.0	11.6	15.5
Imports f.o.b. ($ billion)	−6.5	−3.6	−3.3	−3.1	−4.8	−7.0	−9.2	−10.9	−16.6
Foreign debt ($ billion)	15.7	17.3	19.7	21.1	19.6	19.2	19.1	24.7	27.3
Foreign debt (% of GDP)	48.0	71.1	102.7	119.3	81.1	63.2	44.8	47.4	38.0
Gross national savings ratio (%)	8.2	1.8	2.6	12.2	21.8	24.5	25.2	25.5	23.3

Source: Banco Central de Chile and Instituto Nacional de Estadisticas.

to strength over a period of more than ten years and at the time of writing there is no sign of it weakening. The rate of annual GDP growth in the 1990s has averaged 7 per cent – about twice the average rate achieved in the 1960s. The accompanying table shows the trend of some of the key macro-economic indicators for 1981-96. In addition to the growth of GDP, there have been strong improvements in exports, savings and investment. At the same time, unemployment, inflation and debt (as a proportion of GDP) have been falling.

However, there are still serious problems facing the country. The infrastructure of roads, railways, ports and airports needs much more investment – more, as in other parts of the world, than the public sector has been able to provide, even with the benefit of a rapidly growing economy. Agriculture, particularly production of wheat and livestock, faces growing international competition, lower prices and rising costs. The problem of providing adequate health and public education remains intractable: private health insurance schemes finance first-class facilities for the minority which can pay for them, but the rest who cannot must rely on run-down public hospitals and clinics where little improvement is noticeable, despite the extra funding provided by the elected governments since 1990. Education presents similar dilemmas: the literacy rate is high and basic educational levels are comparable to those in much richer countries, but maintaining a successful economy in the 1990s and beyond will call for more people educated to higher standards and the state system apparently cannot keep up with the demand.

The fundamental social and political problem is to strike the right balance between pursuing the economic efficiency needed to produce the highest possible rate of growth and meeting the social need, backed by increasing popular demand, to ensure that the benefits of growth are fairly shared. Although in the 1990s there has been real improvement for poorer Chileans in the form of more jobs and better pay, their aspirations are still decades away from being satisfied. The poor may be somewhat less poor, but the rich are still taking far larger shares of the available wealth. The uncomfortable fact is that millions of Chileans still live in poverty and the contrast between the affluent lifestyle of the best parts of Santiago and the neighbouring shanty towns is stark. This is one of the principal subjects of political debate both within the *Concertación* and between the *Concertación* and the opposition. The problem is familiar to people in developed countries, but it is striking that it should be debated in very similar terms in a country like Chile which is still thought by many to belong to the developing world.

Probably the most obvious difference between the present condition of Chile and the state of affairs in developed Western countries is the fact that there is almost no welfare system for the millions still living outside the market economy or at its margins. According to the exponents of free market, or neo-liberal, economics the only remedy for this problem is more of the same treatment. They argue that only greater efficiency and more determined exploitation of Chile's comparative advantages can create the wealth needed, and suggest that greater overall prosperity will bring its own solution. At present, voices which argue for any alternative policy are surprisingly few in Chile – as in the British Labour Party or the Democratic Party in the United States. Ideas about redistribution of wealth, expanding the public sector or obliging the private sector to concentrate more on its social responsibilities are considered heretical. It seems that all political leaders are now neo-liberals and only concerned to mitigate the harsher effects of free market economics. Advocates of fundamentally different policies are rarely heard.

Constitutional reforms

Eduardo Frei, though often accused of ineffectiveness or drift in economic and social matters, has certainly made strong efforts to push through the constitutional reforms for which the *Concertación* has pressed since its formation. The *enclaves autoritarios*, authoritarian enclaves, which he was still seeking to remove in 1997 were the nine designated senators who have until now joined with the Right in the Senate to oppose almost all changes to the Pinochet legacy; the inability of the President to replace the Commanders-in-Chief; and the bi–nomial electoral system with its built-in bias in favour of minority parties. These constitutional changes all require more than simple majorities in Congress for approval and it has never yet been possible to achieve that degree of support in the face of opposition from the Right and the designated senators.

President Frei put these key reforms at the head of his agenda yet again, and was expected to have a better chance of success in the second half of his Presidency. This was because some of the occupants of the non-elected seats in the Senate would retire and have to be replaced by 1998, and if the blocking group of designated senators was not removed before then by agreement, Frei himself would be able to influence the choice of their successors. He could, in effect, use this objectionable feature of the 1980 Constitution as the method of changing it.[2]

Relations between the civil and military establishments and personal relations between the President and General Pinochet have been smoother than they were during the Aylwin administration. The most difficult and protracted crisis arose when the two former DINA commanders, Contreras and Espinosa, who had been convicted and sentenced to imprisonment for their part in the assassination of Letelier (even if after a twenty-year delay) refused to surrender to the authorities. Espinosa was soon imprisoned but Contreras, with active cooperation from the Navy as well as the Army, used various excuses to avoid imprisonment for many months. Eventually, however, he was surrendered and began to serve his sentence in a specially constructed prison.

By 1997, there was no longer any great pressure on Pinochet to step down as Commander-in-Chief before the end of his 'constitutional' term of office in March 1998. As the old soldier aged, he showed slightly more inclination to fade away and had become mainly concerned to do so with honour and at a moment of his own choosing. Strange though this may seem to many people outside Chile, he was well respected not only by the large minority who supported him in the plebiscite in 1988 but also by a number of others who have come to admire the contribution which he made to the rebuilding of their country's economy. Many still abominate him, but the majority of Chileans have a certain respect for his achievements.

On 10 March 1998, General Pinochet formally handed over command of the Army to General Ricardo Izurieta[3] at an ostentatious and emotive military parade but against a background of furious protest from all his unreconciled enemies. The next day

[2] In fact, the block of newly designated senators still seemed to be sufficiently strong at the beginning of 1998 to prevent constitutional amendments getting through the Senate.

[3] Izurieta was not Pinochet's first choice to succeed him as Commander-in-Chief, but was selected by President Frei as an officer who had no particular involvement in the 1973 coup or its aftermath.

he took his seat as a Senator for life – as allowed by the Constitution for former Presidents of the Republic – and thereby became, in effect, permanently immune from prosecution. The manner of his departure and the fact that the Minister of Defence resigned in the process, underlined yet again that there were still *enclaves autoritarios* in the Chilean political system.

Pinochet and his unconditional supporters still argued that the coup of 1973 had been entirely justified by the collapse of the democratic system. Whatever the judgement of history on this, or on the methods employed thereafter, Pinochet could claim with justice that the socio-economic model created by the military government (and consolidated by its successors) had proved its success and was indeed being adopted even by formerly socialist countries. Commenting on whether this could have been achieved in Chile under a democratic government, he said that he would 'leave that to the judgement of historians and specialists', but was proud to have led a government which brought in these reforms in a small country like Chile before they were adopted in the rest of the world. He also acknowledged that none of them could have succeeded without the sacrifice and efforts of the ordinary people of Chile.

International and regional links

On first assuming the Presidency, Eduardo Frei said that Chile's primary concern in international relations would be to focus on its own region and the development of political and economic cooperation in the Americas. This has been the field in which his administration has shown most energy and had most success. As already noted, in 1996 Chile achieved an association agreement with Mercosur and a Free Trade Agreement with Canada, and signed a framework agreement with the European Union. These were major steps forward in stabilising some of the main export markets and therefore assuring the momentum of economic growth. The United States market, which took some 14 per cent of Chilean exports in 1995, remains outside the system of trade agreements built up since 1990. However this is of less importance to Chile now than in former times and relations with immediate neighbours in the Southern Cone are probably more important. The Frei administration has pursued policies of integration with neighbouring countries – particularly with Argentina – as one means to this end. Without making any territorial concessions, these policies include practical arrangements favouring Brazilian and Bolivian access to ports on the Pacific (which would of course be in Chile's interest as well). The proposal for a major new port at Mejillones in Antofagasta province could provide a solution for Bolivian ambitions to regain access to the Pacific, although it sometimes appears that both Peru and Bolivia have an interest in keeping their claims in existence for their own internal political reasons.

Investment by the private sector is also seen in Chile as an attractive form of 'integration' with its neighbours. In the 1990s there have been large outflows of capital to all the Southern Cone countries and to Brazil; and if this continues it is likely to have important effects on Chile's foreign policy. Since 1990 Chilean companies have invested more than $10 billion in the Southern Cone, more than 60 per cent going to Argentina. Normally the motives are purely commercial (for example, Chilean industrial companies and banks seeking to broaden their operating or manufacturing base within their immediate region), but there are also ambitious schemes for joint venture infrastructure projects. These projects are often presented as steps towards creating a fully integrated single economy in Latin America, but it is unlikely that this is genuinely seen by any of the countries concerned as either practical or desirable. Western Europe is far further along this road than Latin America, where feelings of national identity and separateness remain very strong – not least in Chile.

Neither the twentieth century's two world wars nor the Cold War from the 1940s to the end of the 1980s had anything like the same impact in Latin America as in Europe and other continents. Chileans, in spite of having been ideologically divided in the Cold War epoch, have never felt the same pressing need to unite with neighbours to resist a common enemy as did European countries. National sentiment, at times verging on xenophobia, remains strong throughout Latin America. Chilean nationalism, particularly when brought face to face with its mirror-image across its borders or indeed with 'Yankee imperialism', is certainly not ready to embrace the idea of political federation let alone fusion with other nation-states.[4]

[4] This seems to be another point of similarity between Chile and Britain. Are

Towards the millennium

If most of the constitutional reforms which President Eduardo Frei has made a prime objective have been achieved by the end of his term of office in the year 2000, the third democratically-elected President of the post-Pinochet era will inherit an established and truly democratic constitution and Chile will have fully resumed its long tradition of constitutional governments operating under the rule of law. Its democratic record has had fewer interruptions in more than 160 years of independence than most Latin American and many West European countries – East European, Asian and African countries are not even in the same league.[5]

As the next presidential election approaches, there will be a prolonged struggle inside the *Concertación* for nomination as the presidential candidate in 1999. In 1997 there were already several hats in the ring and no doubt more will appear. Much the most popular in public opinion polls was Ricardo Lagos, leader of the PPD and a highly successful Minister of Public Works in the Frei administration. As a member of the Socialist Party, Lagos is still distrusted by people on the political Right, but more for his old associations than for his record in office under Aylwin and Frei. To all appearances he was a pragmatic social democrat, but whether he would succeed in winning sufficient support among the Christian Democrats, still the majority party inside the *Concertación*, remained to be seen. If the Christian Democrats insist on nominating one of their own number to stand in 1999 for the *Concertación*, there will certainly be a period of great strain. It would seem most unwise to risk the disintegration of a political coalition which has won power honourably and exercised it with

---

the Chileans 'the British of South America' because they, like the British, are more isolated from the continent to which they logically seem to belong and thus have an unusually strong sense of national identity and feel the need to pursue their destiny independently of others?

5 Western liberals are on shaky ground in criticising the imperfections of the 1980 Chilean Constitution. For example, those critics in Britain who question the purity of this Constitution on the grounds that there is a block of nine 'designated senators' who can obstruct constitutional and other reform must agree that the British House of Lords, entirely unelected and with a much higher number of designated 'life peers', is much less pure when considered in democratic terms.

some success for ten years. Preserving a winning combination ought to be first objective of the politicians involved, but it is not unknown for this advantage to be thrown away at critical moments in politics.

In any event the parties of the Right would again be looking for a candidate of their own and might succeed in uniting behind a charismatic leader.[6] However, the Right has little hope of success in a presidential election unless it can appeal to a wider section of the population than the traditional one-third which has voted for it. Its best hope might well be the possibility that the Christian Democrats would at some stage split into a right and a left wing and that the former would prefer to form a new electoral coalition with moderate parties on the political right than to continue in any kind of alliance with the Socialists.

The most likely prospect for Chile at the beginning of the twenty-first century is 'more of the same'. If economic growth continues with the same momentum for the rest of the 1990s, this is by no means a bad outlook. The total government expenditure on public services and welfare could continue to increase steadily and still remain at the level of 20-22 per cent of GDP at which it has been running since 1989. The pursuit of 'growth with equity' could continue slowly and steadily for many more years. And this might be preferable to any attempt to accelerate improvement or social change by more radical means, which would risk damaging the country's new-found economic health. Having survived the economic storms and bitter ideological conflicts of the last part of the twentieth century, Chile can move ahead in calmer waters into the twenty-first. The greatest political risk would be a renewed outbreak of confrontational politics.

Will it be different this time?

'Given Latin America's history, it is a brave – or foolish – person who attempts to predict its future. Too often foreigners (and Latin

[6] Neither the RN nor the UDI leaders who were in office in 1997 seemed likely to fit this bill. One favoured outsider in the race was the successful *alcalde* of Las Condes (a prosperous part of Santiago), Joaquin Lavín, who was a strong force in the UDI and might conceivably be accepted by the RN. However, even if the two parties unite wholeheartedly, they have no serious chance of winning a presidential election without mobilising other support.

Americans themselves) have believed that stability and prosperity lie around the corner. Too often these hopes have been dashed as yet another boom turned to bust.'

— *The Economist*, 9 December 1995

There are good reasons to think that for Chile it will be different this time. The steady growth of the late 1980s and the 1990s has not been based simply on high commodity prices for minerals and other primary products. Some commodities which Chile exports (copper, fishmeal, fruit, wood pulp etc.) have had low prices for parts of this period. There has not been a boom of the traditional kind and growth has been based on more durable foundations. The pattern of Chile's exports is no longer dominated by minerals but is widely diversified, as are its export markets.

As a result of the long process of economic reconstruction and modernisation started by the Chicago Boys in the 1970s, the Chile of the 1990s also has most of the necessary ingredients for financial stability: high savings, strong and productive investment and an efficient financial sector. These structural changes were not of course achieved at the first attempt but only after the economic collapse of 1982/83, and the pragmatic application of free market ideas thereafter. General Pinochet and his successive Ministers of Finance must have the main credit, but the *Concertación* governments of the 1990s have also played an important part in maintaining and refining successful policies and consolidating the national economic performance on that basis.[7]

Is this beguiling picture of political and economic stability and greater prosperity for all too good to be true? The vision could be spoilt by many factors outside the control of a small country far from the rest of the world but heavily dependent on it. As so often in the past, any world recession would hit Chile harder than most because of its heavy dependence on exports. In any case, the globalisation of the world economy must certainly increase the vulnerability of the whole world to economic upheaval in any one part. Threats of this sort might overwhelm almost any national economy, but Chileans can feel that these risks are similar

[7] For an extended discussion of this question, see Patricio Meller's *Un Siglo de Economía Política Chilena* (Editorial Andres Bello, Santiago, 1997), particularly chapter 4.

to those acts of God – earthquake, volcanic eruptions, droughts and floods – which they have so often experienced over the centuries.

Apart from earthquakes or global economic upheavals, there are self-generated threats which can be countered or at least mitigated by wise policy. Probably the weakest aspect of the civilian governments of the 1990s (as of the military governments that preceded them), has been their failure to make a decisive impact in reducing the number of people living on the margins of the Chilean economy. Even if, as the *Concertación* leadership claims, such marginalised people are much less numerous in the second half of the 1990s than they were at the beginning, this problem continues to be the most serious facing the country. Whatever political group is in power in the year 2000, this will be at the top of its agenda.

The other problem which must have high priority is how to improve the quality of education available to the bulk of the population, particularly in the skills which will be needed to build new technology-based industries in the coming years. This same problem faces many much more developed countries and it is a sign of Chile's new status that it should also be seen as one of the country's most serious problems. Basic literacy is high (95 per cent in 1992, compared with 99 per cent in Britain and 87 per cent in Mexico) and the Chilean élite are highly educated. But secondary, vocational and technical education is not yet of a sufficient standard to release all the talents available. A strong drive to raise educational standards and spread them more widely is vitally important not only to enable the national economy to compete more effectively but also to enable many more of the Chilean people to earn a better living by their own work. Without a major effort to release the full potential of individuals, Chile will continue to be over-dependent on the minerals and other primary products which have been its economic mainstay for most of its history. The wealth generated by those industries was sufficient to support a small landowning élite in the eighteenth and nineteenth centuries. After 1880, the bonanza based on nitrates enabled a growing commercial and professional middle class also to enjoy a relatively high standard of living. But these natural resources alone have not been and never can be enough to provide an acceptable standard of living for all the Chilean people, and few of them have hitherto had the necessary level of education to earn it.

In the last two decades of the nineteenth century, Chile had the opportunity to build a broadly-based and prosperous democracy. The nitrate wealth which came under its control then could have been used differently (it is only fair to add that almost no other country would have done much better at that time). The opportunity was allowed to slip and the will to build up the country as a whole was overlaid by sectional and personal interests in the early part of the twentieth century. Almost a hundred years later, a similar opportunity exists. Chile has not discovered a new source of tangible wealth such as sodium nitrate, but its economy is one of the best-organised and most efficient in Latin America and among the top twenty or so in the world. Barring acts of God and global recessions, this small country, even if still unevenly developed, will in future face the problems of other developed countries rather than those of the underdeveloped world from which it has emerged.

The talk now is that by the year 2005 Chile could reach the same level of prosperity as Southern European countries. It is entirely feasible, and it could aspire to that while still maintaining stability. Some of its business leaders and economists believe that the country's destiny is to become a Latin American version of the Asian 'tiger economies' such as Singapore, Taiwan or even South Korea, which would place it high in the international league tables (as measured by the usual economic indicators). However, others might be more inclined to agree with the great majority of Chileans themselves in rejecting this barren statistical paradise.

In some ways Chileans are more northern in spirit than Latin. Their hispanic instincts are not primarily Andalusian but closer to the Basque and to the spirit of Galicia in north-western Spain. They also have about them something of the English (and the Scots and the Irish) but as much or more of the German, the French, the Italian and the southern Slav. But despite all these ethnic additives, the Chilean people are not by nature deeply imbued with the European work ethic, let alone with North American 'consumerism', or inclined to measure happiness with a material yardstick. Their pursuit of worldly wealth will never be as single-minded as it has become on the opposite side of the Pacific

Ocean. Chileans will always attach as much importance to football, to dancing their *cuecas*, to *vino tinto* and *empanadas*, to beaches and the sea, to horses and to love in all its shapes and forms. Human beings, and Chileans as much as any, need these things in order to be happy. None of us can live on gross GDP per head and the weighted trade index.

Through other eyes

One of the first of northern Europeans to see Chile was the English pirate (or merchant venturer in his own view), Sir Richard Hawkins. On leaving Chilean waters he wrote:

> 'We shaped our course for Arica, and left the kingdoms of Chily, one of the best countries that the sun shineth on: for it is of a temperate climate, and abounding in all things necessarie for the use of man, with infinite rich Mynes of Gold, Copper, and sundry other mettals. The poorest houses in it, by report of their inhabitants, have of their own store, Bread, Wine, Flesh and Fruit; which is so plentifull that of their supperfluitie they supplie other parts: sundrie kinds of cattell; as Horses, Goates, and Oxen brought thither by the Spaniards, are found in heards of thousands, wilde and without owner.'[8]

Four hundred years later a more ironic and pessimistic picture is presented to us by a Chilean poet, Nicanor Parra, who had fallen out of love with his own country:

> 'It is not true that Chile is bordered by the Andes, by the Saltpeter Desert, by the Pacific Ocean: its just the opposite. It's the Andes that are bordered by Chile, it's the Pacific that reaches the rim of Aconcagua. It's the two oceans that break the monotony of the south country into a thousand pieces.'[9]

Nicanor Parra expresses the scepticism of a native Chilean who felt that his country was disintegrating under a military dictatorship

[8] 'The Observations of Sir Richard Hawkins, Knight, in his voyage into the South Sea, AD 1593' (printed in *Purchas his Pilgrimes* by Samuel Purchas, BD, vol. XVII, chapter XI, Hakluyt Society).

[9] Nicanor Parra, 'The Borders of Chile' quoted in that author's bilingual volume *Emergency Poems*, (Marion Boyars, London, 1977).

and had almost lost its identity. His bitter paradoxes are typical of the feelings of many Chilean intellectuals alienated and often exiled in those unhappy years. Now even home-grown sceptics have no real grounds for pessimism about the future of their country. It is just the opposite. There are good reasons not just to hope for better things for Chile in the twenty-first century but also to expect them.

The Colombian writer, Gabriel García Márquez, wiser perhaps than either the Englishman or the Chilean, goes to the heart of the matter:

> Chileans are very much like their country in a certain way. They are the most pleasant people on the continent, they like being alive and they know how to live in the best way possible and even a little more. But they have a dangerous tendency towards skepticism and intellectual speculation. A Chilean once told me on a Monday that no Chilean believes tomorrow is Tuesday, and he didn't believe it either. Still even with that deep-seated incredulity, or thanks to it perhaps, the Chileans have attained a degree of natural civilization, a political maturity, and a level of culture that set them apart from the rest of the region.[10]

[10] Gabriel García Márquez, 'The Death of Salvador Allende', article in *Harper's*, March 1974.

SOURCES AND FURTHER READING

The most comprehensive sources for students of Chile are the *Handbook of Latin American Studies* edited by the Hispanic Division of the Library of Congress in the United States, and the *Fichero Bibliográfico* published in the journal *Historia*, by the Universidad Católica of Santiago. For more general purposes, there is an excellent selected bibliography in the volume on Chile in the World Bibliographical Series by Harold Blakemore (Oxford, 1988). *Chile since Independence*, edited by Leslie Bethell (Cambridge, 1993), contains important and wide-ranging bibliographical essays by each of the contributing British and United States historians (Simon Collier, Harold Blakemore, Paul Drake and Alan Angell).

The following lists include the principal published sources, both in English and Spanish, used for this book. Since it is intended primarily for anglophone readers, there is a strong predominance of books which are available in English. However, the classics of Chilean historiography such as the monumental *Historia de Chile desde la Prehistoria hasta 1891* in 20 volumes by Francisco Antonio Encina, and Diego Barros Arana's *Historia General de Chile* in 16 volumes, are also included with a selection of other books by modern Chilean historians which are only available in Spanish.

This book does not pretend to offer any original research about the history of Chile. In the chapters covering the years up to 1980, it relies entirely on secondary sources and particularly on the recent published work of recognised Chilean and other historians. Unless otherwise stated, the facts and figures quoted are drawn from *Chile since Independence*, part of the *Cambridge History of Latin America*; *A History of Chile, 1808-1994* by Simon Collier and William A. Sater; *Un Siglo de Economía Política Chilena* by Patricio Meller; and *Chile: The Legacy of Hispanic Capitalism* by Brian Loveman.

Among unpublished sources, I have drawn upon a series of interviews with contemporary politicians, writers and business leaders and an important collection of video-taped discussions involving many of the civilian economic advisers and ministers who served in the governments of the Pinochet period between 1973 and 1989. These videos were kindly made available to me by Sr Pablo Baraona, Rector of the Universidad Finis Terrae, who was responsible for creating this archive. My own diaries and my wife's letters to members of our family written from Santiago between 1982 and 1987 have also reminded me of events in those years.

The archives of *El Mercurio* in Santiago and of Latin American Newsletters in London have been particularly valuable for the period 1987-97. The Foreign and Commonwealth Office allowed me to re-read my own formal despatches covering the period 1982-7. The book might have been better, and of more interest to historians, if I had also been allowed to refresh my memory of the much more detailed reports I sent back in those years in several hundreds of telegrams and informal letters. Unfortunately this is still prevented by the 30-year rule.

General History

Barros Araña, Diego, *Historia General de Chile*, 16 vols (Santiago, 1884-1902).

Bethell, Leslie, ed., *Chile since Independence* (Cambridge, 1993).

Bizzarro, Salvatore, *Historical Dictionary of Chile* (1972).

Clissold, Stephen, *Chilean Scrapbook* (London, 1952).

Collier, Simon, and William F. Sater, *A History of Chile, 1808-1994* (Cambridge, 1996).

Encina, Francisco Antonio, *Historia de Chile desde la Prehistoria hasta 1891*, 20 vols (Santiago, 1942-52).

——— and Leopoldo Castedo, *Resumen de la Historia de Chile, 1535-1925*, 4 vols (Santiago, 1954-82).

Galdames, Luis, *A History of Chile*, trans. Isaac Cox (Chapel Hill, NC, 1941).

Loveman, Brian, *Chile, The Legacy of Hispanic Capitalism* (New York, 1979; 2nd edn 1988).

Vial, Gonzalo, *Historia de Chile* (Santiago, 1981).

Geography, Anthropology and Travel Guides

Blakemore, Harold, and Clifford T. Smith, eds., *Latin America: Geographical Perspectives* (London, 1983).

Edwards, Águstín, *My Native Land* (London, 1928).

Faron, Louis C., *The Mapuche Indians of Chile* (New York, 1968).

Instituto Geográfico Militar, Ministerio de Defensa Nacional, *Atlas de la República de Chile* (Santiago, 1970).

Maitland, Francis J.G., *Chile, Its Land and People: The history, natural features and industrial resources of a great South American Republic* (London, 1914).

Martinic, Mateo, *Historia del Estrecho de Magallanes* (Santiago, 1977).

Merrill, Andrea T., ed., *Chile: A Country Study* (Washington, DC, 1982).

Munro, George, *Carretera Austral. Integración de Chile* (Santiago, 1982).

Nurse, Charlie, and Ben Box, eds, *Chile Handbook* (Bath, England, annual).

Passos, John dos, *Easter Island: Island of Enigmas* (New York, 1971).
Pinochet de la Barra, Oscar, *La Antártica Chilena* (Santiago, 1976).
Rudolph, William E., *Vanishing Trails of Atacama* (New York, 1963).
Shipton, Eric, *Tierra del Fuego: The Fatal Lodestone* (London, 1973).
Steward, Julian H., and Louis C. Faron, *Native Peoples of South America* (New York, 1959).
Subercaseaux, Benjamin, *Chile: A Geographic Extravaganza*, trans. Angel Flores (New York, 1971).
Turismo y Communicaciones S.A., *Guia Turística de Chile* (Santiago, annual).

Political History to 1964

Alexander, Robert J., *Arturo Alessandri*, 2 vols (Ann Arbor, MI, 1977).
Bañados Espinosa, J., *Balmaceda. Su Gobierno y la Revolución de 1891* (Paris, 1894).
Bengoa, José, *Historia del Pueblo Mapuche* (Santiago, 1985).
Bauer, Arnold J., *Chilean Rural Society from the Spanish Conquest to 1930* (Cambridge, 1975).
Blakemore, Harold, *British Nitrates and Chilean Politics: Balmaceda and North, 1886-1896* (London, 1974).
Caldera, Rafael, *Andrés Bello: Philosopher, poet, philologist, educator, legislator, statesman* (London, 1977).
Clissold, Stephen, *Bernardo O'Higgins and the Independence of Chile* (London, 1968).
Collier, Simon, *Ideas and Politics of Chilean Independence, 1808-1833* (Cambridge, 1967).
Donoso, Ricardo, *Las Ideas Políticas en Chile* (Buenos Aires, 1975).
Drake, Paul W., *Socialism and Populism in Chile, 1932-1952* (Urbana, IL, 1978).
Guevara, Tomás, *Historia de la Civilización de la Araucania*, 3 vols (Santiago, 1900-2).
Kinsbruner, Jay, *Diego Portales: Interpretative Essays on the Man and his Times* (The Hague, 1967).
Montero, René, *La Verdad sobre Ibañez* (Santiago, 1953).
Pinto Lagarrigue, Fernando, *Crónica Política del Siglo XX* (Santiago, 1970).
Nunn, Frederick, *Chilean Politics, 1920-1931: The Honorable Mission of the Armed Forces* (Albuquerque, NM, 1970).
Pocock, H.R.S., *The Conquest of Chile* (New York, 1967).
Villalobos, Sergio, *Portales. Una Falsificación Histórica* (Santiago, 1989).

Political History since 1964

Alexander, Robert J., *The Tragedy of Chile* (Westport, CT, 1978).

Allende, Salvador, *Chile's Road to Socialism* (London, 1973).

Amnesty International, Reports on Chile (London, 1974-).

Arriagada, Genaro, *Pinochet: The Politics of Power*, trans. Nancy Nirrus (Winchester, MA, 1988).

Bitar, Sergio, *Chile, 1970-1973* (Santiago, 1995).

Cavallo, Ascanio, Manuel Salazar and Oscar Sepulveda, *La Historia Oculta del Regimen Militar* (Santiago, 1988).

Cavallo, Ascanio, *Los Hombres de la Transición* (Santiago, 1992).

Constable, Pamela, and Arturo Valenzuela, *A Nation of Enemies: Chile under Pinochet* (New York, 1991).

Correa, Raquel, and Elizabeth Subercaseaux, *Ego Sum Pinochet* (Santiago, 1989).

Davis, Nathaniel, *The Last Two Years of Salvador Allende* (Ithaca, NY, 1985).

Debray, Régis, *Conversations with Allende* (London, 1971).

Drake, Paul, and Ivan Jaksic, eds, *The Struggle for Democracy in Chile, 1982-1990* (Lincoln, NE, 1991).

Falcoff, Mark, *Modern Chile, 1970-1988* (New Brunswick, NJ, 1989).

Fáundez, Julio, *Marxism and Democracy in Chile from 1952 to the Fall of Allende* (New Haven, CT, 1988).

Fermandois, Joaquín, and Michael A. Morris, 'Democracy in Chile: Transition and Consolidation, 1987–2000', *Conflict Studies*, 279 (London, 1995).

Frei Montalva, Eduardo, *Latin America: The Hopeful Option*, trans. John Drury (New York, 1978).

Furci, Carmelo, *The Chilean Communist Party and the Road to Socialism* (London, 1984).

Garcés, Joan, *Allende y la Experiencia Chilena* (Barcelona, 1976).

Garretón, Manuel Antonio, *El Proceso Político Chileno* (Santiago, 1983).

Gazmuri, Cristián, *et al.*, *Eduardo Frei Montalva, 1911-1982* (Santiago, 1983).

Gross, Leonard, *The Last Best Hope: Eduardo Frei and Chilean Democracy* (New York, 1967).

Henfry, Colin, and Bernardo Sorj, eds, *Chilean Voices: Activists describe their Experiences of the Popular Unity Period* (Hassocks, 1977).

Hojman, David, *Chile: The Political Economy of Development and Democracy in the 1990s* (Pittsburgh, PA, 1993).

Huerta Diáz, Ismael, *Volvería a Ser Marinero* 2 vols (Santiago, 1988).

Inter-American Commission on Human Rights of the Organization of American States, Reports on the Status of Human Rights in Chile (Washington, DC, 1974 etc).

Lagos, Ricardo, *Democracia para Chile. Proposiciones de un Socialista* (Santiago, 1986).

Moss, Robert, *Chile's Marxist Experiment* (Exeter, 1973).

Pinochet, Augusto, *Camino Recorrido. Memorias de un Soldado*, 3 vols (Santiago, 1991-4).

——, *El Día Decisivo* (Santiago, 1982).

Politzer, Patricia, *Miedo en Chile* (Santiago, 1991).

Prats Gonzalez, Carlos, *Memorias. Testimonio de un Soldado* (Santiago, 1985).

Rettig, Raúl, *et al.*, *Informe de la Comission Nacional de Verdad y Reconciliación*, 3 vols (Santiago, 1991).

Roxborough, Ian, *et al.*, *Chile: The State and Revolution* (London, 1977).

Sigmund, Paul, *The Overthrow of Allende and the Politics of Chile, 1964-1976* (Pittsburgh, PA, 1978).

——, *The United States and Democracy in Chile* (Baltimore, MD. 1993).

Smith, Brian, *The Church and Modern Politics in Chile* (Princeton, NJ, 1982).

Valenzuela, Arturo, *The Breakdown of Democratic Regimes: Chile* (Baltimore, MD, 1978).

Valenzuela, Samuel, and Arturo Valenzuela, eds, *Chile: Politics and Society* (New Brunswick, NJ, 1976).

——, *Military Rule in Chile: Dictatorship and Opposition* (Baltimore, MD, 1986).

Varas, Florencia, *Conversaciones con Viaux* (Santiago, 1972).

Verdugo, Patricia, *Caso Arellano. Los Zarpazos del Puma* (Santiago, 1989).

——and Carmen Hertz, *Operacion Siglo XX* (Santiago, 1990).

Whelan, James R., *Out of the Ashes: Life, Death and Transfiguration of Democracy in Chile* (Washington, DC, 1989).

Foreign Relations; Diplomatic and Military History

Arriagada, Genaro, *La Política Militár de Pinochet* (Santiago, 1985).

Avila Martel, Alamiro de, *Cochrane y la Independencia del Pacifico* (Santiago, 1976).

Barros, Mario, *Historia Diplomática de Chile, 1541-1938* (Barcelona, 1970).

Branch, Taylor, and Eugene Propper, *Labyrinth* (New York, 1982).

Burr, Robert N., *By Reason or Force: Chile and the Balancing Power in South America, 1830-1905* (Los Angeles, 1965).

Davis, W.C., *The Last Conquistadores: The Spanish Intervention in Peru and Chile, 1863-1866* (Athens, GA, 1950).

Dinges, John, and Saul Landan, *Assassination on Embassy Row* (New York, 1980).

Edwards, Jorge, *Persona Non Grata: An Envoy in Castro's Cuba* (London, 1976).

Fermandois, Joaquín, *Chile y el Mundo, 1970-1973* (Santiago, 1985).

Francis, Michael J., *The Limits of Hegemony: US Relations with Argentina and Chile during World War II* (Notre Dame, IN, 1977).

Grimble, Ian, *The Sea Wolf: The Life of Admiral Cochrane* (London, 1978).

Jensen, Paul, *The Garotte: The United States and Chile, 1970-1973*, 2 vols (Aarhus, Denmark, 1988).

Morris, Michael, ed., *Great Power Relations in Argentina, Chile and Antarctica* (London, 1990)

Muñóz, Heraldo, *Las Relaciones Exteriores del Gobierno Militár Chileno* (Santiago, 1986).

Nunn, Frederick, *The Military in Chilean History* (Albuquerque, NM, 1986).

Orrego Vicuna, *Francisco, La Participáción de Chile en el Sistema Internacional* (Santiago, 1974).

Petras, James, and Morris Morley, *The United States and Chile: Imperialism and the Allende Government* (New York, 1975).

Pike, F.B., *Chile and the United States, 1880-1962* (Notre Dame, IN, 1963).

Sater, William F., *Chile and the United States: Empires in Conflict* (Athens, GA, 1990).

——, *Chile and the War of the Pacific* (Lincoln, NE, 1986).

US Senate Staff Report of the Select Committee to Study Government Intellegence Activities, *Covert Action in Chile, 1963-1973* (Washington, DC, 1975).

West, Nigel, *The Secret War for the Falklands* (London, 1997).

Economic and Social History

Angell, Alan, *Politics and the Labour Movement in Chile* (London, 1972).

Bardon, Alvaro, *et al.*, *Una Decada de Cambios Economicos. La Experiencia Chilena, 1973-83* (Santiago, 1985).

Barría, Jorge, *El Movimiento Obrero en Chile* (Santiago, 1971).

Blakemore, Harold, *From the Pacific to La Paz: The Antofagasta (Chili) and Bolivia Railway, 1888-1988* (London, 1990).

Correa, Enrique, and Jose Antonio Viera Gallo, *Iglesia y Dictadura* (Santiago, 1986).

Edwards, Sebastián and Alejandra, *Monetarism and Liberalization: The Chilean Experiment* (Chicago, 1991).

Ffrench-Davis, Ricardo, *Políticas Económicas en Chile, 1952-70* (Santiago, 1973).

——— and Ernesto Tironi, eds, *El Cobre en el Desarrollo Nacional* (Santiago, 1974).

Fontaine, Arturo, *Los Economistas y el Presidente Pinochet* (Santiago, 1988).

Foxley, Alejandro, *Para una Democrácia Estable* (Santiago, 1985).

International Bank for Reconstruction and Development *Chile: An Economy in Transition* (Washington, DC, 1980).

Lavin, Joaquín, *La Revolución Silenciosa* (Santiago, 1987).

Loveman, Brian, *Struggle in the Countryside: Politics and Rural Labour in Chile, 1919-73* (Bloomington, IN, 1976).

Mayo, John, *British Merchants and Chilean Development, 1851-1886* (Boulder, CO, 1987).

McBride, George M., *Chile: Land and Society* (New York, 1936).

Meller, Patricio, *Un Siglo de Economía Política Chilena, 1890-1990* (Santiago, 1996).

Miller, Rory, *Britain and Latin America in the Nineteenth and Twentieth Centuries* (London, 1993).

Monteón, Michael, *Chile in the Nitrate Era: The Evolution of Economic Dependence, 1880-1930* (Madison, WI, 1982).

Ortega, Luis, 'Economic Policy and Growth in Chile from Independence to the War of the Pacific' in Abel and Lewis, eds, *Latin America: Economic Imperialism and the State* (London, 1985).

Pinto Santa Cruz, Anibal, *Chile, un Caso de Desarrollo Frustrado* (Santiago, 1962).

Steenland, Kyle, *Agrarian Reform under Allende: Peasant Revolt in the South* (Albuquerque, NM, 1978).

Tironi, Eugenio, *Los Silencios de la Revolución* (Santiago, 1988).

Veliz, Claudio, *Historia de la Marina Mercante de Chile* (Santiago, 1961).

de Vylder, Stefan, *Allende's Chile: The Political Economy of the Rise and Fall of the Popular Unity* (Cambridge, 1976).

Travel, Personal Reminiscences and Miscelleaneous Classics

Bitar, Sergio, *Isla 10* (Santiago, 1988).

Bowers, Claude G., *Chile Through Embassy Windows* (New York, 1958).

Boyd, Robert Nelson, *Chili: Sketches of Chili and the Chilians during the War, 1879-1880* (London, 1881).

Cassidy, Sheila, *Audacity to Believe* (London, 1977).

Chatwin, Bruce, *In Patagonia* (London, 1977).

Darwin, Charles, *Narrative of the Surveying Voyages of H.M.S. Adventure and H.M.S. Beagle between 1826 and 1836*, vol. III (London, 1839).

Edwards, Jorge, *Adios Poeta* (Santiago, 1990).

Ercilla y Zúñiga, Alonso de, *La Araucana* (Buenos Aires, 1977).

Fergusson, Erna, *Chile* (New York, 1943).

Graham, Maria (Lady Calcott), *Journal of a Residence in Chile during the year 1822: And a Voyage from Chile to Brazil in 1823* (London, 1824).

Hall, Captain Basil, *Extracts from a Journal Written on the coasts of Chile, Peru and Mexico in 1820, 1821, 1822* (Edinburgh, 1824).

Herivel, E.B., *We Farmed a Desert* (London, 1957).

Hofmann, Adriana, *Flores Silvestres de Chile*, 2 vols (Santiago, 1979).

Horne, Alistair, *Small Earthquake in Chile* (London, 1972).

Johnson, A.W., *The Birds of Chile and adjacent regions of Argentina, Bolivia and Peru*, 2 vols (Buenos Aires, 1965-7).

Lambert, C.J., *Sweet Waters. A Chilean Farm* (Greenwood, CT, 1975).

Lucas Bridges, E., *The Uttermost Part of the Earth* (London, 1948).

Miers, John, *Travels in Chile and La Plata*, 2 vols (London, 1826).

Neruda, Pablo, *Memorias. Confesio Que He Vivido*, trans. Hardie St Martin (London, 1977).

———, *Canto General* (1950).

———, *Selected Poems: A Bilingual Edition* (New York, 1972).

Parra, Isabel, *El Libro Mayor de Violeta Parra* (Madrid, 1985).

Pring-Mill, Robert, *Pablo Neruda: A Basic Anthology* (Oxford, 1975).

Russell, William Howard, *A Visit to Chile and the Nitrate Field of Tarapacá* (London, 1890).

Shipton, Eric, *Land of Tempest: Travels in Patagonia, 1958-1962* (London, 1963).

Spooner, Mary Helen, *Soldiers in a Narrow Land – The Pinochet Regime in Chile* (Berkeley, CA, 1994).

Swale, Rosie, *Back to Cape Horn* (London, 1986).

Ure, John, *Cucumber Sandwiches in the Andes* (London, 1973).

INDEX